International Environmental Policy

International Environmental Policy

Interests and the Failure of the Kyoto Process

Sonja Boehmer-Christiansen

Reader of Environmental Politics, Department of Geography, Hull University, UK

Aynsley Kellow

Professor, and Head of the School of Government, University of Tasmania, Australia

Edward Elgar

Cheltenham, UK • Northampton, MA, USA

Published by
Edward Elgar Publishing Limited
Glensanda House
Montpellier Parade
Cheltenham
Glos GL50 1UA
UK

Edward Elgar Publishing, Inc.
136 West Street
Suite 202
Northampton
Massachusetts 01060
USA

A catalogue record for this book is available from the British Library

Library of Congress Cataloging in Publication Data
Boehmer-Christiansen, Sonja.
    International environmental policy : interests and the failure of the Kyoto process / Sonja Boehmer-Christiansen, Aynsley Kellow.
        p. cm.
    Includes index.
    1. Environmental policy—International cooperation. 2. Environmental risk assessment—International cooperation. 3. Greenhouse gases—Government policy—International cooperation. 4. Air—Pollution—Government policy—International cooperation. 5. Global warming—Economic aspects. I. Kellow, Aynsley J. (Aynsley John), 1951– II. Title.

GE170 .B64 2002
363.7'0526—dc21

                                                                                    2002072175

ISBN 1 84064 818 X
Printed and bound in Great Britain by MPG Books Ltd, Bodmin, Cornwall

Contents

List of abbreviations   vi
Preface   ix

1   Introduction   1
2   The international environmental policy process:
    increasing complexity and implementation failure   13
3   Energy interests, opportunities and uneven burden-sharing   33
4   The Kyoto process   53
5   The failure of principled discourse   85
6   Institutionalizing scientific advice: designing consensus as a
    policy driver?   116
7   The suppression of scientific controversy   148
8   Baptists, bootleggers and the Kyoto process   176

Bibliography   187
Index   205

Abbreviations

ABARE	Australian Bureau of Agricultural and Resource Economics
AGBM	Ad Hoc Group on the Berlin Mandate
AGGG	Advisory Group on Greenhouse Gases
AIJ	Activities Implemented Jointly
AKE	Energy working group of Deutsche Physikalische Gesellschaft
AOSIS	Alliance of Small Island States
APEC	Asia–Pacific Economic Cooperation Forum
BAU	Business as usual
BNFL	British Nuclear Fuels Limited
CAN	Climate Action Network
CCGT	Combined cycle gas turbine
CDM	Clean Development Mechanism
CFCs	Chlorofluorocarbons
CHE	UN Conference on the Human Environment, Stockholm, 1972
CO_2	Carbon dioxide
COP	Conference of the Parties
COW	Committee of the Whole
CSE	Centre for Science and Environment (India)
CSIRO	Commonwealth Scientific and Industrial Research Organization (Australia)
ECOSOC	Economic and Social Council of the United Nations
EITs	Economies in transition
ENGO	Environmental non-governmental organization
EPA	Environmental Protection Agency (USA)
ESRC	Economic and Social Research Council
EU	European Union
FAO	Food and Agriculture Organization (UN)
FAR	First Assessment Report
FCCC	Framework Convention on Climate Change
FGD	Flue gas desulphurization
FOE	Friends of the Earth
G-77	Group of seventy-seven 'non-aligned' nations
GARP	Global Atmospheric Research Programme
GATT	General Agreement on Tariffs and Trade

GCM	General circulation model
GEC	Global Environmental Change (Programme, UK)
GEF	Global Environment Fund
GHG	Greenhouse gas
GWP	Global warming potential
HEP	Hydro-electric power
HFC	Hydrofluorocarbon
IAEA	International Atomic Energy Agency
ICSU	International Council of Scientific Unions
IEA	International Energy Agency
IGBP	International Geosphere Biosphere Project
IGCC	Integrated gasification and combined cycle gas turbine
IGO	Intergovernmental organization
IIASA	International Institute of Applied Systems Analysis
IMI	International Meteorological Institute
INC	Intergovernmental Negotiating Committee
IPCC	Intergovernmental Panel on Climate Change
JI	Joint Implementation
JUSCANZ	Japan, USA, Canada, Australia and New Zealand group of countries
JUSSCANNZ	Japan, USA, Switzerland, Canada, Australia, Norway and New Zealand group of countries
LDCs	Less developed countries
LIA	Little Ace Age
LRTAP	Geneva Convention on Long-range Transboundary Air Pollution 1979
LULUCF	Land use, land use changes and forestry
MARPOL	Convention for the Prevention of Dumping by Ships 1973
MCA	Medieval climate optimum
MEA	Multilateral environmental agreement; monoethanolamine
MIT	Massachusetts Institute of Technology
NAFTA	North American Free Trade Agreement
NAS	National Assessment Synthesis (USA)
NASA	National Aeronautics and Space Administration (USA)
NCAR	National Center for Atmospheric Research (USA)
NGO	Non-governmental organization
OECD	Organization for Economic Cooperation and Development
OPEC	Organization of Petroleum Exporting Countries
PFC	Perfluorocarbon
QELRO	Quantified emission limitation and reduction objective
SCOPE	Scientific Committee on Problems of the Environment (ICSU)
SAR	Second Assessment Report

SDP	Social Democratic Party (Germany)
SF_6	sulphur hexa-fluoride
SPM	Summary for Policy-makers
TAR	Third Assessment Report
UNCED	UN Conference on Environment and Development
UNCHE	UN Conference on the Human Environment, Stockholm, 1972
UNEP	United Nations Environment Programme
WEC	World Energy Conference
WG I, II, III	Working Groups I, II, III (IPCC)
WMO	World Meteorological Organization
WRI	World Resources Institute
WTO	World Trade Organization
WWF	Worldwide Fund for Nature

Preface

It is one of the distinguishing features of the scientific debate over climate change that those who contest the prevailing orthodoxy of the Intergovernmental Panel on Climate Change (IPCC) are often called 'sceptics', and this is meant to be a pejorative term. Scepticism, however, has long been central to the scientific endeavour.

We have written this book out of a commitment to scepticism. We are sceptical for two reasons: after decades of observing environmental policy and politics, we are convinced that effective policy cannot be made against the interests of nations and people, especially businesses and employees – ironically, interests least represented when multilateral environmental agreements are negotiated, but all too apparent at the level of the nation-state. Second, we question the claim that international environmental treaties can be based on 'consensus' science as long as fundamental research questions remain unresolved, which may be for a very long time. When knowledge remains fundamentally incomplete, precautionary policy in particular will tend to drive policy towards the interests of short-term winners, ultimately enhancing global conflict unless there is genuine sharing. Consensus policy is one thing, but an 'underpinning' consensus among selected scientists and sciences funded by policy-makers is quite another. In arguing that science remains too uncertain and interests too diverse to justify the Kyoto Protocol as envisaged by its advocates, we have adopted an unpopular stand against a large amount of scientific, social scientific and legal literature, which will certainly not be welcomed by environmentalists. We still consider ourselves as supporters of environmental protection, but as politically unlikely to be achieved by use of 'green' rhetoric and selectivity. The green 'movement', if it wants to remain effective, needs to become politically more sophisticated.

In taking our stand we have been helped by many people in research and government, only some of whom we can mention. Sonja Boehmer-Christiansen owes much to all the IPCC scientists she was able to interview and observe during the early 1990s, including Sir John Houghton and Robert Watson. She has acted as a reviewer for its Working Group III, the experts with the solutions, since the mid 1990s. On the sceptical science side, she learnt from the astro- and space physics communities to which her late husband Dr Peter James Christiansen belonged, and more recently benefited from discussions with critical

Russian environmental scientists, especially Professor Kirill Ya Kondratyev. As editor of *Energy & Environment*, she has published many of the critical voices, not because she knows them to be right or highly 'acclaimed' by their peers, but because she felt that official journals in Europe in particular were ignoring critics. Our confidence in scientific scepticism is maintained not only by personal belief but also by contact with an informal global e-mail network that included a few IPCC authors and supporters and a self-selected group of sceptics, including well known IPCC critics such as Fred Singer, John Daly, Richard Courtney and Nigel Calder, as well as a number of German, Scandinavian and Australian scientists from several disciplines. Few have changed sides; the debate continues with little financial help for sceptics and their fundamental objections to 'climate prediction' by simple mathematical computations. However, no single hypothesis to counter the IPCC 'consensus' has so far emerged, nor is it being funded.

The seeds of doubt about climate models as policy tools were sowed early in our minds, but sprouted well while living with research communities that included not only fusion and plasma physics but, increasingly and more directly, the social and natural sciences. Sonja benefited from two UK Economic and Social Research Council (ESRC) grants which allowed her to study the IPPC during its early years, and then observe how the climate threat was picked up for aid and trade purposes by international financial institutions. The Leverhulme Trust helped to fund a visit to Australia in 1998, and the Mawson Centre of the Geography Department (University of Adelaide) is thanked deeply for providing a friendly base for the study of Australia's climate policy. The Lavoisier Group of the Australian Parliament is thanked for funding her travel to and in Australia in 2000 to discuss climate policy with policy-makers and stakeholders. Aynsley Kellow wishes to thank Stuart Harris for inviting him (on behalf of the Academy of Social Sciences in Australia) to present a paper to a Joint Academies Forum on Climate Change in 1997, and thus draw out his interest in climate change. David Robertson and Alan Oxley subsequently extended similar invitations. Meg McDonald and Howard Bamsey, both former Ambassadors for the Environment in Australia, provided valuable insights into the Kyoto process. Aynsley also learned much about the impact of climate change policy while acting as a consultant to Sinclair Knight Merz on compliance with Kyoto. In the end, however, taxpayers must be thanked most. It is primarily in their interest that this book is written.

Observing the behaviour of the UK government and the European Union (EU) on climate policy has remained a major research interest since the late 1980s. In this context Sonja would also like to thank Gavin Watson, once closely involved in European environmental policy-making, for valuable insights. Few 'outsiders' realize how effectively a small, dedicated number of unelected civil servants and their scientists 'on tap' are able translate their common visions and interests into a policy option 'sold' as ethical-scientific imperative. At least in the UK during the 1990s, funding 'the environment' became increasingly controlled by public servants seeking, apparently, policy-relevant knowledge and *de facto* diverting the academic community from studying other problems. Scientists working for governments institutions would often talk only in confidence, itself an indication that climate change debates were being (self-) censored for political reasons. Many thanks must therefore go to many unnamed colleagues and friends in several countries who have discussed 'climate change' research and policy with us. Many keep their doubts strategically to themselves; even more are by now believers.

1.   Introduction

The prospect of rapid climate change has generated many possible global responses. Such responses might entail attempts to adapt to the effects of climate change. Or they might entail actions which will minimize climate change, provided of course that this is anthropogenic in origin, and thus susceptible to human control.

Since the mid-1980s efforts have been made to mitigate or combat global warming by reducing the emission of greenhouse gases (GHGs), particularly carbon dioxide (CO_2) generated by the combustion of fossil fuels, in particular coal and oil. The international legal context for these efforts is provided by the Framework Convention on Climate Change (FCCC, 1992) and its Kyoto Protocol (KP, 1997). Negotiations, after stalling in late 2000, have finally succeeded, at least partially, with the 'mini-Kyoto' protocol agreed (without the USA) in Bonn in July 2001 and later that year in November in Marrakesh. An intergovernmental agreement to go forward has indeed been reached, but in much watered-down form and with many important decisions again deferred. The refusal of the political leaders of the USA, the largest emitter of GHGs, to join is seen in America as a principled stand against UN dominated globalization and has been justified with reference to economic unfairness and scientific uncertainty. In contrast, the European Union and the United Kingdom have been whole-hearted supporters of the Kyoto process which is supported by a 'scientific consensus'. What is going on scientifically and politically? Why has the Kyoto Protocol, designed ostensibly to prevent dangerous anthropogenic planetary heating, been embraced by so many governments, industrialists, scientists and environmentalists in Europe and even, more cautiously, by governments in most developing countries – while being rejected by the USA and regarded with caution by other countries such as Japan, Canada and Australia?

For climate change, states formed into negotiating blocs and agreed in Kyoto to a number of differentiated reduction targets for industrialized nations which amounted to a 5.2 per cent reduction over 1990 emission levels of greenhouse gases. But many details were left to be finalized, and in subsequent rounds of negotiation the collective 5.2 per cent cut was reduced to an effective reduction in emissions of about 2 per cent at the sixth meeting of the Conference of the Parties to the FCCC (COP-6), which broke down without agreement in The Hague in late 2000 but was concluded eight months later in July 2001 in Bonn.

Both mitigation, which has dominated the debate so far, and adaptation, which is now creeping into it, raise issues which are central to politics, in part because anthropogenic (or human-induced) climate change, if serious as well as real, raises questions about the distribution of liability, of costs and benefits, and hence of global competitiveness and political stability. Even adaptation responses raise questions about who should research solutions and who should pay for them. Questions just as difficult arise if naturally occurring climate change were to take place at a rate which makes gradual adaptation – that is change without drastic intervention – difficult or prohibitively costly. We live in an interdependent world and therefore should aid neighbours who are unable to cope when catastrophe befalls them. But if such disasters have human origins, then the claim by the victims on those who cause the problems is stronger. Attribution of causality is therefore the essence of any attempt to impose legally binding obligations.

But, although devising and implementing policies and determining the allocation, first, of blame and then, in particular, of costs, are all fundamental political activities usually undertaken through the agency of government, government is absent at the global level. Here, governance without a single government is required (see Rosenau, 1995). How then should courses of action be devised and chosen, and costs and benefits be allocated: for example, in the case allegedly as 'global' and 'dangerous' as global warming? International relations theory suggests some insights, stressing the value of shared norms and understandings of science, of cause and effect, to help bring disparate parties together. Yet, as we will show, strong normative and causal discourses were insufficient with Kyoto, which came down to a negotiation of interests. In order to get a deal that had some prospect of Kyoto receiving sufficient ratifications to enter into force, the EU and G-77 and China had to concede so much ground to Russia, Japan, Canada and Australia that the gross reductions in CO_2 emissions required were close to zero, with sinks and trading of 'hot air' resulting from Russia's post-communist economic collapse serving to meet targets.

In the absence of government as a single sovereign actor, global governance cannot rely upon the imposition of coercion which is fundamental to government at the level of the nation-state, although some nations are subject to coercion by others. The international system cannot readily even rely upon majority voting – even by substantial majorities – since those not in agreement are sovereign states. Faced with the classic options of 'exit, voice or loyalty' (Hirschman, 1970), states might simply choose to exit from the deliberative process by which a scheme of governance is to be devised. Should one nation choose exit over voicing disagreement or adhering to the dominant view, the whole scheme is threatened. This is especially so if the party departing is a significant player, but any departure risks being copied by others.

Regardless of whether international treaties make provision for voting, actual voting is the exception: one which is actively avoided. The threat to call a vote becomes in itself an important bargaining device, used not just by those who might win the vote, but also as a disruptive threat by the likely losers, because voting is likely to shatter the consensus which lies at the heart of international agreements, including those on environmental problems, usually referred to as multilateral environmental agreements (or MEAs). Consensus is difficult to achieve, especially among the over 180 diverse members of the United Nations. For this reason, the negotiation processes have been described as analogous to a convoy of ships, which can move only at the speed of the slowest boat (Sand, 1990). Not only is the speed of the negotiation process limited in this way to ensure that all parties are 'brought along' together, but there is a qualitative corollary to the 'slowest boat problem': what can be agreed often reflects the 'lowest common denominator'. The negotiations themselves put a premium on certainty (about damage and costs) and the reduction of complex issues to simple visions, thus creating a difficult environment for scientific advice to flourish, but encouraging verbal ambiguity and legal flexibility.

The challenge in developing responses to climate change and other global environmental problems is thus one involving pace of progress, quality of outcomes and coping with uncertainty: of achieving a degree of cohesion among disparate actors which will produce worthwhile agreements on a reasonable timetable. The challenge is often described in terms of interdependency norms prevailing over sovereignty norms: the realization by states' parties to negoti-ations that, for whatever reason, it is more important that they cooperate than defend their independence and the interests of those within their borders. But will this strategy work when it remains uncertain whether the resulting agreement has any real effect on the environment? The outcome must remain problematic as, especially if practical implementation takes place over time spans that may be very long indeed, human behaviour and technologies are by no means fully under the control of even the most powerful government. Many governments may also lack the capacity for implementation.

Brenton (1994, 252–9) identifies four forces encouraging international cohesion in international environmental politics: the use of 'toe in the door' negotiating processes; reliance upon science and epistemic communities; the influence of environment non-governmental organizations (NGOs); and what he terms 'environmental altruism', or responding to rhetorical justifications which are difficult to resist. Brenton extends Lumsdaine's (1993) insights about the force of moral suasion in the aid arena to suggest that governments may find it difficult to resist rhetorical injunctions to 'save the planet'. The rhetoric alone 'tends to make politicians and negotiators readier to look for common ground than they would be in other sorts of international negotiation.' (Brenton, 1994, 259). Brenton admits to having had personal feelings of this kind in climate change negotiations, and similar feelings were reported by the chief US negotiator on the ozone issue (Benedick, 1991). But moral injunctions that are difficult to resist are not necessarily a sound foundation upon which to base an international regulatory regime. Certainly, Nadelmann (1990) suggests that prohibition regimes are more successful when they reflect, rather than impose, strong moral positions, and it seems reasonable to suppose the same applies with any strong regulatory regime.

'Toe in the door' negotiating processes are not unique to international environmental politics, and are indeed an example of a fundamental political strategy of the 'thin end of the wedge' – of achieving acceptance of a small, innocuous measure and then expanding it. It forms the basis of Lindblom's (1959, 1979) claim that incremental change can produce rapid progress by dealing with political realities and of Wildavsky's (1984) similar notion in the politics of the budgetary process. In the international context this has been referred to as 'iterative functionalism' (Feldman, 1995), and has been formalized in the model of the development of 'framework' conventions, such as the FCCC. These have little binding content but establish an institutional setting that facilitates the development of shared norms and understandings which later make possible the development of more explicit binding commitments under a protocol to the framework convention. This has been the case with regimes dealing with problems such as acid rain or ozone depletion.

The nature of the negotiating process is thus the adoption of initial agreements whose substantive content is low, but which gave rise to a subsequent series of meetings which are used 'as an opportunity by those countries with environmentally more advanced positions to place pressure on others, both directly and via environmental NGOs, to shift in their direction' (Brenton, 1994, 252). This depends upon the globalization of the news and the uniquely open and public style of international environmental negotiation developed at the 1972 UN Conference on the Human Environment at Stockholm 'which means that NGOs and others can apply their pressure on the right issues at the right time' (Brenton, 1994, 253).

Brenton (1994, 255) also notes that the use of science – sometimes distorted for effect – is important; that and 'the power of a united scientific view to push even unwilling governments into action is now one of the key mechanisms of international environmental cooperation'. Most notably, Peter Haas (1990) has emphasized the importance of epistemic consensus evolving among communities of scientists in the development of a broader political consensus. The emergence of a scientific consensus is seen by Peter Haas as a necessary rather than a sufficient condition for international agreement, although Ernst Haas (1990) is of the view that changing knowledge can lead to a redefinition of interests. Once agreement has been reached and policy commitments have been made, there is a need for science to support it, and this can add to the factors which might have a corrupting influence on science, as the scientific consensus can become a tool for securing additional research funding for scientists. Boehmer-Christiansen (1994a, 1994b), however, has questioned the scientific nature of such consensus if research science is under pressure to deliver in order to justify a policy direction already defined by interests that may be considered precautionary.

The absence of a scientific consensus is seen as more significant than consensus, because scientific disagreements are regarded as likely to be sufficient to limit the prospects for agreement. This in turn tends to lead to pressure on science, or to the selection of 'relevant' or 'sound' science by governments seeking agreement; and the process whereby the Kyoto Protocol to the Framework Convention on Climate Change was developed, we suggest here, is an example of this.

The emergence of a scientific consensus was certainly important in the development of an international response to the problem of ozone-depleting chemicals. From the publication of the first paper suggesting that CFCs might be responsible for depleting the ozone layer, it took little more than a decade for the Montreal Protocol to be concluded, during which time further research had built support for a particular understanding of the problem. The success of Montreal encouraged an attempt to repeat the process for climate change. Mustafa Tolba, Executive Director of the United Nations Environment Programme (UNEP) when the Montreal Protocol was being negotiated, stated that the mechanisms designed for the protocol would be used as the blueprint for the development of a response to the problem of climate change (Benedick, 1991, 7).

SCIENCE, NORMS AND THE KYOTO PROCESS

The equivalent international agreement developed in response to the threat of climate change – the Kyoto Protocol – necessarily saw national interests figure much more prominently during negotiations than had been the case at Montreal, with science proving much less effective in producing consensus. With climate change, the proposed emission reductions have far more serious and pervasive and unpredictable effects on energy supplies and fuel competition than substitution for CFCs, which were produced only by a handful of companies eager to retain advantage in the production of substitutes.

The original Kyoto decision had proven to be too advantageous to the EU, and concessions had to be granted to others in the form of provision for sinks and emissions trading to secure agreement, despite explicit attempts to use science and strong normative arguments to bring non-European parties into agreement. Meantime, in March 2001, the USA effectively exited the Protocol, rendering not just its effectiveness but its relevance to the climate change issue problematic.

Does this suggest that we should discount the importance of epistemic consensus as a factor in the development of political agreement? We shall suggest in this book that we need not discount totally the views of Peter Haas (1990); on the contrary, the pressure for consensus among scientists was great but could not overcome the many issues of equity and practical implementation raised by the proposed solutions. But, as we shall show, not only did interests feature more prominently with climate change than with ozone depletion, but the science of climate change itself (*contra* ozone) has been inescapably tied up with the play of interests from the outset. Rather than a scientific consensus evolving gradually as more and more research was conducted, as it did with ozone, institutional means were developed to *produce* a scientific consensus in the expectation that this would be decisive in producing a political consensus in favour of action on climate change – and action of a particular kind at that. An international organization, the Intergovernmental Panel on Climate Change (IPCC), was specifically established to generate a consensus that could be presented as being 'scientific'. We shall discuss to what extent this label is merited.

With ozone, in other words, science was essentially an independent variable, and the consensus it produced a dependent variable. With climate change, we suggest, causality has been more confused simply because human understanding of climate, its natural variability and impacts remains limited and contested among several disciplines. The epistemic community on climate change science is self-selected and is dominated by a few governments with strong atmospheric-science/climatology research capacities and space lobbies: the United States, the United Kingdom, Sweden, Canada, Japan, Germany and Australia. Most of these countries also have in their national interests a prominent component of interests such as oil companies, whose gas holdings are made more valuable by restrictions on coal (USA, UK, Canada). The nuclear programmes and industries of some are similarly advantaged (USA, UK, Canada, Sweden, Japan, Germany), and some had heavily subsidised coal industries that they wished to close but needed political support to do so (UK, Germany). The UK and Germany have been particularly advantaged by the form of international commitments negotiated thus far. Climate change also seemed to require action which reinforced policies aimed at providing both energy security and taxation revenues. Australia is unusual in this company, because (uranium exports aside) restrictions on the emission of greenhouse gases represent considerable costs, and its scientific commitment has thus conflicted with its national interests.

The scientific endeavour of climate research itself has thus resonated strongly with significant national interests, but science itself has also been an interest. The threat of anthropogenic climate change has led governments collectively to spend billions of dollars on climate research, based largely on computer modelling rather than empirical research, much of it redirected from studies which might have had more immediate returns in predicting natural variability, such as droughts. This has created a 'grant-dense' environment for climate change science, and especially meteorology, which was institutionalized domestically and internationally in a well-established intergovernmental organization and quickly, if reluctantly at first, made this part of its global research agenda funded by national governments. The geological and space sciences are still attempting, with little success, to enter this field. Many dedicated research centres for climate change modelling have been created and the 'science politicians' involved in both the allocation and securing of funds have set priorities which can exert a powerful pull on research. Climate change policy became in large part research policy.

We consider that this milieu has meant that the science of climate change is no longer 'pure', but also reflects, rather than simply drives, politics. The need for 'relevance' and the dependence of society on those who have an interest in there being a problem has left decision-makers dangerously exposed to the possibility of Lysenkoism on a global scale: Soviet scientist Trofim Lysenko set the science of genetics back years in the USSR by advancing the false theory that improvements in things such as milk production could become acquired characteristics which could be inherited by successive generations – a theory which (though false) resonated loudly with Marxist–Leninist ideology.[1]

It is not that we consider all climate science to be on a par with Lysenko's genetics – far from it. Nor do we reject the possibility that anthropogenic GHG emissions *might* have an impact on future climate. Rather, we are sceptical about greenhouse science as it has been funded and used for policy purposes – as we think everyone should be of *all* science. And we consider that climate change science is riddled with interests to the extent that it has much less power as a force for consensus than was the case, for example, with ozone, asbestos, ionising radiation or even acidification of surface waters.

We shall argue that the attempt to construct a scientific consensus has involved the science politicians in attempting to impose a political consensus on states. This attempt itself has certain attributes that seem to require that the science should be responded to in a particular way. The science politicians, in other words, have sought to impose a particular problem definition and solution on society. This, they seem to think, will trump the powerful interests that would otherwise block action. The proposed solution is one which 'demands' emission reduction rather than adaptation strategies, even though (should their own predictions prove correct) emission reduction is likely to be futile! This problem definition closely tied to the solutions was particularly attractive politically because some solutions were already available and had been proposed initially not to reduce emissions from fossil fuel combustion, but to replace fossil fuels that had either become too expensive – the oil shocks of the 1970s – or were allegedly threatened by rapid depletion, according to the 'limits to growth' discourse of the 1970s.

Any emission reduction measures likely to be politically possible may well prove futile if CO_2 has indeed a long residence period in the atmosphere – in excess of 100 years (the contrarians say 20 or 30 years) – so that accumulated CO_2 *already emitted* together with that emitted over the next century will raise levels in the atmosphere. The 5.2 per cent cut agreed to in Kyoto would (even if achieved) quickly be wiped out by growth in emissions by developing countries. The IPCC argues that a 60 per cent reduction in total global emissions would be required to stabilize atmospheric CO_2 levels. Given this assumption, there is a fundamental flaw in the case that compels us to pursue vigorously emission reductions: unless CO_2 emissions are slashed by at least half, CO_2 levels will continue to rise and (if the predictions of the scientists and energy forecasters in the IPCC consensus are correct) climate change will inevitably ensue. There is a strong argument, therefore, that dangerous change should be slowed a little, but that adaptation and longer-term technological change are surely more important priorities. Why then the enormous, if so far only very partially successful, effort to reduce emissions undertaken at the global level?

If the IPCC scientific consensus proves correct, some adaptation to climate change is inevitable. Hence a response strategy focused primarily on emission reduction would seem to be flawed. The most important policy issue would appear to be one of how to respond (in the face of uncertain science) to the possibility of climate variability – with a strong regional dimension – which might be exacerbated by human activity. Climate is inherently variable and unpredictable; it has changed greatly over geological time scales and much apparent unusual climate behaviour is merely created by omitting from the picture earlier periods when change has been even faster than today, without any human presence (Gorshkov and Gorshkov, 1998; Berner and Streif, 2001). Avoidance of climate change is an impossibility. It is by no means clear that attempting to prevent climate change is the best strategy, and an ability to provide economically the means to adapt to and absorb climate variability is central to any response strategy. Many see emission reduction as likely to be driven more by technological change, such as the development of more energy-efficient devices such as fuel cells, than by policy, and particularly by policies which have high costs that might limit our collective ability to meet the costs of adaptation. These policies do, however, add another interest to an already complex circle of international, national and subnational actors, namely bureaucratic agencies that have been enabled to acquire information, count emissions, administer, tax, and regulate activities giving rise to GHG emissions to an extent quite unusual in an era of deregulation and privatization.

Yet the thrust of the international policy process remains weighted overwhelmingly towards reduction strategies. Why? We suggest that the reason lies in an understanding of interests primarily related to energy which infuse both the science of climate change and the moral arguments invoked to give the science force. We suggest in this book that the Kyoto process has not been successful because it is based upon an assumption that a scientific consensus and strong moral injunctions will be sufficient to drive international policy. We argue that the negotiation of the Kyoto Protocol was a triumph for an interest-based explanation *because* of, rather than despite, the provision of science and normative arguments which were employed. This was because both the science and the normative arguments reflected the play of some powerful interests, and were being employed to push the direction of the process not just towards emission reduction rather than adaptation, but towards policy instruments which favoured some national or economic interests at the expense of others.

Under these circumstances, science and normative arguments had less force than suggested by many accounts of international environmental politics, ironically because the international system has 'learned' that scientific consensus tends to amount to a consensus negotiated between selected scientific institutions dependent on official funding and eager to exclude competing disciplines, and that strong normative arguments can do only so much to drive actors towards accepting 'interdependency' rather than 'sovereignty'. Kyoto also revealed that, at the end of the day, there is little policy which is solely 'environmental', as the issue had important implications for many other policy areas, which brought in other interested actors. It is not so much that interests were stronger than they were in the ozone case, and the scientific and moral forces were thus insufficient, but that the scientific and moral interests exerting themselves in favour of Kyoto reflected (to a much greater extent than with ozone) the interests of those who would benefit from restrictions being placed on selected emissions.

This conclusion, which we shall argue in detail, accords with other recent studies of international environmental politics, where a more nuanced understanding of the place of science and norms is emerging. To give but one example, according to Ronald B. Mitchell (employing discourse analysis), through international treaties states redefine their rights in areas of common jurisdiction and these redefinitions of rights then redefine sovereignty. But the key question in an anarchic international system concerns whether – and under what circumstances – *de jure* redefinitions of sovereignty alter the *de facto* practices of sovereignty that harm the environment (always assuming that there is general agreement on what is 'harm'). Mitchell (1998, 275) suggests that: 'The success of efforts to alter sovereign *practice* by redefining sovereign *rights* depends, at least in part, on the form of discourse used to justify the redefinition.' Drawing on the work of Goldstein and Keohane (1993) and Sikkink

(1993), Mitchell distinguishes between 'instrumental' (or interest-based) discourse, causal (or science-based) discourse, and 'principled' (or morals-based) discourse.

Mitchell suggests that instrumental discourse will only result in reluctant states accepting new norms of sovereignty if that discourse coincides with new patterns of power and interests that would 'force' them to accept such norms anyway. Available solutions each have their own champions in the form of interests pushing not only for solutions which advantage them, but also for *problems* which advantage their solutions – in the manner of Cohen *et al.*'s (1972) notion of problems and solutions meeting in the 'garbage can', or Winner's (1977) notion of adapting ends to available means. Scientific (or 'causal') discourse will only prevail over short-term interests when sufficient scientific consensus and acceptance of that consensus persuades decision-makers to focus their attention on 'how nature will respond to their actions rather than on how other states will respond' (Mitchell, 1998, 283). He also warns, and we agree, that not only does moral (or 'principled') discourse often fail to lead to the acceptance of new principled beliefs, but it is likely to be counterproductive, leading states to reject new norms of sovereignty unless more direct, material incentives encourage their acceptance.

Note that Mitchell focuses on a distinction between *de jure* redefinitions of sovereignty and the *de facto* practices of sovereignty, which point to an increasing focus on international policy-making rather than just international politics – a focus (introduced from policy studies at the domestic level) on implementation and outcomes, rather than on whether interdependency norms prevail over sovereignty norms. Unlike 'high politics', the 'low politics' (Hoffman, 1966) of which international environmental regulation is so typical requires that we move beyond politics to policy, and consider the terms of 'global governance' (Soroos, 1986). Scholars such as Hanf and Underdal (1998) have suggested that the importance of science and norms might be limited only to particular stages of the international policy process, such as initiating negotiations rather than the process of devising workable solutions, and our findings here support that conclusion. (More on this in Chapter 2.)

Implementation is not just a process which must follow treaty adoption and accession. It is a process which may impact significantly on the negotiating process itself. It has been observed in studies of negotiations between nations in the European context that the tough and detail-minded negotiators are those who later tend to implement decisions correctly, while those who are most ready to compromise tend to have poor records of compliance (Weiler, 1988, 355–6). Laxity in implementation allows those nations least supportive of high levels of protection to sign agreements, knowing that they can drag their feet on implementation (Eichner, 1997). Many accounts of the development of MEAs ignore implementation and therefore miss an important dimension, not just for issues of compliance, but for the implications of a low probability of compliance with agreement.

At the time of writing, the Third Assessment Report (TAR) of the IPCC has just been released. While it contains a large number of 'scenarios', the one which has been given prominence by IPCC Chairman Robert Watson is one which shows an alarming rate of global warming: 5.8°C over the next century. This result, generated from computer models, is the most extreme: it assumes that sulphate aerosols which cool the atmosphere will be controlled but that CO_2 will not, and economies will continue to be extremely heavily dependent on fossil fuels, with economic growth rates that seem unrealistic even if desired. Watson and other IPCC spokesmen have made statements accompanying the release of TAR to the effect that these predictions make it imperative that nations implement the Kyoto Protocol reductions: advice we consider quite improper as 'scientific' advice. We suggest on the basis of the analysis which follows that this was a misguided political attempt to use science to trump interests. Not only did it lead to an outcome in Bonn in 2001 widely regarded as a failure, but it runs the risk of being one cry of 'Wolf!' too many.

PLAN OF THE BOOK

We see the Kyoto process as having been modelled on the stages outlined by Brenton, but argue that this ignores both the need to negotiate interests and important stages in the international policy process. Specifically, the model ignores both implementation and an important distinction between policy initiation (where science and principled discourses can help initiate action) and policy adoption (where instrumental discourses are needed). The Kyoto process, by allowing reliance on normative arguments and science to spill over in to policy adoption, actually marginalized the instrumental discourses needed to develop practical policy instruments, resulting in what Hanf and Underdal (1998) call the vertical disintegration of policy. We shall argue for this in detail in Chapter 2.

In Chapter 3 we set out the nature of the most significant interests in the Kyoto process, and then show in Chapter 4 how they were central to the negotiation. Chapter 5 examines the principled discourse employed in the Kyoto process, arguing that the use of such discourse was made by agents which did not rise above the interests at stake. We also maintain that the science in the Kyoto process failed to overwhelm interests, partly because the attempt to create an institutional consensus was also mixed up with various interests, partly because – despite these efforts – the science was inconclusive, and partly because even settled science neither suggests nor demands any particular response and thus has limited power to produce a policy consensus. We make reference throughout to examples of peer-reviewed science which point to possible sources of error in the IPCC consensus. We explore the development of the IPCC in Chapter 6, arguing that the body institutionalizes not just a scientific consensus, but a certain kind of consensus intended to produce a certain kind of policy response. We provide some examples of this in Chapter 7, before arguing in Chapter 8 for our conclusion: that reliance on strong normative and causal discourse in the Kyoto process, rather than helping produce a consensus in favour of a workable response to climate change, actually contributed to an outcome widely seen as disappointing.

NOTE

1. Trofim Lysenko rejected the 'dangerous Western concepts' of Mendelian and Darwinian genetics and evolution in favour of somewhat bizarre Lamarckian views that, under a socialist system, cows could be trained to give more milk and their offspring would then inherit these traits (see Cole, 1983). Heisenberg's uncertainty principle had received similarly short shrift in Soviet science. Claus and Bolander (1977) have noted the key features of Lysenkoism which can be seen in the politicized science of today: a necessity to demonstrate the practical relevance of science to the needs of society; the amassing of evidence as substitute for causal proof as the means of demonstrating the 'correctness' of the hypotheses; ideological zeal supplanting devotion to science, so that dissidents could be silenced as enemies of the truth. Manipulating data to support the ideological cause was permissible, since this was a higher truth.

2. The international environmental policy process: increasing complexity and implementation failure

Robert Putnam (1988) once characterized the problem faced by governments as international actors as being that they had to play 'two-level games'. They simultaneously have to play at two boards, but each with its own logic and set of rules: the international arena, where treaties are negotiated, and the domestic arena, where treaties are ratified.

We suggest that climate change negotiations are incomparably more complex than this. Putnam was writing from a top-down, United States perspective, where the separation of powers at the federal level is a significant factor. The executive branch of government can sign treaties, but they can be ratified only if supported by a substantial majority in the legislative branch of government (by a two-thirds majority of the Senate). Nevertheless, the politics of ratification is important for even those nations where such formal scrutiny by the legislature is not present. This is because the decisional logic that might carry negotiators to the point of consensus in the international arena might also take them some distance beyond the preferred national position when viewed subsequently in the cold light of day.

Putnam was also writing predominantly about what Hoffman (1966) referred to as 'high politics', or politics concerning the very existence of the state: defence, foreign policy, law and order. Such issues relate primarily to undertakings by states themselves, that is with immediate power to behave in a particular way as actors in the international arena. Little further action is required beyond the stage of ratification, except for states to adopt the required behaviour as international actors, respect the borders of others, and occasionally go to war. Increasingly, however, international politics deals with matters of international regulation, or what Hoffman referred to as 'low politics'. Agreements of this kind require much more than ratification and compliance by a single state: the adoption of domestic legislation to put in place policies to deliver on international commitments, and the subsequent implementation of those policies to produce desired outcomes. Both stages may arouse major domestic challenges and divert large amounts of national resources to unwanted policy realms.

In addition, and of major importance to the intensity of political processes, is the simple fact that 'Nature' cannot act for itself. Nature's 'interests' are by no means clear but must enter negotiations entirely through the perceptions of those human groups that make it to the negotiation table. This makes diverse ideas about the natural world, its value, vulnerability and, for some people, even its 'rights', part of intergovernmental relations. For decades now, and perhaps most sharply illustrated during the Law of the Sea negotiations of the 1970s, environmental protection has been used as an argument to advance both exclusive sovereignty, the rights of the coastal state for example, and shared sovereignty, over deep ocean resources, for example.

As part of 'low politics', it therefore makes sense to talk of an international policy process that encompasses much more than just decision-making at the international level plus the politics of ratification. Environmental issues are the foremost example of the need for this approach, and not just because non-governmental organizations (NGOs) are active at most levels and stages of this international policy process. It also no longer makes much sense to talk only in terms of whether in international arenas states are willing to allow 'interdependency norms' to prevail over 'sovereignty norms'. Many writers (for example, Mitchell, 1998, 275) still account for the development of MEAs in these terms, but agreements like the FCCC and the Kyoto Protocol contain features which can no longer be accounted for thus. They attempt the detailed specification, monitoring and even enforcement of policy instruments at the international level and, beyond mere ratification, the adoption and implementation of domestic policy measures which will give effect to these agreed policies. The question is not just whether states are prepared notionally to set aside sovereignty here, but whether they will in the end be prepared to ratify the MEA, adopt the implicit policies it requires, and then implement faithfully those requirements. This raises the issue of the internal powers, the capacity of states to comply, and at times even understand the obligations entered into, as well as the implications for international relations of the development of global enforcement regimes.

Marvin Soroos's (1986) 'global policy framework' illuminates many of the developments and processes occurring at the international level for which conventional theories of international relations – with their focus on power relations between states – have been unable to account. This framework consists of three elements familiar to students of the policy process at the domestic level: the global agenda, which focuses on the factors which affect the development of international agendas (and issue definition); global policy processes, which focus on actors, processes and arenas within which policy-making is conducted; and the global response, which examines policy outputs, compliance and effectiveness (what in policy studies would be called implementation and evaluation). Most states are reluctant to cede sovereignty to international treaty secretariats or other intergovernmental organizations (IGOs) to undertake implementation. Developing countries in particular are sensitive to anything which hints of neo-colonialism and during the negotiation of the Montreal Protocol opposed giving the secretariat power to make on-site inspections on its own initiative (Kosken-niemi, 1996, 243). In the negotiation related to the 'flexible mechanisms' of the Kyoto Protocol, these same countries insisted that the definition of sus-tainable development would rest with them individually. The nation-state is thus important not just for ratifying treaties, a process which is necessary for them to enter *into effect*, but for taking actions (passing laws and providing administrative machinery) to *make them effective*. International policy outputs are little more than pieces of paper, accompanied perhaps by some resources to assist developing countries.

All this exposes the inadequacy of Putnam's concept of 'two-level games' to account for the development of international regulatory regimes for envi-ronmental issues as examples of 'low politics'. But even Soroos's 'global response' element tends to blur the fact that (with 'low politics' issues) ratifi-cation must be followed by a full round of domestic policy-making, involving both policy adoption and implementation. The 'global response' usually consists of actions by the numerous states' parties to agreements which entail the adoption and implementation of a policy to give effect to the international regulation. Different treaties are more or less proscriptive in detailing how this response should look, leaving states' parties at least some scope for matching responses to their own circumstances.

This chapter argues therefore that for governments dealing with such issues the situation is much more complex and there are at least four levels to the games which must be played. (We could, of course, break the domestic policy process down further into numerous stages using one or other of the models of the policy process, paying attention to the particular nature of each state, its development, natural resource endowment and historical experience – all factors that shape the geopolitics of environmental regime development.) This complexity of 'reality' is central to an understanding of why the results of MEAs have been widely regarded as disappointing, and the distinction between 'policy outputs' and 'policy outcomes' – which in some cases may be decades in the future for environmental outcomes – though usually neglected by the international relations literature, which is commonplace in the public policy literature, is central to our analysis.

We can add to this complexity even further by distinguishing between envi-ronmental outcomes (such as stabilizing climate) and non-environmental ones, usually immediate and expected in the shorter term, closely related to interests and therefore more likely to be the 'drivers' of policy than the uncertain environ-mental aspirations. Often the non-environmental outcomes are driving the politics.

PROBLEMS WITH MULTILATERAL ENVIRONMENTAL AGREEMENTS

Previously, the major concern over MEAs was that they were doomed to move at the speed of the slowest boat and be formulated according to the lowest common denominator (Sand, 1990). This causes many scholars to view sovereignty as the cause of the environmental *problematique* (see, for example, van der Lugt, 2000), but holistic talk of 'ecological interdependence' and the need for 'ecological sovereignty' to counter sovereignty as conventionally understood would appear to embody an idealism so far from the current 'world of states' as to be of little assistance in either interpreting the world or, as Marx made the point, changing it. This is not to downplay the importance of interdependency, nor to deny that the state's interests might extend beyond national territory, but we suggest it overstates the prospect that any alternative to sovereignty could yield better environmental outcomes. After all, as far back as Aristotle, it has been acknowledged that that which is of common concern receives the least attention, and there are alternative ways of responding to common pool resources than establishing some overarching global Leviathan in the interests of 'ecological sovereignty' (Ostrom, 1990) – were that prospect even likely.

The slowest boat/lowest common denominator analogy was meant to imply that such agreements took too long to develop and were not sufficiently stringent, given the perceived urgency of the global environmental crisis. The greatest concern now is not that strong measures cannot be developed but that those that are will, in Wynne's (1987, 5) words, 'simply flutter in mid-air as symbolic gestures'. The prospect for effective global environmental governance is not promising. Martti Koskenniemi (1996, 236) has summarized the situation in the following terms:

> the gap between law in books and how states act may now appear wider than at any other time in history – the more rules there are, the more occasion there is to break them. After years of active standard-setting, global and regional organizations stand somewhat baffled in front of a reality that has sometimes little in common with the objectives expressed in the inflated language of their major conventions and declarations.

It is difficult to disagree with this assessment if one surveys the various international instruments which have been concluded since 1972, and it was the prevailing view at the UN General Assembly Special Session to review progress on implementing Agenda 21 held in June 1997 (see Sandbrook, 1997). Contrary to early hopes of environmentalists that their cause would unite the inhabitants of this 'fragile' planet, the experience since seems to suggest continuity of competition for resources. Differential levels of wealth and technology, highly varied resource endowments, including access to environmental sinks, merely add a new dimension of conflict and the need for painful and painstaking negotiations.

Such negotiations also serve other, often purely political objectives and are successful in this regard because the environment is a relatively new issue and is less institutionalized than many issue areas, and there is much use of normative arguments to run other agendas through the relatively unstructured environment arena. Other agendas can thus readily obtrude into the environment arena: in the case of Kyoto, it was in the end about trade, aid and energy competitiveness rather than just about climate change.

There have been some successes, such as the Geneva Convention on Long-range Transboundary Air Pollution (LRTAP) 1979 and its protocols, which have substantially reduced acid rain from sulphur oxides, the emission of volatile organic compounds and particulates, although how much of the apparent success is attributable to international agreements and how much to technological change remains uncertain (Underdahl and Hanf, 2000). The London Dumping Convention and the Convention for the Prevention of Pollution by Ships 1973 (MARPOL) also appear to have delivered improved environmental outcomes. Decisions under the International Convention for the Regulation of Whaling 1946 appear to have saved several whale species from extinction and the Convention for the Protection of the World Cultural and Natural Heritage 1972 has extended protection to numerous sites of natural or cultural importance nominated by national governments for inclusion on the World Heritage list.

David Vogel (1997, 567) has argued that a pattern is now emerging from the considerable scholarly literature on factors that promote effective international environmental governance. He notes that many of the most effective agreements are regional rather than global, and address specific, highly visible and commonly acknowledged problems of cross-border pollution, usually of air or water. They typically involve a limited number of countries, impose costs on only a few industries and affect primarily countries generously endowed with financial resources and administrative capacity. The examples he gives of relatively successful MEAs are Montreal, LRTAP, MARPOL (London), the Oslo, Helsinki and Paris Commissions, and the Mediterranean Action Plan. Among those rated as less successful by Vogel have been the Convention on International Trade in Endangered Species, the International Tropical Timber Agreement, the Bonn Convention on Migratory Species, and the Convention on Biological Diversity. All these have required parties to bear substantial internal costs, including political ones. In contrast, we note that there have been behind-the-scenes attempts to suppress any discussions of the regional aspects of climate change under the Kyoto Protocol in the belief that this might reduce perceptions of a common threat, with some areas gaining (the Arctic, for example, and even the UK, where a bit less rain and more sunshine would be appreciated, or more winter rain in Australia).

There have been problems, even with the more successful instruments. The Montreal Protocol is widely seen as having slowed the destruction of the ozone layer and an end to the problem is apparently now in sight. However, its 'double standards' provisions permitted continuation of the use of ozone-depleting substances in developing countries, and there are frequent reports of a large black market in illegal CFC refrigerants smuggled from exempt countries and sold in those industrialized countries where they have been phased out. Nevertheless, the apparent success of Montreal led many, rather unwisely, to see it as a model for future development of MEAs, most particularly for the development of responses to the prospect of climate change. For example, as we noted in Chapter 1, Mustafa Tolba, Executive Director of UNEP when the Montreal Protocol was being negotiated, stated that the mechanisms designed for the Protocol would very likely become the blueprint for the institutional apparatus for climate change.

The Montreal negotiating process demonstrated the four characteristics which Brenton (1994, 252–9) has described as being the four 'forces for cohesion' in international environmental politics (and which we noted in Chapter 1): the use of 'toe in the door' negotiating processes such as framework conventions and subsequent protocols; reliance upon science and epistemic communities; the influence of environmental non-government organizations (ENGOs); and what he terms 'environmental altruism', often responding to ethical justifications which are difficult to resist. The force of moralistic rhetoric has undoubtedly been enhanced by the linkage between environment and development forged by the Brundtland Report and the use of the discourse of 'sustainable development'. The latter replaced the largely unsuccessful 'north–south' rhetoric of the 1970s, so that many MEAs now have double standards provisions and provisions for 'capacity building', 'technology transfer' and 'clean development mechanisms'. The Global Environmental Facility, for example, almost assumes that, by providing highly directed environmental aid, it is thereby advancing sustainable development (Boehmer-Christiansen and Young, 1997). This has transformed the discourse of many MEA negotiations into one containing a higher level of redistributive rhetoric; but, while it has perhaps helped enhance the pace of negotiating processes, it has done little to improve the quality of the policy instruments produced. Rather, in the case of the Convention on the Law of the Sea and the Basel Convention, and now the Kyoto Protocol, this emphasis on redistributive obligations has excluded the USA, which has declined to ratify these instruments.

Ambivalent Science

Brenton (1994, 255) notes that the use of science (sometimes distorted for effect) is important – that 'the power of a united scientific view to push even unwilling governments into action is now one of the key mechanisms of international environmental cooperation'. We do not deny this, but raise questions about the possible misuse of science. The danger here clearly is that if this significance of science is accepted, then such a united view may be created or constructed for the sake of agreement, thus harming scientific research as well as policy. The use of ecocentric and biocentric interpretations of ethics by environmental NGOs in particular (Laferrière, 1996), but increasingly also by environmental bureaucracies, means that the power of science and that of ethical arguments have become dangerously related. However, ecocentrism is not easily brought into harmony with the desires and procedures of international political processes which may well be strong enough to use (or even misuse) these systems of ethics rather than being 'converted' by them.

Central to this understanding of what facilitates the development of MEAs is the significance accorded to the building of epistemic consensus concerning science and policy (P. Haas, 1990). The Intergovernmental Panel on Climate Change was therefore accorded a central place in the development of the Framework Convention on Climate Change, with the parties committing themselves to future action on the basis of future IPCC findings. IPCC pronouncements have indeed been closely synchronized with FCCC-related negotiations, with the 'concern' expressed by its spokesmen and hence the threat image generated by some of its model scenarios intensifying as the obstacles to agreement increased (see Chapters 6 and 7). While under Article 2 of FCCC, the parties committed to no more than a vague undertaking to stabilize concentrations of GHGs at a level which would prevent dangerous anthropogenic interference with the climate system, they also committed to review their commitments at the First Conference of the Parties (COP-1) in Berlin in 1995 and regularly thereafter in the light of the best available scientific information. Having undertaken such a review they are *legally bound* (under Article 4.2(d)) to take appropriate action which may include the adoption of amendments to the commitments. The Berlin Mandate which led to the negotiation of the Kyoto Protocol was thus effectively decided by the IPCC rather than the COP.

This technique of toe-in-the door negotiating processes involves using devices known as 'creative ambiguity' and 'iterative functionalism' in framework agreements (Feldman, 1995), which allow parties to sign vague, open-ended commitments that may be hardened over time, for example, as new knowledge emerges. This has undoubtedly politicized the science of climate change, in contrast to Montreal, where a greater degree of scientific consensus emerged over a decade and on an issue that was much simpler and less dependent on the creation of institutions designed to produce a consensus.

We argue here that this politicization of 'global warming' science limited the power of epistemic consensus and this in turn allowed interests to play a more significant and divisive role. Further, much of the political force of the scientific consensus has relied upon the use of arguments derived from the precautionary principle to overcome the uncertainties and gaps in knowledge, but such a principle has many subjective interpretations, with the degree of precaution selected varying according to interests. The effect was that science, *contra* E.B. Haas (1990), was able to do less to redefine interests than might have happened had its case been stronger and less open to suspicion.

Indeed, subsequent analysis of Montreal has also stressed the much more significant role played by interests in the development of that MEA (Sprinz and Vaahtoranta, 1994), such that epistemic consensus is perhaps better seen as a necessary but by no means a sufficient condition for the successful development of an MEA. For example, central to the change in position of the USA in the negotiation of the Montreal Protocol was the awareness that US chemical manufacturers held patents on substitutes for CFCs (Sebenius, 1992; Sprinz and Vaahtoranta, 1994, 94). There was a similar pattern with negotiations on acid rain, in which Germany and Sweden represented 'third party interests', since both had substantial environmental industries for the removal of sulphur emissions and subsequently became major exporters of these technologies on the European market (Boehmer-Christiansen and Skea, 1993).

There are some sceptical voices about the potential of science to serve as the basis of agreement in international politics, including our own (Skolnikoff, 1993). Waterton and Wynne (1996, 422) have suggested that science is an ambiguous force for both alienation and standardization, yet is also a source of binding authority, and that this is especially evident in the environmental policy domain, 'an issue whose ostensibly scientific character is enriched with human symbolic meanings and energies'. There is a temptation in international negotiations to seek common ground in science as the 'global' authority it seems to embody cannot be questioned. This is to overcome the tensions created because norms, interests and institutions vary considerably between nations, as do levels of affluence. The latter are likely to influence whether concern is greater, for example, for infectious diseases such as malaria, or for peregrine falcons which might be affected by insecticides such as DDT (see Kellow, 1999). Local differences and idiosyncrasies (and perceptions of environmental risk) make for divisions between nations and the 'universalistic frameworks of science and modernity' that hold out the promise of consensus (Waterton and Wynne, 1996, 422; see also Boehmer-Christiansen, 1999b).

Waterton and Wynne also note that 'quantification' and 'objectification' can provide a kind of abstraction from the 'messy and deeply complex contextual factors' which could equally be described as political, structural, cultural and institutional factors. In support of their view they cite Porter (1995, 86), who has argued that: 'The remarkable ability of numbers and calculations to defy disciplinary and even national boundaries and link academic to political discourse owes much to this ability to bypass deep issues.' But the power of numbers, science and technical frameworks to provide a unifying discourse is much diminished when interests are closer to the surface and the numbers are revealed as 'spin'.

The advantages of this 'superficiality through science' in reducing complexity may reflect political weakness rather than technocratic influence, and clearly there are limits to its force, particularly in the face of powerful interests.

INFLUENCE OF INTERESTS AND THE INTERNATIONAL POLICY PROCESS

Interests are accepted as a motivating factor in many approaches to politics, and 'interests' is usually taken to refer to pecuniary stakes (profitability, market access, job opportunities, compliance, fiscal, and so on) – all legitimate and related to human well-being rather than of just immediate benefit to a company or corporate actor.

The influence of those motivated by interests is not spread evenly throughout the international environmental policy process, a factor which is important in understanding the differences between our four arenas. While, as Lindblom (1977) has suggested, business enjoys a 'privileged position' in politics, this privilege has in the past at least been confined mostly to the domestic level and does not transfer well to the international level. This rather simple and obvious point is often overlooked in accounts of the development of treaties such as Kyoto, but it has profound consequences for an understanding of the international environmental policy process.

Lindblom's analysis of the power of business identifies three factors which give it such a degree of influence that he concludes it enjoys a privileged position. The first factor relates to the structural dependence of the state on business. Structural dependence theory suggests that the state enjoys a degree of autonomy from business power but in a market system is structurally dependent on private sector profitability. State managers depend on popular support and legitimacy, which in turn depends on jobs and prosperity in the private sector and the ability to fund government programmes from taxation revenue. In an era of globally mobile capital, states have to compete with each other to attract investment, and thus are driven 'to act on behalf of, rather than at the behest of, business' (Levy and Egan, 1998, 342) which gives business its 'privileged position'. International organizations are not subject to these structural dependencies and are not as open to influence. For this reason, they make less attractive targets for business influence, and when business does exert its influence in international negotiations it may come too late, and so it seeks to try to contest regulation at the national level (ibid., 343; Kellow, 2002).

The UN bureaucracy is not directly dependent for revenues upon healthy national economies and is above any competition to attract capital; it is thus insulated from the economic consequences of international policies to the extent that this is a source of concern to some observers (Levy and Egan, 1998, 347). Levy and Egan note that despite the vast resources potentially available to business groups, their influence has not thus far overwhelmed that of environmental NGOs at international negotiations (ibid., 45). Their influence is also weakened by the diversity of industry interests which often prevents business from acting as a cohesive bloc (ibid., 346). While the rhetoric in environmental politics at the international level is often redistributive and accentuated by linkage with development issues, the policies adopted are usually regulatory – in the terminology of Theodore J. Lowi (1964) – and thus they frequently divide business along sectoral lines; peak business groups such as the International Chamber of Commerce are frequently thus split. Even within sectors the interests of coal, oil and gas producers are substantially different when confronted by climate change policies, since they each give rise to progressively fewer emissions, with fuel demand switching to gas providing the easiest way of achieving substantial emission reductions.

The second factor to which Lindblom attributes the superior bargaining resources held by business at the domestic level is its command over the knowledge and practical expertise which is necessary to the development and implementation of effective policy. Only business possesses the detailed knowledge, both technical and economic, which is crucial to the success of any policy. Governments, for example, usually know very little about the cost curves confronted by industry and are therefore unable to predict the response and therefore what the outcome of any policy measure might be. But IGOs are not responsible for implementation, which must be undertaken by national governments, so this form of leverage is also diminished in the international arena. Indeed, the implementation of MEAs is an area of considerable concern.

Finally, Lindblom argues that business has a superior ability to mobilize resources when compared with other groups. This factor does not appear to hold with international environment politics, where NGOs have substantial budgets which not only are comparable to or larger than those of business groups, but are also larger than intergovernmental organizations, such as UNEP, and which may come from governments seeking allies. In part, this unwillingness of business to commit resources in the international arena probably reflects other factors which make this arena less propitious than the domestic route (Kellow, 2000, 2002; Boehmer-Christiansen, 1999a). Returns on funds invested in political activity are likely to be higher at the domestic level for business, so it is less likely to invest internationally. But regardless, as we shall show later, environment NGOs are by no means the poor relations of business when it comes to the resources they can bring to bear in international politics.

For all these reasons, environment NGOs have been the more effective transnational actors than are individual corporations, sectoral groups or peak business associations. NGOs advocate international regulation because they recognize that many states would not take strong action without international agreement because of the structural dependence of the state on capital, and unilateral action is likely to result in high costs for little environmental benefit (Levy and Egan, 1998, 355). And, although this ignores Vogel's (1995) analysis of the *advantages* which might lie in a 'first mover' strategy if only domestic approaches can subsequently be successfully internationalised, at the international level the balance of influence appears to have remained with the NGOs, possibly because of their close links with the media and a greater general trust by the public in their pronouncements. For this reason, business groups can frequently be found supporting international regulations which internationalize their domestic regulatory disadvantage. This either ensures that international competitors face the same disadvantage or that export opportunities are created for those who can meet the new international standards because they have been required to do so domestically. As Sandbrook (1997, 649) notes, transnational corporations often want rules to be harmonized, and have an interest in spreading effective international regulation to maintain competitiveness (to avoid being undercut on environmental costs). Rather than deploying a moralistic discourse which has the effect of excluding business, he sees a need to 'bring the private sector into the discourse'. But the temptation to marginalize or even demonize business can be strong, and while this might make broad agreement more achievable, it does not bode well for the development of workable, practicable policy.

With climate change, we suggest that this picture is not quite accurate, because business interests are more diverse than with many other MEAs. There are business interests (such as gas, nuclear and renewables) which are advantaged by policies to restrict the emission of CO_2 so that the obvious disadvantage for business as represented by, say, coal producers is not the whole picture (see Chapter 3). Indeed, strong principled discourses in favour of action on climate change may privilege and enhance the power of some business interests.

Environment NGOs are more likely than business groups to be international actors not only because the arena is less propitious for its business opponents, but because it is also more favourable for them. Formal provision for NGOs is made within the UN system, with Article 71 of the UN Charter providing for 'suitable arrangements' to be made for consultation with NGOs concerned with matters within its competence. Economic and Social Council (ECOSOC) Resolution 1296 (XLIV) of 23 May 1968 governs these arrangements (Willetts, 1982). The UN now even recognizes NGOs which are active in only one country

(Willetts, 2000). The international arena is more favourable to NGOs because the functions they can perform for IGOs translate into influence and income. ENGOs are able to provide lobbying and information and arguments not just at international meetings, but at the national level, where UNEP cannot lobby without violating Article 2(7) of the Charter, which forbids intervention in matters essentially within the domestic jurisdiction of any member state.

Even without this impediment to domestic-level lobbying in its constitution, however, it is doubtful whether UNEP possesses either the resources or the capacity to be effective in such a role since it faces problems of severe overload. The transnational activities of ENGOs are, for this reason, important to the development of MEAs, and, whatever the motivations of ENGOs, they assist UNEP greatly by being able to campaign for proposals in areas where UNEP cannot go. Princen and Finger (1994, 5–6) point out that NGO participation in the development of the Montreal Protocol (and subsequent MEAs) was actively encouraged by UNEP, and the same pattern can be found with other MEAs such as Basel and Climate Change. Willetts (1996) has shown how they were quite deliberately harnessed by Secretary-General Maurice Strong at both the Stockholm and Rio conferences, and then how access was limited post-Rio in the Commission for Sustainable Development.

At the international level, therefore, the relative advantage of environment and business groups tends to be the *reverse* of that which obtains at the domestic level. Business interests have good relations with some national delegations in the climate change arena, but these are based primarily on congruence of interests between industries and nation-states (Levy and Egan, 1998, 344). The climate change case, according to Levy and Egan (ibid., 348), suggests that, while business is active at the international level in trying to influence regulatory outcomes, 'such action in this arena, rather than eclipsing the national state, is largely channelled through it, and is frequently directed toward blocking strong international action'.

The environment NGOs also enjoy an advantage in 'discursive power' in the international arena, where 'blame and shame' rhetoric (and even moral blackmail) is often employed, assisted by the linkage forged with international redistributive politics. Sandbrook (1997, 646) has noted that in the Commission for Sustainable Development, 'attendance is made up of environment ministries or the UN representatives who play out the same games in every forum. There is very little evidence of the finance or big economic players.' Sandbrook is critical of populist writing which tends to portray corporate players always as villains (see, for example, Korten, 1996). Nevertheless, the redistributive discourse dominant at the international level remains much more suited to the tactics of 'blame and shame' used by environment NGOs than are the overtly interest-based claims of business.

Yet the force of moral suasion can be powerful (Shue, 1995). Governments find it difficult to resist rhetorical injunctions to 'save the planet', which 'tends to make politicians and negotiators readier to look for common ground than they would be in other sorts of international negotiation'. Shue (1995, 456) argues that any sharp dichotomy between interests and ethics is misleading, and that 'Ethical judgments are inextricably embedded in international affairs.' Ethical claims, often resting on the false and dangerous assumption that these are universally legitimate, are routinely smuggled into what are advanced as explanations, and they sometimes 'change the outcome of the calculus from what it would have been if only one's own interests, such as national interest, were considered.' Shue warns that we should not assume that interests and ethics always (or even usually) clash: 'When they clash and when they converge upon the same answer, are precisely the questions' (ibid.). Shue notes, however, that much of the power of the environment movement comes from its ethical claim to be 'acting in defence of what they take to be the interests of the environment itself or of elements of the environment, such as endangered species and endangered ecosystems' (ibid., 457–8). This often provides it with a discursive advantage against business, especially as long as the question of who has to pay is not raised. As Walker (1994, 675) notes, it is difficult to specify who actually has the authority to act in the name of rainforests and dolphins, but NGOs have certainly managed to stake a more convincing claim here than business, which is thus marginalized.

This suggests that some of the very factors which are 'forces for cohesion' (especially science-based normative discourses) in international environmental politics might actually be responsible for disappointing outcomes. We appear to be confronting a dilemma involving the 'problem of the slowest boat' and the 'problem of the lowest common denominator'. How may attempts to speed up the convoy be prevented from diminishing the quality of the policies adopted?

This trade-off is likely to occur, however, because the stronger are the principle-based discourses which might force the pace of negotiations, the weaker the position of business interests and thus the instrumental discourses that are usually expected to deliver the solutions. They are already weaker than in the domestic arena because of the lack of influence through structural dependency. Here the lack of responsibility at the international level for implementation becomes so important, for (as Lindblom, 1977 notes) the practical knowledge on which successful implementation depends, would usually translate into influence. Rather, the marginalization of business now adds to the lack of concern with policy realism.

In a subsequent chapter we shall suggest that there is a radical, principle-based discourse in environmental (and climate change) politics which runs parallel to 'mainstream' politics. It is suggested that the main groups of parties in the Kyoto negotiations found it difficult to come to terms because they were essentially operating in these different discourses. But our immediate concern is to try to explain why factors that are widely seen as helping to achieve international consensus might *de facto* diminish the quality of the same agreements. We do so by drawing on the approach of Kenneth Hanf and Arild Underdal.

A MODEL OF THE INTERNATIONAL ENVIRONMENTAL POLICY PROCESS

The international policy process does not end with the signing of an international agreement and neither can its implementation be reduced to a matter of 'ratification' or even 'compliance'. As Hanf and Underdal (1998, 150) note, 'The "implementation game" has more often than not been neglected in studies of international cooperation, or analyzed only in terms of factors encouraging or curbing defections from the agreements entered into.'

Hanf and Underdal base their analysis on two fundamental assumptions: that 'issues determine politics'; and that 'politics determine policy'. They suggest (ibid., 151) that what comes out of a decision-making process will depend on *'who* are involved and *how* decisions are made'. They note that, unlike the issues of 'high politics', the new issues of international regulation, such as environmental problems, are of particular salience to some subgroup or segment of society, and often involve regulation of the behaviour of corporations or citizens. They argue that *scope* and *symmetry* are the significant aspects of problem structure which shape the set of actors, the configuration of preferences and the choice of decision-making arena(s).

Their two *ceteris paribus* assumptions are, first, that as subgroup concentration of the issue salience increases, the involvement of sector agencies and interest organizations tends to increase, while the roles of foreign affairs agencies and to some extent legislatures and political parties tend to decline (scope). This is consistent with a move to Lowi's regulatory policy and away from redistributive policy. Second, the less symmetrical is the impact of a problem on a particular society, the more domestic conflict it is likely to generate, activating a larger number and a broader range of actors, and hence retarding or preventing implementation, or even successful negotiation. Because 'conflict tends to generate its own stakes' this also can move issues upwards to higher levels in organizational hierarchies (ibid., 153).

Data from Norway and Sweden support the first assumption, but have less to say about the second. The existence of conflict seemed to be a major factor in determining the involvement of political parties, 'idealistic' NGOs and *ad hoc* campaigns in international affairs, but *not* for business and labour NGOs, which appeared to thrive slightly better in 'calm waters'.

Looking at the climate change issue, Hanf and Underdal distinguish four stages of policy-making at the international level:

1. Consensual problem 'diagnosis' takes place. (We agree that this stage is important but do not see why this should be 'consensual'; whether this is the case will depend very much on the nature of the problem and the scope of any proposed solutions.) A common understanding that 'something must be done' may develop. 'Cures' at this stage are described in only general terms and the domestic impact of emerging alternatives is hard to determine. Environmental agencies predominate and problem definition is often linked to the research agendas of science institutions.
2. Negotiations get under way. A broader range of agencies is brought in to develop and consider options and the foreign affairs agency is likely to conduct the negotiations. It is at this stage that the providers of potential 'solutions' may have a major effect on directing policy, and this may add to the direction already suggested by research. We will refer to the 'unholy' alliance between research science and technological solutions already available, but possibly uncompetitive without policy assistance.
3. As the negotiations move beyond the framework convention stage, attention will shift to specific policy measures and instruments, the societal impact of which will be more determinate and differential. Specialized domestic agencies and interest organizations will see their interests as substantially affected and are likely to claim a more substantial role in policy-making. Consideration of implementation intrudes into policy-making.
4. Implementation: domestic agencies might succeed in taking over much of the action and the problem might be redefined. What started out as a 'grand design' to control GHGs is likely to become a matter of energy pricing or industrial restructuring, new energy taxes, and new or shifting subsidies.

Especially because international negotiations proceed slowly, we argue that these stages should not be seen as strictly sequential; in fact they frequently take place simultaneously, though not with equal impact, on national negotiations – again with national and intergovernmental bureaucracies as gatekeepers.

Hanf and Underdal suggest that implementation of internationally agreed policies to reduce GHG emissions in future requires the development of policy measures which will tend to involve concentrated costs and distributed benefits – the variant of Lowi's regulatory policy which can be referred to as regulation in the public interest (see Kellow, 1988). This may well produce the pattern of implementation labelled 'symbolic policy' by Edelman (1964), since the common good (in this case the global common good) is poorly represented, while business again enjoys its privileged position at the national level. Hanf and Underdal note that such policies are least likely to be adopted and implemented, unless the issue takes on symbolic significance and becomes the subject of strong political mobilization. They note that the remoteness in time of the benefits of environmental protection compared with the immediacy of the costs exacerbates this problem. But we would add that not all immediate impacts are costs, and there are also many possible benefits: revenue for government, bureaucratic turf battles to be won, larger research budgets, and so on. Where these immediate benefits are strong or even already realized nationally such parties are more likely to support the advancement of MEAs.

What Hanf and Underdal further fail to consider, however, is that the discourse of international processes can have a higher symbolic content than that at the domestic level. If so, this will help extend and reinforce this vertical asymmetry between international and domestic arenas and *de facto* aim at little more than redistributing political-bureaucratic power at this level between inter-governmental bodies and between national bureaucracies. They do note, however, that (at least for some kinds of international problems) there is a risk of what Underdal (1979, 7) had earlier called a *vertical disintegration of policy*: 'a state of affairs where the aggregate thrust of "micro-decisions" deviates more or less substantially from what higher-order policy goals and "doctrines" would seem to require' (Hanf and Underdal, 1998, 157).

Hanf and Underdal (ibid., 159) suggest that implementation is a *third* level to be added to Putnam's two, with its own political logic and dynamics, which might cause *involuntary* defection by states from their international obligations through lack of state capacity (both political and administrative), and that such defections might be as frequent and as interesting as deliberate 'cheating'. They subsequently make reference to *three* stages of policy-making at the domestic level: ratification, translation into national legislation, then implementation (ibid., 161). We consider that implementation concerns directly and immediately shape ratification – and, indeed, impact upon the negotiation process itself, with the likelihood of ratification increasing the degree of scrutiny given to negotiating proposals. Hanf and Underdal (ibid., 162) argue that:

> Each of these sets of decisions will be the focus of political interest and pressure from those sectors in society for which the agreement entails costs and benefits. Each phase can involve a different pattern of interaction among governmental and societal actors.

These three domestic stages can be added to the three they identify in the international 'policy adoption' process, so that they are in effect suggesting that the making of policy on the regulatory issues of 'low politics' such as climate change involves the playing out of 'games' at *six* levels. The argument here is that the dynamics of the arena within which international environmental policies are initiated have characteristics (reliance on scientific simplification and moral suasion) which produce asymmetry with the development of detailed policy responses. They do so because they marginalize the very interest-based players on whose participation (and instrumental discourse) the crafting of a detailed, workable and politically acceptable policy instrument actually depends.

This carries through to the (domestic) arena in which these policies must be given effect. The asymmetry is likely to be highest when the moral suasion and scientific reductionism, which might well be functional during initiation, spill over into the arena where policy development occurs, further marginalizing those interests whose effective participation is likely to be needed to inject some policy realism. There is then a danger that such policies will suffer from implementation failure and are likely to contain flaws which will result in unanticipated (and even counterproductive) consequences.

We therefore suggest a model of six-level games if the three domestic stages of Hanf and Underdal are added to the three they describe at the international level. Each of these could be further broken down in accordance with any number of policy process models, but it seems preferable that we provide some simplification in the interests of parsimony.

At the international level, the key distinction would appear to be that between policy initiation, where science and morality combine to increase the pressure on parties to negotiate, and international policy adoption, where the practical knowledge possessed by economic actors would be beneficial. Unfortunately, there is substantial scope for these actors to be discursively disenfranchised if the strong moral tone of initiation and framework convention spills over into policy adoption or protocol development (unless, of course, they can join the discourse because it advantages their interests). Business groups that are discursively disadvantaged, in these circumstances, may be tempted to effectively withdraw from the field and save their efforts for the domestic arena, where business occupies its privileged position – unless its interests are aligned with the positions advanced by the thrust of negotiations.

But this assumes that there is a conflict between economic interests and environmental goals, and central to the argument in this book is the point that this need not be the case and rarely is, once the non-environmental impacts of policies are considered, since they include subsidies, competitive advantage, market access, new opportunities to employ people or new legal competences. The Kyoto negotiations promised relative (if not absolute) advantage for some parties, and normative and scientific arguments thus worked to the advantage of their net interests. Such parties were encouraged to continue the moralistic and scientific discourse that would ultimately weaken productive negotiations. The structure of normative arguments and scientific simplification offered the temptation of a hegemonic position to these interests (principally the European Union) in the negotiations and thus heightened the vertical disintegration of climate policy.

Ratification, domestic policy adoption and policy implementation must occur in a setting where business may be more influential relative to environmental NGOs than for international policy adoption. This vertical imbalance between the international policy adoption and domestic policy implementation arenas, where it occurs, encourages disappointing outcomes in international environmental policy, as policies continue to be adopted in processes where reductionism, moral suasion and constructive ambiguity can produce agreement at the expense of practicality. As we noted in Chapter 1, ambiguity has long been seen as *destructive* to effective policy outcomes at the domestic level; its positive potential in assisting consensus at the international level poses a dilemma. But, worse still, we suggest that the very prospect of implementation failure can assist the development of international consensus.

In the European Union, environment ministers are often relatively weak members of the cabinets of national governments, and returning from Brussels or some other negotiation with a new international requirement (regardless of whether there is any commitment to implement it) tends to give them leverage against their economic colleagues or promise new competences that may be removed from subnational levels. There may thus be some unreality about many commitments which conflict with, rather than coincide with, economic interests of the EU members and other parties likely to be represented by environment ministries and foreign affairs officials, rather than including economic agencies. In contrast, other countries (such as Australia and the UK) develop whole-of-government negotiating positions from the outset, either because they have net interests in a rules-based international order (Australia) or because such behaviour is the accepted norm (UK). In both cases, such states will tend to implement what they accede to; they will therefore tend to be much harder-nosed negotiators, and differences in domestic constitutional arrangements will make different demands upon them. Canada, for example, requires unanimity among the provinces before it can ratify any treaty, and this will cause problems with Kyoto because of the oil and gas interests of provinces like Alberta. In the UK, on the other hand, there must be unanimity between ministries, but local authorities are not consulted.

CONCLUSION

While the processes by which MEAs are developed and perhaps eventually implemented could be specified in multi-stage process models derived from the public policy literature, it seems that we can account for the outcomes widely considered to be disappointing, at least to environmentalists and some bureaucracies, with a simpler model, warning, however, that it might require reinterpretation and adjustment for specific cases.

With this model, we propose that by means of reducing environmental problems to their scientific components, stripped as much as possible of the contextual detail (which is likely to divide nations) and combining these with the persuasiveness of moral arguments, the international policy process is initially assisted. However, this alone is much less likely to overwhelm interests in later policy development, especially when these concern major future impacts and investments and when we deal with virtual (forecast) rather than real, experienced problems. Precaution remains a dubious aid to agreement here, especially as domestic 'games' must also be negotiated successfully if good outcomes are to result. As the time and domestic politics dimensions become much stronger, permanent intergovernmental institutions may well be needed, with resources, to keep the ship afloat and moving anywhere. However, this is not easy to achieve as many economic interests are disadvantaged at the international level and are less likely to invest in political activity at that level than at the domestic level. If they are excluded from the international policy adoption game – the very process where their practical knowledge is most needed – they are more likely to withdraw to a game where they enjoy greater advantage and seek to block domestic policy adoption and implementation.

We hope to show that this pattern is apparent in the FCCC and Kyoto Protocol, where powerful economic interests are at stake but remain disunited, as some expect to benefit from implementation. It is also apparent in the amendment to the Basel Convention, which bans trade for recycling. Here the moral arguments mounted by NGOs were particularly powerful, with few willing to contest the claims of 'toxic colonialism' and support the view that such trade was an important source of secondary raw materials for many developing countries. Yet this factor and extensive domestic-level lobbying have at the time of writing restricted ratifications of the amendment to only 25, including both the European Union and seven of its members (Kellow, 1999).

This contrasts with the latest developments in the regional Geneva Convention LRTAP where, combined with EU directives, interests in tightening and widening regulations are now shared among governments. These developed over time, as 'cleaner technology' options with trade potentials have appeared, and NGO pressure and public attention have both largely ceased. New pollutants have been included without major public debates.

The blame and shame tactics employed by environment NGOs, calling business interests 'reptiles' or 'climate killers' (in the case of climate change negotiations) or 'toxic criminals' (in the case of Basel) might create advantage for these actors, and might even facilitate the conclusion of a framework agreement – but at considerable cost: the exclusion of those whose practical insights, whose instrumental discourse, might improve the quality of the policy instrument and who are likely to exercise their considerable power in domestic games to produce subsequent implementation failure if they are marginalized.

Yet, even with the Basel Convention and the Geneva Convention, strong moral discourse worked to the advantage of some economic interests. For example, bans of the export of hazardous waste amounted to the equivalent of trade protection for domestic waste processing industries; and the increasing costs of burning coal were to the advantage of gas and nuclear power, both keen either to enter or to remain in the market place at that time. This dimension of environmental policy measures, advantaging interests rather than amounting only to disadvantage for economic interests, is even more marked with climate change, as we shall see.

The answer to the problem of how to improve outcomes from MEAs would appear to be to redress this vertical asymmetry – to find ways of getting better participation by business in international arenas while enhancing the participation of environment groups at the domestic level – as well as getting the science, if not right, then at least less biased, so that interested parties and principle-based actors cannot misuse uncertain knowledge for their own, conflicting ends as easily as in this case.

3. Energy interests, opportunities and uneven burden-sharing

In order to understand why the Kyoto process ran into the sand it is necessary to consider critically what was at stake: how various interests were impacted by the Protocol, what Kyoto sought to achieve, and what the chances were of achieving the commitments contained within it.

Kyoto, if ratified, will make very little difference to future accumulation of GHGs and thus the possibility of anthropogenic climate change. However, it is meant to be only a first step, and the need for the other steps leading to very much greater net emission reduction must be considered. Very profound changes in human life styles and consumption patterns would be needed and/or major technological changes world-wide. Who is to accomplish such change in politically acceptable ways and would the benefits be worth the costs and pains? Or is the climate threat intended to be no more than an incentive for these first small steps with unknown regional impacts?

One model-based estimate was that by 2100 Kyoto would reduce an increase in mean global temperatures of 2.1°C by a mere 0.2°C – a very small difference indeed. To achieve this insignificant result, it would have shaved perhaps 2 percentage points off growth in GDP in Annex I countries (Annex I includes the industrial nations – essentially the OECD members plus the former Soviet Union and Eastern Bloc) – a sizable amount over 100 years, and about $250–500 per capita per annum. If Kyoto is an insurance policy, it will be an expensive one. Richard Lindzen (2001) has put it that: 'If we view Kyoto as an insurance policy, it is a policy where the premium appears to exceed the potential damages, and where the coverage extends to only a small fraction of the potential damages.'

To put this in perspective, the annual opportunity cost of Kyoto would have been perhaps as much as $350 billion: a sum which might have been spent on adaptation, or on buying goods and services, perhaps those produced by developing countries and thus assisting their economic development. Or it could have been used to wipe out the debt of the 41 poorest countries (*The Times*, 19 July 2001). Just $70 billion could give all Third World inhabitants access to basic necessities such as health, education, clean water and sanitation (*Guardian*, 16 August 2001). But the impact would have varied between Annex I parties and between industrial sectors. As we shall see, these interests were significant in that national positions were reflective of these variations, and also of various opportunities Kyoto provided for enhancing competences or justifying revenue measures.

Significantly, there were marked differences between the costs for the European Union (EU) and those for the other parties, such as the USA, Japan, Canada, Australia and New Zealand, which formed themselves into a negotiating group known as the 'Umbrella Group'. EU Environment Commissioner Margot Wallström reported that a Commission study indicated that compliance for the EU would cost it only 0.06 per cent of GDP, and even less if emissions trading were allowed (*Frankfurter Allgemeine Zeitung*, 17 July 2001). It is not important whether this analysis was accurate, because it is the perceived economic impact which is important in determining negotiating stances, but it is significant that the perceived difference between the EU and the rest of the western industrial nations listed in Annex I of the FCCC (even allowing some discount for Commissioner Wallström's enthusiasm) was *two orders of magnitude*.

It is important to set out the nature of the interests involved in the Kyoto process, and that is the task of the present chapter. It is also important to understand the way in which different parties' national interests were constructed by various factors relating to their economies and energy systems, as well as by their recent histories and the manner in which seemingly arbitrary factors that were built into the structure of the negotiations came to advantage some interests over others. Thus, for example, the use of 1990 as the base year against which future emissions would be measured structured advantage for some actors. It assumed hegemonic significance in the way in which the negotiation proceeded, because it could not effectively be revisited and a more neutral date substituted.

We shall first examine the crucial role of interests in the key withdrawal of the USA from the Kyoto process, and then turn to consider how the restrictions on the emission of CO_2 central to the Protocol would have impacted differentially on different interests. We focus on both the nuclear and fossil fuel industries, making some observations about renewable energy in the process. As we shall show, it is important to distinguish between different kinds of fossil fuels in doing so, because while the popular perception is that all fossil fuel interests are disadvantaged by CO_2 emission reduction policies, some are actually advantaged, at least in what is for climate the short term, but the long term for the normal business planning horizon.

THE FAILURE OF THE KYOTO PROCESS

The Bush Administration's decision to withdraw from the Kyoto process was a triumph of interests over the green ambition of Kyoto. US withdrawal will, however, by lowering the demand for carbon credits, reduce the likely inflow of investment funds to industrializing countries, as a result of the constraints of binding targets and the relative cheapness of emission reduction in some countries, and reduce the expectations of carbon traders and carbon consultants. Clearly, the only nations remotely likely to meet the target without trading were those, such as the UK, Germany, Russia, Ukraine and other economies in transition (EITs), where economic collapse or energy restructuring for thoroughly economic reasons had produced substantial windfall reductions in CO_2 emissions. Any other outcome in future would have required politically impossible interventions in national economies, with political consequences that could not be foretold. In the end, too many hoped to benefit either from global warming itself, and hence had little incentive to act at great cost to themselves, or from current investments in advocated solutions.

Moreover, one of the factors which undermined Kyoto most of all was the low probability that any of the Annex I parties could realistically deliver on their commitments other than by serious economic decline. At the time of the Third Conference of the Parties (COP-3) in Kyoto, US emissions were already almost 10 per cent above 1990 levels, and were rising at about 1.2 per cent per annum. Even in the UK, some future rise was expected again. Given the momentum which comes from long lead times in the energy sector, it was always clear that the USA was unlikely to meet its Kyoto target, which was at least 25–30 per cent and perhaps as much as 40 per cent below 'business as usual' (BAU). Umbrella Group member Australia was already at +17 per cent by 1999 and had been estimated at the time of Kyoto to be heading for +30 per cent by 2010 under BAU. The BAU estimate by the European Commission for the EU was about +6 per cent, meaning that the Kyoto target for the EU was in reality about –14 per cent (Gummer and Moreland, 2000). But this compares with an effective cut of –20 per cent for Australia and around 30 per cent for the USA.

Some EU members were just as badly affected: for example, the Netherlands at +17 per cent in 2000 over 1990 as opposed to the target it has accepted of –7 per cent. There is clearly no way in which the Netherlands would be able to meet its target without emissions trading. A German–Dutch study by the research bodies Ecofys and the Fraunhofer Institute in October 2000 predicted that the EU's emissions would increase by 7–8 per cent on 1990 levels by 2010 compared with the 8 per cent reduction to which it had committed under Kyoto (*Reuters*, 19 October 2000). Within Europe, only the UK was likely to meet its target.

Some parties had an interest in a deal being made, provided there were generous provisions for emissions trading. Russia hoped to make $4 billion per annum by selling rights to 200 million tons of carbon dioxide, for which it would have surplus quotas at $20/ton, although at that time quotas traded on the Chicago market were then fetching only about 10–20 cents/ton (*Moscow Times*,

18 May 2001). Similarly, the potential for credits to be earned through sink creation and management varied enormously between parties. The ratio of all sinks created by human-induced activities to national emissions in 1990 – which gives an indication of the value of sinks to various parties – varied between 1 per cent for the Netherlands to 81 per cent for New Zealand (GACGC, 1998, 6). For Germany the ratio was only 3 per cent.

This points towards there being substantial asymmetries in the distribution of costs and benefits associated with reducing emissions of CO_2 in the energy sectors of parties and in the opportunities each had for gaining credits through sink creation. Where the parties stood on the various issues under negotiation was inevitably going to be affected by where they sat, in terms of interests. The USA withdrawal from Kyoto, therefore, was not just a reflection of lobbying on the part of the fossil fuel industry, as several NGOs have suggested. According to this view, Exxon's $1.2 million contribution to George W. Bush's election campaign is supposed to have been crucial in determining US national interests. The *Guardian*, for example, ran this line under the headline: 'How the high priests of capitalism run roughshod over fears for the planet' (*Guardian*, 19 April 2001).

This view is naively simplistic. Not only does it misrepresent the structural manner in which business power influences governments, but it also overlooks the substantial and very real differences of interest between the USA (and its Umbrella Group partners) and the EU detailed above. It also assumes that fossil fuel interests are undifferentiated, whereas oil is advantaged with respect to coal by Kyoto, gas to oil, nuclear to fossil fuels, and so on. The interests are nowhere near as simple as the *Guardian*'s headline would have us believe and entirely ignores EU desires to reduce its very high, and possibly growing, dependence in energy imports.

Bush's decision was to drive a stake through the heart of Kyoto as far as the USA was concerned. Despite rhetoric to the contrary, his presidential rival Al Gore Jr (had he won the election) would not have effectively done much different, given the hostile nature of the Senate which would have to ratify the Protocol. Kyoto under Gore would have been, as it was under the Clinton Administration, 'undead', hence the 'vampire' metaphor above. But Bush was emboldened both by continuing scientific scepticism, which was more visible in the USA than in Europe, but also by a range of possibilities which, thanks to the US interest position, looked more attractive to him than to any European leader. This was so in a direct political sense, also, because whereas most European governments were of a social democratic complexion and were seeking to harvest the green vote which posed a threat to their hold on power, Bush was a conservative politician who had actually come to power assisted by the green vote. Without the bleeding of support from Gore to Green Party candidate Ralph Nader, Bush most certainly would not have won the 2000 presidential election.

One factor which provided support to Bush's more explicit interest-based approach was an influential paper from one of the leading greenhouse scientists which suggested that the focus on CO_2 and thus energy competitiveness was misplaced and unnecessary. James Hansen, who had done much to get the greenhouse bandwagon rolling in 1988 with his testimony to a congressional hearing, published a joint paper in August 2000 suggesting that, while CO_2 was the main GHG, non-CO_2 GHGs were collectively just as significant, and that it might be easier both technically and economically to reduce emissions of methane, nitrous oxide, CFCs, tropospheric ozone and aerosols such as carbon soot rather than necessarily focusing on emissions of CO_2 (Hansen *et al.*, 2000). This point was made to Bush by Senators Hagel, Helms, Craig and Roberts in their letter to him of 6 March, to which Bush responded on 13 March, foreshadowing his decision to quit Kyoto.

Anthropogenic radiative forcing resulting from increases in well-mixed GHGs from about 1750 to the year 2000 is estimated to be 2.43 Wm^{-2}. Of this 1.46 Wm^{-2} is estimated to come from CO_2, 0.48 Wm^{-2} from methane, 0.34 Wm^{-2} from halocarbons (HFCs substituted for CFCs under the Montreal Protocol plus perfluorocarbons and sulphur hexafluoride), and 0.15 Wm^{-2} from nitrous oxide. In addition, however, the increase in tropospheric ozone has added 0.35 Wm^{-2} and black soot from fossil fuel combustion 0.20 Wm^{-2}. In total therefore, the non-CO_2 forcings amount to 1.52 Wm^{-2}, or about the same as CO_2, which underscores Hansen's point that it might be preferable and more cost-effective to concentrate mitigation efforts on these non-CO_2 factors. Combined with the emerging technology of CO_2 removal and sequestration (already happening in Norway, admittedly helped by a $45/tonne carbon tax) and advances in nuclear energy, Bush could both believe that Kyoto was not the best answer and see economic reasons for so believing.

The Bush Administration's initiatives on climate change, announced in early July 2001, included $120 million for climate research to address the uncertainties highlighted by a National Academies of Science report. It included sink creation schemes in El Salvador, Brazil and Belize. But it also included an agreement with an international team of energy companies (BP-Amoco, Shell, Chevron, Texaco, Pan Canadian, Suncor Energy, ENI, Statoil and Norsk Hydro) to develop technologies for carbon dioxide capture from fossil fuel plants.[1] These options not only appeared reasonable to the Bush administration, they looked preferable to an international agreement which was structured so as to favour the EU, perhaps by as much as two orders of magnitude.

To understand why the interests of the USA and the EU were so markedly different in relation to the proposed Kyoto obligations, we must look at the relative natural energy resource endowments and thus at the politics of nuclear energy and coal in Europe.

RECENT NUCLEAR POLITICS IN EUROPE

It has become questionable whether even Germany, which once claimed for itself the role of environmental vanguard on the climate change issue, had any realistic hope of meeting its target, despite massive subsidies to alternative energy technologies and the imposition of unpopular 'eco-taxes'. The government of Helmut Kohl had set for Germany a target of a reduction of 40 per cent by 2020, but (as we shall see) that was set with the political goal in mind of building support for nuclear energy. Subsequent to Kyoto, a Social Democrat–Green Coalition government was elected in 1998; it did not commit to the Kohl target, but rather to a 25 per cent reduction in CO_2 by 2005, essentially because it was also committed to phasing out nuclear energy and 40 per cent was an even more unrealistic target under that scenario. We shall explore this linkage between climate change and nuclear energy in Germany further below, but Germany was not the only nation in which this linkage was forged.

The Toronto conference on 'The Changing Atmosphere: Implications for Global Security' in 1988 followed a call for a convention by the International Geosphere Biosphere Project (IGBP) and International Council of Scientific Unions (ICSU) scientists at Villach (see Chapter 6). In sponsoring the conference, Canada was advancing two linked agendas, one environmental, the other economic. Canada was concerned about acid rain from SO_2 emissions from across the border in the USA, and a call for action on CO_2 (that is, less coal burning) reinforced their calls for action on acid rain. But Canada also had an economic interest in the nuclear industry which would be advantaged by a sudden move away from fossil fuels. This interest lay in Canada's important place as a major uranium producer, but also as a supplier of this technology, because Canada had developed the CANDU reactor and was eager to develop export markets. European participants at Toronto such as Wolf Häfele were also attracted to this agenda, because anti-nuclearism had become the foundation of the European green movement, especially in German-speaking countries which did not possess nuclear weapons. (France remained aloof.) In Sweden the early anti-acid rain efforts were supported by the Left because the loss of heavy fuel oil in generation was to be replaced as soon as possible by nuclear energy.

Canada had both nuclear technology and uranium for which it sought markets, at home as well as abroad. Ontario Hydro, for example, was seeking approval for a controversial \$65 billion nuclear expansion programme from 1986 in the face of two decades of environmental opposition. The Ontario government had signed long-term take-or-pay uranium contracts in excess of that required by existing reactors costing in excess of $400 million. Energy prices had collapsed in 1986 and the domestic and export market for CANDU reactors was in need of assistance. The nuclear capacity of Ontario Hydro could produce electricity to sell into the US market, which became increasingly open after the conclusion of the North American Free Trade Agreement (NAFTA). Ontario Hydro voluntarily mothballed a thermal power station, simultaneously setting a good example to the USA on acid rain and strengthening the justification for its nuclear programme, and its planners at this time indicated considerable willingness to try to meet the 'Toronto Targets' (Kellow, 1996). Canadian provinces such as Quebec, Manitoba and British Columbia also had substantial hydro resources and saw the USA as a potential market after the conclusion of the Free Trade Agreement.

The nuclear accident at Chernobyl in Ukraine in April 1986 had profound consequences for climate change politics in Germany, because climate change had been inseparable from nuclear politics even before the former became an issue. Surprisingly, Chancellor Schmidt, when opening the European Nuclear Conference in Hamburg in May 1979 (shortly after the nuclear accident at Three Mile Island in the USA, which had threatened to stall German efforts to implement its nuclear programme), stated that he believed that it was conceivable that GHG emissions might soon evoke discussions 'equally as emotional as those about the exact consequences of Harrisburg' (cited by Hatch, 1995, 415). This context was of central importance in the emergence of early concern over global warming in Germany, and the politics certainly ran ahead of the science (see also Cavander and Jäger, 1993). The case against fossil fuels and high sulphur coal in particular was strengthened by the growing alarm over *Waldsterben*, or forest dieback, attributed (if wrongly) to acid rain (Boehmer-Christiansen and Skea, 1991). The Social Democrats and the Greens used a proposed massive expansion in coal-fired capacity as the basis for their commitment to *Ausstieg,* or nuclear phase-out, for their 1988 election platforms, while Kohl's Christian Democrats, long supporters of nuclear power, leapt at the opportunity the threat of climate change provided.

But whereas the coalition partners had opposed nuclear power a decade previously and proposed expansion of the coal sector as an alternative, they were by 2000 committed to phasing out nuclear energy while at the same time cutting CO_2 emissions by a quarter. It was agreed in 2000 that Germany's 19 nuclear stations, generating about a third of its electricity, would be phased out over 25 years. How it could possibly achieve this while reducing CO_2 emissions by a quarter created a credibility problem internationally for Germany, and thus for the European Union.

German credibility was not helped by a statement from Economics Minister Werner Mueller just after the US withdrawal from the Kyoto process that he did not consider the target could be met. Mueller stated: 'Following the atomic

phase-out plan, by 2020 nuclear energy as a primary energy source will prac-
tically be gone. Thus a CO_2 reduction of 40 per cent by 2020 is hardly possible'
(*Reuters*, 2 April 2001). Plans to do so had been based on GDP growth of only
1 per cent per annum, whereas Mueller, a former energy executive and non-
partisan minister brought into the government to strengthen its business
credentials, predicted that growth would be double this in the medium term,
leading to higher emissions growth. This was immediately denied by the Environment Ministry (*Reuters*, 3 April 2001), but the effects of nuclear policy were
already becoming apparent, with the 29-year-old 640 MW reactor at Stade
owned by E.ON scheduled for closure in 2003 and likely to be replaced by a
gas-fired plant, using Norwegian gas supplied by Statoil (which would thus be
responsible for CO_2 emissions resulting from gas production). While gas-for-
coal substitution can reduce GHG emissions, gas-for-nuclear would increase
them. Moreover, chemical plants owned by Akzo Nobel and Dow Chemical
currently used cheap steam from the nuclear plant, and steam from gas would
be more expensive (and less available if produced in a high efficiency combined
cycle gas turbine plant) (*Reuters*, 20 February 2001).

The German nuclear decision calls into question the credibility of future
German reductions in CO_2 emissions, and illustrates the fact that climate change
politics has (as Helmut Kohl intended) provided considerable structural
advantage for the nuclear industry. Many conservationists have seen the possibility of restrictions on fossil fuel combustion as a factor which will fire the
renewables/efficiency market, but, despite Chernobyl, so far the largest effect
has been to stimulate a flagging nuclear industry.

While this revival has been most apparent in Annex I countries without major
political opposition to nuclear energy *since* Kyoto was negotiated, it was already
evident as Kyoto was being negotiated. Nuclear power facilities were considered
for inclusion in the Clean Development Mechanism (CDM) during post-Kyoto
negotiations and while there had not been an order for a new nuclear plant in
the USA for 20 years, there were active nuclear programmes in France and
Japan. The market was expanding in Asia, Central and Eastern Europe. In
Eastern Europe alone there were 37 unfinished reactors, and the upgrade-and-
refurbishment market was worth US$50 billion. In addition, some governments
were looking to replace older Soviet-built reactors. Romania, for example, was
in the process of commissioning five (Canadian) CANDU reactors. Slovakia had
signed a US$856 million deal with a consortium headed by Siemens AG and
Framatome SA for reactor upgrades. Westinghouse was installing new control
systems in reactors in the Czech Republic (Gailus, 1996). In addition to further
expansion of coal-fired generation capacity, China was planning to commission
12–14 reactors by 2010 – about 20,000 MW of capacity.

The conclusion of Kyoto has accelerated this nuclear revival. Finnish utility
Teollisuuden Voima Oy (TVO) is planning Finland's fifth nuclear reactor, a

1600 MW facility, directly citing Kyoto as a justification (*The Times,* 15 December 2000; *Reuters*, 26 March 2001). Mauno Paavola, chairman of TVO, has stated that nuclear power is making a comeback because of climate change, and has noted that there is often a contradiction between public posturing and private practice on the nuclear issue, with Sweden *increasing* nuclear production despite its stated aim of phasing it out by 2010.

Support for nuclear energy has also re-emerged in the UK, with the Conservative Party (*Observer*, 29 October 2000) supporting it and even the *Independent* (16 December 2000) suggesting that environmentalists needed to rethink their opposition because of climate change. The UK has recently given the much contested go-ahead for a MOX plant at Sellafield. Its emissions were almost 10 per cent below 1990 levels in 2000, but are predicted to rise so that they will be only 7 per cent below 1990 by 2010 and 2 per cent by 2020. The UK's Kyoto target under the European bubble was –12.5 per cent, and the government had committed to –20 per cent by 2020, so further effort was needed. By May 2001 British Nuclear Fuels Ltd (BNFL) and British Energy were both calling for a return to nuclear power, and the Labour Government's 2001 election manifesto had dropped its 1997 pledge to block the building of any new nuclear stations (*The Sunday Times*, 20 May 2001). Japan went further and approved a 2740 MW nuclear station planned by Chugoku Electric Power (*Reuters*, 17 May 2001).

In May 2001 the US nuclear operator Exelon announced plans for the first nuclear reactor ordered there in 20 years (*The Financial Times*, 23 May 2001) and the Bush Administration's energy plan included a prominent role for nuclear energy. Exelon, the largest US nuclear operator, hoped to commence the construction of a new Pebble Bed Modular reactor (reportedly faster, safer and cheaper than conventional reactors) within a year (ibid.). The Pebble Bed Modular reactor was being developed in collaboration with BNFL in South Africa. Public opinion had swung around considerably on the issue from the years after Three Mile Island, and support for the nuclear option in California had doubled to 59 per cent since 1984, helped as much perhaps by failed deregulation and rolling outages as by concern over climate change (*Reuters*, 24 May 2001). These moves were supported by bipartisan legislation introduced into the US Congress on 3 May to facilitate this nuclear revival. The Nuclear Regulatory Commission was relicensing the 103 existing reactors and was expected to extend the 40-year licences of all by 20 years (*Reuters*, 21 April 2001). At the international level, the International Energy Agency indicated that climate change had altered the future outlook for nuclear energy (*Reuters*, 2 May 2001).

The harsh realities of governing, as opposed to opposing, are causing difficulties for the German Green Party. Even the issue of the nuclear phase-out split the Greens, because associated with it was a resumption of shipments of reprocessed waste from La Hague in France; this mobilized green protests against Green Party complicity in the decision (*The Daily Telegraph*, 25 March 2001). The Greens were thus caught between those who opposed waste shipments and those who saw that GHG emissions would inevitably rise as a result of the gradual phase-out. And while the EU opposed the inclusion of nuclear energy in the Clean Development Mechanism (CDM) during the first commitment period, it annoyed Greenpeace by pushing a scheme to finance at least six nuclear reactors in China (*ABC News Online*, 20 June 2001).

This boost for nuclear power comes at a time when technological innovation is making it more competitive. The US nuclear industry estimates that nuclear construction costs would need to fall to $1,000/kW before they were competitive. The most recent nuclear station in the UK (Sizewell B, commissioned in 1995) cost almost $4,000/kW, but Westinghouse had reduced its costs to $1,440/kW and it could hit the crucial $1,000 mark if the new AP1,000 water-cooled reactor is approved by US regulatory authorities (*The Financial Times*, 26 June 2001). But gas prices are rising, and this will advantage nuclear energy. The UK is expected to be importing as much as 15 per cent of its gas by 2006, compared with 2 per cent in 2001, and much of this is likely to come from high-risk areas such as Algeria, Iran and Russia.

THE FOSSIL FUEL SECTOR AND ENERGY SECURITY

Nuclear and hydro aside, climate change creates winners and losers *within* the fossil fuel sector – a point often overlooked. Gas is advantaged in relation to black coal, as is oil, and black coal in relation to brown coal (or lignite). Various fossil fuels have a differing carbon content, and so switching to a lower carbon fuel –where possible – is in most circumstances the most painless way of achieving substantial reductions in the emission of CO_2. Such switching is least likely, at this time, in the transport sector but affects electricity generation greatly. As oil companies are frequently owners of gas resources, which is a co-product of oil or a product frequently found during oil exploration, the willingness of most oil companies to adopt a position on the climate change issue which environmentalists might favour and the split of corporations such as BP and Shell from the Global Climate Coalition was perhaps not surprising. After all, oil is a premium fuel for transportation and is likely to be affected much less than fuels such as coal and gas which are close substitutes. Oil is also less carbon-intensive per unit of energy, so climate change advantages the oil companies' oil and gas interests at the expense of coal.

The way in which the climate change issue impacts upon different fossil fuel sectors can be illustrated by considering a comparison developed for the evaluation of a new 800 MW coal-fired power station constructed at Millmerran, near Brisbane, Australia (Sinclair Knight Merz, 1998, 5–30). The station was

designed by Bechtel Corporation for Intergen, its joint venture with Shell, with
state-of-the-art advanced boiler firing using supercritical steam temperatures,
and can thus be regarded as being at the cutting edge for black coal stations. The
comparison between the design performance for this station and three different
technological approaches is shown in Table 3.1. The three other technologies
are conventional pulverized black coal, combined cycle gas turbine (CCGT)
and coal using integrated gasification and combined cycle gas turbines (IGCC).

Table 3.1: Fossil fuel alternative technologies comparison

Alternative technology:	Coal: advanced boiler	Pulverized coal	Combined cycle-gas	IGCC[a]
Type of power technology	Super-critical steam	Sub-critical steam	Advanced frame GT[b]	Advanced frame GT[b]
Nominal size (MW)	800	800	800	800
Fuel	Coal	Coal	Natural gas	Coal-gas
CO_2 emissions (kg/MWh)	846	881	422	1,007
Capital cost (US$/kW)	750	700	350	>1,200

Notes:
[a] IGCC = integrated gasification and combined cycle gas turbines.
[b] GT = gas turbine.

First, it is significant to note that generation from the proposed station is
likely ultimately to displace that at older black coal stations, which emit CO_2
at rates in excess of 1,000kg/MWh, or brown coal stations, where the rate is in
excess of 1,200kg/MWh. The new station will generate electricity with CO_2
emissions (respectively) 15 per cent and 29 per cent lower than such stations.
This is indicative of the manner in which retirement of old plant and its replace-
ment over time with new technology is likely to produce significant reductions
in emissions of CO_2 regardless of the fate of the Kyoto Protocol.

The second point to note is that advanced boiler design offers about a 4 per
cent reduction in CO_2 emissions for a 7 per cent increase in capital costs over
new conventional pulverized coal firing, so the selection of the better technology
will depend upon both fuel prices and the cost imposed on any externality, such
as CO_2. In the case of Millmerran, relatively low fuel costs plus the prospect
of some value being placed on CO_2 emissions was sufficient to induce the
owners to choose the more efficient technology.

Third, even the best coal technology results in approximately twice the emissions of CO_2 per unit of electricity that results from combined-cycle gas turbine combustion. This is the basis of the substantial reduction in CO_2 emissions in the United Kingdom following the post-1990 'dash to gas'. In the UK context, coal was expensive and gas at that time very cheap. Further, privatization increased the effective cost of capital by moving investment in electricity generation from the low rates of public sector investment to the private sector; with CCGT plant requiring only half the capital per MW of capacity, the drivers of the dash to gas can be seen to have been both fuel costs and capital costs. The prospect of a price attaching to CO_2 emissions increases the relative advantages of this form of generation, thus substantially privileging gas.

The final point to note from this table is that a significant new coal-utilization technology, the integrated gasification combined cycle gas turbine, is actually *worse* in terms of CO_2 emissions because of the amount produced during the process by which coal is gasified. There might be other environmental advantages in using this technology but its contribution to GHG emission reduction is not one of them.

Coal is therefore at a considerable disadvantage (in addition to its particulates and acid gases problem) compared to gas in terms of GHG emissions, and there is little immediate prospect that CO_2 removal and disposal technology will provide much relief. The collection of CO_2 from large-scale combustion plants already occurs at about five plants in the USA, but this occurs to produce CO_2 for commercial sale so recovery rates are not an issue. It is important to remember, however, that CO_2 is currently a commercial product: there is a producing well in Australia, and CO_2 is used to inject into oil fields to enhance production. The use of such oil or gas reservoirs to sequester CO_2 is possible, and costs are likely to be around US\$10/tonne (McMullan, 1996, 54). Storage in deep aquifers has been proposed (estimated at \$50/tonne) as has on-site storage in specially constructed spheres (\$75/tonne), although these techniques are unlikely to be attractive when compared to forest sinks. Deep ocean dumping is attractive in capacity terms, but while it is technically feasible in theory, cost is likely to be high.

These costs are in addition to those associated with removing CO_2 from power station emissions. Scrubbing with monoethanolamine (MEA) or advanced oxygen firing are feasible, but at about an 80 per cent cost penalty. However, much of the cost of MEA scrubbing is involved in the flue gas desulphurization (FGD) which must be undertaken first. The cost penalty might not be so large with low sulphur coals, and if FGD were not required the cost of electricity from MEA-scrubbed Australian coal would be raised by about 30 per cent. Removal of CO_2 from emissions is at a relatively early stage of development, and would not yet appear to be cost-effective when compared with alternatives such as sequestration in sinks. Norway, with a carbon tax of about

$45/tonne, is developing capture and storage in aquifers under the ocean. But without such taxes, and with the probable oversupply of commercial CO_2 as a result of climate change policies, such technologies are not likely to become commercial. However, a large amount of research is underway, for example, under OECD/IEA Clean Coal Research, a commitment which in itself can be counted among the interests in support of the Kyoto process.

The differences between the EU and parties such as the USA, Canada and Australia were perhaps most stark on the question of the cost of coal, the fossil fuel most at issue with the negotiations. Because coal results in more GHGs released for a given amount of energy produced than other fossil fuels, it would be the energy source most disadvantaged by restrictions in the Kyoto negotiations on CO_2 from energy utilization. Since the cost of coal production for electricity generation in Germany and the UK was approximately four times that in Australia, the USA, South Africa and Indonesia, a positive economic benefit could be expected from switching from coal to other fuel sources in Europe, whereas it was a cost for other countries.

Prime Minster Thatcher might have done much to break the power of the mining unions in the mid-1980s, and the productivity of coal mining in the UK doubled between 1980 and 1990, but only at the cost of a producer subsidy which rose from $26/tonne in 1986 to $75/tonne in 1990. This subsidy was reduced to $18/tonne between 1990 and 1993, increasing productivity by about another 50 per cent and halving domestic coal production. But it still represented a level of productivity which was only a quarter of that prevailing in the USA and Australia. The situation was even worse in Germany, where productivity was essentially static from 1980 to 1992, and the producer subsidy per tonne of coal almost doubled from $62 in 1986 to $115 in 1993. The power of the mining unions in Germany has prevented any meaningful attempts to reduce this subsidy, which costs around DM8 billion per annum. Other countries had substantial subsidies for coal mining, including Japan, which by 1993 was paying a subsidy of $126/tonne of coal produced domestically – about five times the price at which it was buying its coal from Australia (see Australia, 1997; Anderson, 1995; Anderson and McKibbin, 1997).

In short, there were substantial differences between the parties concerning the the price of coal which were reinforced by concerns over energy security, since many nations clearly were paying such large subsidies because strategic concerns reinforced the demands of coal producers and mining unions.

Price is not the sole energy concern in Europe, however. Balance of payments concerns also drive energy policy for most EU members, because they must import oil. Fears over the impact of OPEC-led oil price rises in the 1970s, for example, was an important driver of the technocratic decision in France to move to nuclear energy (Feigenbaum, 1985).

ENERGY EFFICIENCY AND RENEWABLES

While the positive benefits of climate policy for the nuclear industry are perhaps the most stark, largely because opposition to that energy source has in the past been the most vehement, the climate change issue has created other winners, and it has been especially useful where political opposition to siting facilities has been important, including opposition to renewable energy forms such as hydroelectricity. For example, the Canadian Hydropower Association, in a press release on 19 February 2001, used Kyoto to argue for an expansion in hydroelectric construction in Quebec, Manitoba and British Columbia, stalled by environmental opposition for a decade (see Kellow, 1996). Kyoto has the potential not so much to 'trump' these other concerns, by playing a card of a different suit such as economics (after all, economic arguments are explicitly rejected by many green advocates): the power of climate change is that it is a powerful card within the same suit of environmental concerns. It imposes the notion of 'opportunity cost' in their own *numéraire* upon environmental activists, who customarily enjoy the luxury of single issue politics free from the constraints of opportunity cost.

The market for energy efficiency and renewable energy has also continued to grow, but the nuclear expansion has dwarfed the renewables market. The world wind turbine market (of which Denmark has 60 per cent) was only about 600 MW per annum in 1997 when Kyoto was signed. (The national wind turbine programme commenced in 1979 and employs about 15,000 workers, but it still supplied only about 5 per cent of Denmark's electricity in 1996.) Low oil and natural gas prices in the 1990s had been bad news for the alternative energy industry in the USA, where 13 of California's biomass power plants had shut down by 1997 and the state's wind power companies were laying off staff. While solar water heating was viable, solar electricity generation was competitive only in remote locations, and the world solar cell market was then currently only about 81 MW per annum. It was growing rapidly but coming off a very low base. Climate change was therefore clearly helping the nuclear industry much more than the renewables industry. The appropriate NGOs in this area, the US and European Business Councils for a Sustainable Energy Future (which represented industries such as renewable energy, natural gas, co-generation, energy services, home appliances and insulation) were active on the climate change issue (French, 1996, 253).

In addition to having a strong interest in phasing down its coal industry and attempting to support its nuclear industry, Germany's national interests on climate change include a significant component which reflects the substantial investment in environmental technologies in the early 1980s. This formed part of Chancellor Kohl's response to the emergence of green politics, so-called 'Green Keynesianism', which included the adoption of the *vorsorgeprinzip*, a forerunner of the precautionary principle used to justify preventative action to protect the environment (see Boehmer-Christiansen, 1992a).

Much of this investment was in energy efficiency and alternative energy in response to the 1979 oil crisis, and it shaved about 1 per cent per annum off energy consumption in Germany throughout the 1980s. By the mid-1990s this ecological modernization had produced almost 1 million jobs in the environmental technologies sector (almost as many as in the motor vehicle industry), and the successful export of the *vorsorgeprinzip* as the precautionary principle into international agreements both protected the domestic market and helped develop export markets. The collapse of oil prices in 1986 jeopardized this investment, but the emergence of the climate change issue then helped to justify investments and regulations in support of 'alternative' energy that did not emit CO_2. But Germany's 'ecological modernization' is showing signs of unravelling, with Eco Bank going into liquidation and handing in its banking licence and the children of the baby boomers showing less enthusiasm for paying higher prices for 'ecologically sound' products (*Frankfurter Allgemeine Zeitung*, 5 July 2001).

The UK and Germany are installing substantial numbers of wind generators and solar panels. It is not just the economics of these options which requires support, but also their acceptability on environmental grounds in large-scale proposals, as opposition has emerged on the basis of noise, visual amenity and avian mortality. Again, it is instructive to consider alternative energy in the context of the Millmerran coal-fired station, because the comparison involves a sub-tropical location with high levels of solar radiation and strong coastal winds (including favourable sea breezes).

Typically, wind turbines are clustered into 'wind farms' of 5–50 MW capacity, with each turbine rated at 100–300 kW. There are two major environmental concerns: the land lost to the wind farm, and the threat to local bird populations from the turbines. The land loss is required for the wind farm, and there is reduced opportunity for other uses due to noise and safety. Low frequency noise from wind generators can travel substantial distances. Access roads and construction can cause erosion and require constant maintenance. To generate the 800 MW comparable with the Millmerran station, about 1,100 wind turbines would be required over a land area of between 2,300 to 4,600 hectares. Power would however only be available from 25 to 75 per cent of the time, depending on wind conditions. To extract the same energy as that generated by the Millmerran Project, about double this capacity would therefore be required. The capital costs of wind energy are about $1,000/kW (excluding land costs). Wind is the closest to being competitive with conventional sources of electricity generation.

Turning to solar energy from photovoltaic cells, in the Brisbane area the average total horizontal surface solar radiation is approximately 3.5 kWh/m^2-

day in the winter and 7.0 kWh/m^2-day in the summer. With a typical conversion rate of 10 per cent, a surface area of about 2,300,000 m^2 would be required in the winter and about 1,100,000 m^2 in the summer for a nominal generation of about 800 MW. Concentrating or tracking mechanisms could potentially reduce this area. However, electric power would only be generated during daylight hours; storage mechanisms such as pumped hydro would be necessary to maintain generation over daily periods. The capital cost of this technology is about US$7,000/kW and while it is commercially viable in remote, off-grid locations, it is far from competitive with conventional electricity generation and is unlikely to be so with foreseeable improvements in conversion efficiency.

The primary type of large-scale power production for solar thermal energy is through a series of tracking parabolic concentrators. These systems can produce steam from 100° to 400°C which can be used in a steam turbine generator. Typical size of this technology is within a 7–10 MW range. The area for collection is similar to photovoltaic. Capital costs are above US$1,000/kW. Solar power using thermal technology is also only available during daylight hours. Solar water heating and passive solar building design are cost competitive.

The land requirements of these technologies is perhaps the most significant drawback. Their considerable footprint means that sites with insignificant alternative economic uses are preferable (solar energy generating electricity is solar energy which is lost to agricultural production or other biological processes) – precisely the kind of land which is of ecological significance, because it is remnant vegetation which has survived precisely because it would not favour productive agriculture. In the USA, the Mojave Desert has been used for solar energy, provoking opposition from conservation groups which point out that it is a wilderness that is considerably despoiled by the technology. Opposition to wind generators has emerged from similar quarters because of their effects on bird life. Both these technologies have escaped scrutiny in the past because of their small scale of application, but their increasing success, which has depended substantially on climate change policy, is beginning to remind populations that there is no such thing as an energy technology with zero environmental impact.

While championing alternative energy sources allows politicians to respond to the demands of green voters, there are strong economic and environmental grounds why such technologies will not prove to be adequate to the task of producing the GHG reductions that climate change policies appear to demand. It is true that their producers have interests that are advantaged by climate policies, and in the case of countries like Denmark, with its dominance in the world wind turbine market, that will translate into the determination of its national interest position in international politics. But for the foreseeable future, even the laws of thermodynamics are running against renewables other than hydro. They simply cannot provide energy on the scale required to replace the substantial reliance modern industrialized nations place on coal and other fossil fuels.

ENERGY OR CARBON TAXES

Under the SDP–Green Coalition government, Germany has introduced an 'ecology tax' which will currently run until 2003; the Greens want the government to commit to extending it, a move Chancellor Gerhard Schroeder has resisted. While the multibillion dollar revenues have been hypothecated to support the failing pension scheme, the tax is highly unpopular, with polls showing around 80 per cent of Germans opposed to it (*Reuters*, 6 March 2001). While Kyoto provides an external justification for the tax, this level of unpopularity does not bode well for continued support for either it or (ultimately) Kyoto, which again poses an international credibility problem for Germany. The eco-tax provoked protests by truck drivers, taxi operators and farmers in October 2000, when oil prices rose as a result of OPEC production cuts, and relief measures were immediately announced for those worst hit. But Chancellor Schroeder intended to increase the eco-tax in 2001. Despite these taxes, Germany is still criticized by environmental groups for continuing to subsidize its coal industry by around DM8 billion per annum (*Reuters*, 19 October 2000). In the United Kingdom, a Climate Change Levy (which is energy- and not CO_2-based) introduced in 2001 would cost business £100 million, even after offsetting reductions in insurance levies, and is highly unpopular. Promising to abolish it did not gain many votes for the Tories in the 2001 election, but Prime Minister Tony Blair has been back-pedalling and is now accused by environmentalists of wanting to rejuvenate the nuclear industry (*The Independent*, 2 April 2001).

The conclusion of an international treaty governing energy was important for the European Union because it would establish both enhanced competence and strong political support for a European energy tax. Attempts in the early 1990s to institute such a tax had failed.

The taxation issue is also central to climate change politics. Europe generally has high energy taxes, not just because they provide a significant source of revenue, and not just out of a desire to encourage energy conservation and innovation. Oil is cheap in the USA and proposals to tax it have proven politically unpopular, but Australia follows a policy of export parity pricing for its domestic production, precisely to ensure that the correct signals are sent to the market about rates of depletion and the competitiveness of conservation and alternatives. There is also a substantial taxation component to fund road construction and maintenance. Nevertheless, petroleum prices at the pump for

European motorists are about double those in Australia, such that widespread protests were a feature in the UK and continental Europe in late 2000 as an OPEC production cut drove prices even higher.

TECHNOLOGY AND ECONOMIC CHANGE

Climate change policy has boosted the renewables industry substantially, largely with the help of public funds or 'incentives', and will continue to do so. But the big winners have been, and will continue to be, hydro and gas compared with coal, and nuclear compared with all others, especially because it emits no GHGs and (unlike hydro) is not restricted by the availability of suitable sites while uranium ore is plentiful and nuclear fuel can be recycled or even produced from weapons-grade plutonium. Climate change simultaneously boosts renewables, gas and nuclear energy while providing a strong rationale for ending coal subsidies in European countries such as Germany. Moreover, it provides countries which have pursued high energy taxes for balance of payments reasons not just with political support for such unpopular measures, but with the opportunity to try to export their relative disadvantage by requiring through international treaty an effective tax on coal relative to other energy sources. Simultaneously, it provides political reinforcement for policies to redress energy security issues, which generally involve policy instruments that are politically unpopular.

Moreover, it provides a moral basis for attempting to spread the additional costs of energy security and competitiveness across trading partners. For example, the European Parliament called for the EU to launch 'initiatives' under the World Trade Organization to prevent countries that do not ratify Kyoto from gaining competitive advantages, especially in the energy products sector (*Environment News Service*, 6 July 2001).

Climate change politics thus entails a Faustian bargain for environmentalists because, while it provides a definite boost to renewable energy and conservation, such approaches ultimately cannot provide the answer to the energy needs of modern societies without substantial (and hence unlikely) changes to their economic bases. While the preferred technologies of environmentalists are undoubtedly advantaged, the nuclear industry, gas industry and oil industry are all advantaged compared with coal (in that order). To the extent that the Annex I parties to the Kyoto Protocol have different resource endowments, such that the economics of these various energy sources vary considerably, we can see that there are substantial differences in the national interests of each party. But it was also the way the nature of the energy systems of parties varied over time which was significant, because the selection of 1990 as the base year for emission reductions impacted differently upon different parties.

The choice of the base year of 1990 against which emission reductions would be measured constituted a major problem for Japan, among others. It was included in the FCCC non-binding collective Annex 1 commitment, where it was not particularly threatening, but it logically became established as the base year for individual, binding reduction commitments, and it created advantage and disadvantage when applied at the level of the individual nation. For example, poorly endowed Japan had made a concerted effort after the oil crises of 1973 and 1979 to improve energy efficiency, but this effort came before 1990 and as a result Japan had 'picked the low-hanging fruit' in energy efficiency and now found itself closer to the zone of diminishing marginal returns. In contrast, significant EU nations like Germany and the UK were advantaged by the selection of 1990 as the base year for emissions.

Germany was favoured by 1990 because the Treaty of Unification was concluded in October of that year, and reunification was followed by a dramatic collapse in the former, almost entirely brown coal dependent, East German economy (the East quickly shut down its nuclear reactors), with economic output contracting 23 per cent in the following year and total primary energy consumption falling by 30 per cent (Boehmer-Christiansen *et al.*, 1993). This economic collapse produced a substantial windfall for Germany in terms of GHG emissions, and further reductions were facilitated by the inefficient base from which further reductions would be made in the east. Similarly, the post-1990 economic collapse of the former Soviet Union and other 'economies in transition' (EITs) has produced similar windfalls which these parties were keen to be allowed to trade under the provisions of Kyoto.

Similar factors were at work in the UK, still well endowed with fossil fuels but either approaching depletion or with very high costs, where 1990 was the year in which the electricity sector was privatized and Prime Minister Thatcher continued her political moves against subsidized, inefficient coal mining which had commenced with the miners' strike in the mid-1980s. Assisted by the relaxation of an EU directive limiting use of gas as a fuel for electricity generation, these factors resulted in a 'dash to gas' based on North Sea reserves. Between 1990 and 1995, 20 per cent of the fossil fuel-fired capacity in the UK was switched from coal to gas, which with modern combined cycle technology gives rise to 60 per cent lower emissions of CO_2 for the same electricity output. As a result, emissions of CO_2 in this sector fell by 12 per cent (Bantock and Longhurst, 1995). By 2000, Britain was generating 38 per cent of its electricity by gas, surpassing coal at 28 per cent and nuclear at 24.5 per cent (*The Financial Times*, 26 June 2001).

Much of the principled discourse emanating from the European Union ignored the self-interested nature of their position. Even within Europe, the UK and Germany attempted to assert moral leadership on the basis of windfall gains. For example, just prior to COP-6 *bis*, German (Greens Party) Environment Minister Juergen Trittin singled out his own country and the UK for praise, but said the rest of Europe was far from honouring its promises (*The Times*, 16 July 2001).

CONCLUSION: INTERESTS AND THE KYOTO PROCESS

For all the high moral tone evident in the pronouncements of participants in climate change negotiations, these are the inescapable realities of the underlying interests. There were two orders of magnitude differences in the perceived costs of compliance between European and non-European Annex I parties in the way in which Kyoto would impact upon their interests, thanks to the mixes of fuel sources and costs which comprised the national interest of each.

The Europeans had (very) expensive coal, which is the worst energy source in terms of GHG emissions. They also had access to relatively cheap gas, not just from the North Sea fields of the UK, the Netherlands and Norway, but from North Africa and Russia. Gas from these sources outside the EU (which includes Norway) had the added advantage of giving rise to production-related CO_2 emissions which would count against the producing nation, not the EU. European governments variously wanted reasons for ending coal subsidies, justifying energy taxes, supporting nuclear energy, and addressing energy security concerns. Various bureaucratic agencies wanted to acquire jurisdictional turf, and the EU Commission in particular wanted to gain competence in the energy field.

The mixes of energy and potential for sinks and emission trading differed substantially between parties. The 'logic' of the climate change issue thus varied substantially from one party to the next, and the parties formed interest-based groups for negotiating purposes. The participants were well aware of this logic, because their national interests were comprised of different combinations of these factors, and their stances throughout the negotiation were heavily influenced by these economic interests. Regardless of what the science says and regardless of the moral arguments which might be mounted, there are enormously powerful interests at stake in climate change policy, and a successful negotiation to produce an international response should have started with this recognition; instead, through ignoring it, it has *ended* with this recognition.

NOTE

1. There is currently commercial recovery of CO_2 in five power plants in the USA. Refined carbon
    dioxide sells in the range of $50–300/tonne, whereas that recovered from energy plants costs
    about $100/tonne (*Sapa-AFP*, 14 June 2001).

4. The Kyoto process

In June 1988 Canada sponsored an international conference on 'The Changing Atmosphere: Implications for Global Security'. This was attended by 340 people from 46 countries, including two heads of state and more than 100 government officials, but it was not an officially sanctioned intergovernmental conference and government participants attended only in their personal capacities. Also attending were many scientists, industry representatives and environmentalists. Despite having no official status, the Toronto Conference issued a statement calling for a global framework convention, the establishment of a 'World Atmosphere Fund' to be part-financed by a levy on fossil-fuel consumption in industrialized countries, and an ambitious 20 per cent reduction in global CO_2 emissions from the 1988 level by 2005. (A target of 60 per cent had been discussed, but Wolf Häfele argued against such a demanding target because the fast breeder reactor would not be ready in sufficient time to achieve this goal.) As we saw in the preceding chapter, nuclear interests were never far below the surface at this conference.

This close relationship between interests and negotiating positions can be observed throughout the whole process, in particular in the negotiation of the Kyoto Protocol and subsequently. While much of the rhetoric surrounding these negotiations suggested that only the fossil fuel industry, OPEC countries and the Umbrella Group were driven by economic interests, such interests were inextricably woven through the positions of all parties. All were seeking both to maximize their interests in the development of international agreements and to reduce the likely costs of compliance, or in some cases use the agreement for economic and political advantage quite unrelated to climate change. In this analysis it is important to distinguish between environmental benefits and non-environmental benefits, such as competitive advantages, revenue raising, and changes in legal competence and political power.

The time scale over which these benefits are likely to accrue is also politically of major importance. Climate mitigation is a hope based on uncertain science (see Chapter 7) while economic benefits can be expected much sooner. Benefits to bureaucracies (jobs, revenue and regulatory competence) and research budgets are immediate benefits and hence likely to be politically attractive considerations.

In this chapter we set out our reasons for this conclusion that interests were of primary importance, outweighing both science and normative discourse in determining the outcome of the negotiation. What follows is not a full history of the Kyoto process, but a brief and necessarily selective account. It is therefore incomplete, focusing on the key negotiating issues and their relation to interests rather than attempting to set out a narrative account of the negotiations. The focus is on Kyoto, rather than the FCCC, but we commence by looking at some features of the FCCC that were to be significant later. (We mention something of the origins of the FCCC in discussing the science base in Chapter 6).[1]

FCCC: A STATEMENT OF PRINCIPLES

In June 1992, 155 countries attending the UN Conference on Environment and Development (or 'Earth Summit') in Rio de Janeiro signed the Framework Convention on Climate Change (FCCC). A further 10 nations signed by the time the treaty was closed for signature in June 1993, and the fiftieth ratification was received in December 1993, triggering its entry into force on 21 March 1994. Ratification of this framework convention has no effect on the Kyoto Protocol, which has yet (at the time of writing) to receive sufficient ratifications to enter into force (see below). The USA has withdrawn from Kyoto, but remains a party to the FCCC.

The objective of the FCCC was the

> stabilization of greenhouse gas concentrations in the atmosphere that would prevent dangerous anthropogenic interference with the climate system. Such a level should be achieved within a time-frame sufficient to allow ecosystems to adapt naturally to climate change, to ensure that food production is not threatened and to enable economic development to proceed in a sustainable manner. (Article 2)

The vast knowledge requirements and the legal and institutional difficulty of defining 'dangerous' need hardly be stressed, but these raised even then the possibility of the treaty not being implementable.

The FCCC set out principles to guide parties in taking action and contained some general commitments, the most important of which was a non-binding commitment by those parties listed in Annex I (industrialized nations) to stabilize GHG emissions at 1990 levels by 2000. These were seen as initial commitments only and the Convention established a framework for the periodic review of commitments in the light of the objectives of the FCCC, new scientific findings and the effectiveness of national climate change programmes. The issue of reliably measuring these emissions had yet to be resolved.

The Principles of the Convention were spelled out in Article 3. The first of these was that parties should protect against climate change on the basis of equity and the 'common but differentiated' responsibilities of parties and their respective capacities. Developed countries were to take the lead (Article 3.1) and the specific needs and special circumstances of nations which would have to bear disproportionate burdens should be given full consideration (3.2). Parties should pay particular attention to the vulnerability of developing countries (3.2) and cooperate to promote an economic system that results in sustainable economic growth, particularly in developing countries (3.5). The precautionary principle was cautiously adopted, with an undertaking not to use the lack of full scientific certainty as a reason to postpone efforts to address climate change (3.3).

Parties also agreed that policies should be cost-effective and comprehensive (3.3), covering all relevant sources, sinks and reservoirs of GHGs as well as adaptation, and cover all economic sectors. The parties also recognized that economic development was essential for countries to be able to adopt measures to address climate change (3.4) and agreed that policy measures should not constitute a means of arbitrary or unjustifiable discrimination or a disguised restriction on international trade (3.5). Policies were to be appropriate to the specific conditions of each party (3.4).

The general commitments (under Article 4) are vast and read like a strategy for fundamental social change directed from above. They include commitments to adopt national programmes for mitigating climate change, to develop adaptation strategies, to promote sustainable management and conservation of GHG sinks, to integrate climate change concerns into the development of other policies, to cooperate in technical, scientific and educational matters and to promote scientific research and the exchange of information – taking into account 'their common but differentiated responsibilities and their specific national and regional development priorities, objectives and circumstances'.

However, the stabilization commitment (at 1990 levels by 2000) was for Annex I parties only, namely developed countries and 'economies in transition' – essentially, the former Soviet Union and Eastern European countries. Significant was a commitment to limit GHG emissions 'with the aim of returning individually or jointly to their 1990 levels these anthropogenic emissions of carbon dioxide and other greenhouse gases not controlled by the Montreal Protocol' by 2000 (Article 4.2(b)). Not only was this implicit target inclusive of non-CO_2 GHGs, but it explicitly provided for differentiated responses among Annex I parties, taking into account differences in starting points and approaches, economic structures and circumstances, resource bases, available technologies, and so on (Article 4.2(a)). And in a proviso of importance to some countries such as Australia, Article 4.10 required parties to take into account the situation of individual parties:

with economies that are highly dependent on income generated from the production, processing and export, and/or consumption of fossil fuels and associated energy intensive products, and/or the use of fossil fuels for which such parties have serious difficulties switching to alternatives.

It is important to note, therefore, that this non-binding commitment was a *joint* one for Annex I parties, that differentiation was explicitly provided for, and that all GHGs, rather than CO_2 alone, were included. This first point is significant, because many statements by NGOs and others during the Kyoto process referred to the performance of individual countries against the FCCC commitment, as if this was a commitment target accepted at the level of the individual nation. It never was an individual commitment, and the singling out of individual nations as being '*x* per cent' over this target was clearly an attempt to bring pressure to bear. That this commitment was in fact met was due largely to the collapse of former communist economies, including East Germany, and the restructuring of the energy sector in the United Kingdom. There had been little deliberately accepted pain in the name of climate change policy. The singling out of Annex I parties which had not individually met a stabilization target was fuelled by resentment that other Annex I countries had not done enough – even though the implicit target was achieved.

So the Kyoto process continued to create structural advantage in the negotiation process for some interests, as had already commenced with the FCCC. Of particular significance was the way the structure of the negotiations favoured the European Union and disadvantaged other parties, including Australia, the USA and Japan. The selection of 1990 as the base year for emission reductions favoured some players where the post-communist economic collapse and energy restructuring produced windfall reductions for reasons unrelated to climate change policy.

The European Union was able to use these windfall gains to secure agreement within Europe for the proposal for a 15 per cent reduction target for Annex I parties. It did so by securing the right to have a single European reduction target within which the targets for member nations could be differentiated (the so-called 'European Bubble' or Burden Sharing Agreement). The windfall gains of Germany and the UK could thus be used to allow increases, not just for the less affluent nations such as Greece, Portugal and Spain, but also for Sweden, which would have difficulty reducing GHG emissions while acting in accordance with the 1979 referendum decision. This called for the phasing out of nuclear electricity generation, which provided 37 per cent of its total energy needs. Sweden was therefore given a target of +5 per cent within the EU bubble, although Swedish industry thought that +50 per cent might be a more realistic figure. Similarly, France had made the move to nuclear electricity over the preceding two decades and was able effectively to exempt itself from reductions under Kyoto, whereas Japan, which was in a comparable position, was unable to do so and ultimately had to accept a binding reduction target.

The significance of 1990 for the EU raises the question of where the selection of this year as the base for negotiations came from. The first use of 1990 as a base year did indeed come from the EU and was developed in October 1990 on the eve of the Second World Climate Conference (Collier, 1996, 125). It was then walked into the final meeting of the Intersessional Negotiating Committee developing the FCCC for signature at Rio by the UK and the USA, as the target for non-binding stabilization measures for Annex I parties. It is clear that this was not an innocent move, at least on the part of the UK, which had earlier sought in acid rain negotiations to have a base year for emissions adopted which would suit its interests (Sprinz and Vaahtoranta, 1994, 102). It was well known in UK energy circles that only after 1990 would emission reductions, including of CO_2, begin to result from the switch to gas.

The European Union was therefore keen to argue for uniform reduction targets for the rest of Annex I, while retaining for itself the flexibility of trading off serendipitous reductions in the UK and Germany against *increases* or zero targets for other EU members. All the while, it could occupy the high moral ground by proposing the largest reduction target of all Annex I countries at 15 per cent of 1990 emissions and criticize others not being as generous and such good global citizens. Some of this achievement was undoubtedly paid for by the many coal miners who lost their jobs and were facing significant reductions in quality of life.

There was an additional agenda at work for the European Commission in putting together the European Bubble: the expansion of jurisdiction or competence. Non-EU parties in the Kyoto negotiation were understandably concerned about who would be responsible for compliance under the EU Bubble. If Germany did not deliver on its cuts against which Portugal was granted an increase, would Germany or Portugal be accountable? The obvious answer was to make the European Commission responsible, and so the Commission expanded its competence in the area of energy policy and possible EU taxation, for an energy or carbon tax had been a Commission proposal since the early 1990s and remained on the table.

The construction of the problem as one of finding a way to reduce *current* emissions also conveyed considerable advantage to the same European players which benefited from the selection of 1990 as the base year for reduction targets: Germany and the UK. Despite the fact that industrialized countries had made a greater contribution in causing the climate change problem historically, their governments managed to avoid any responsibility for this. This arose because of the long residence time of CO_2 in the atmosphere of an estimated 50–200 years. GHG emissions today have the potential to cause problems because they will continue to accumulate in the atmosphere, so the problem is not just one of flows but of stocks, as the economists would put it. Current elevated levels of atmospheric CO_2 are usually attributed to the partial accumulation of this gas emitted since the industrial revolution, which initiated the wholesale shift not only from 'biomass' and other renewable energy sources to fossil fuels, but also from human beings to machines as the main agents of doing physical work. Current emission patterns thus tell us little about who has been responsible for current atmospheric concentrations.

In fact, the UK and Germany are responsible for the largest shares of historic emissions, a point well understood by Brazil when it argued that a differentiated response reflecting historic emissions over the previous 150 years would be the fairest approach (Australia, 1997, 94). The EU managed to define the problem differently: as one in which the clever selection of 1990 as the baseline portrayed current emitters other than the EU as disproportionately responsible for the problem. Its own members, in contrast, would in future be able largely to exempt themselves both from costly policy measures to meet Kyoto targets and from any perception of their 'historical debt'. As the EU could not have been unaware of this, it is important to recall the non-environmental interests driving EU 'concern' for emission reduction (see Chapter 3).

In addition to minimizing its own responsibility for the problem or potential solutions, Europe also sought to use the climate change negotiation process to export its own likely disadvantage in energy competitiveness to other Annex I parties. It did so by attempting to have the negotiations focus on CO_2 rather than other GHGs, since CO_2 impacted on the energy sector and provided advantage to Europe, whereas non-CO_2 GHGs did not provide any particular advantage to Europe or disadvantage to others. It also attempted to block proposals for generous interpretation of sinks, naturally on scientific grounds, and emissions trading, which would allow the economies in transition to gain economically by allowing others to offset their increased emissions against the calculated windfall reductions of the former Soviet Union and Eastern Europe – as the EU itself was able to do under the EU bubble.

Moreover, the EU stood to gain by allowing political aggregation of credits and debits under its bubble but not emissions trading outside Europe, because many of the economies in transition in Eastern Europe had made applications to join the European Union or it was anticipated that they would to seek to join at some time in the future. As they joined the EU, they would thus bring with them a 'dowry' of emission credits – so long as they were not permitted to realise these advantages by trading. This possibility was foreclosed by Kyoto as negotiated.

The European Union sought advantage in other significant ways. For example, its negotiators opposed the inclusion of carbon sinks, both directly within countries and as part of emissions trading. Despite the fact that the principles were quite clearly included in the FCCC, the EU attempted throughout to limit opportunities for addressing atmospheric CO_2 levels through sinks or through reducing activities such as land clearing. As we have seen, the opportunities for doing so are markedly different for Europe and for countries like the USA and Australia. In the latter, substantial land clearing continues to be a significant source of GHGs and relatively vast areas of uninhabited land make sink creation and enhancement not only more possible than in Europe but also more desirable, thus also adding non-climate related interests, such as devising carbon related policies to counter dry land salination in the interests supporting the Kyoto process. Emission trading would not only weaken the need for direct official intervention in the energy sectors of member states, but also undermine the desired emphasis on energy demand management, for example by requiring higher energy efficiency in buildings, cars and appliances. As we shall see, where virtually all parties stood on the key issues in Kyoto depended upon where they sat and what they expected in future.

THE BERLIN MANDATE

The FCCC, like many MEAs, made provision for several matters to be decided on an on-going basis by meetings of the Conference of the Parties (COP) – a clear example of iterative functionalism. The first meeting (COP-1) was held in Berlin in March–April 1995. While the meeting adopted rules of procedure and established subsidiary bodies, one important task was to review the adequacy of the FCCC mitigation commitments in Articles 4.2 (a) and (b). A standing invitation was thus provided for science, apparently, to drive the political process. COP-1 had no difficulty concluding that these commitments were not adequate to achieve the stabilization objective of the Convention, especially as the commitments did not extend beyond 2000.

COP 1 agreed to a negotiating mandate ('the Berlin Mandate') to serve as the basis for further negotiation. The aims were to elaborate policies and measures for Annex I parties and to set targets – specifically, quantified emission limitation and reduction objectives or QELROs – within specified time-frames taking into account differences in starting points, economic circumstances and available technologies, and the need for equitable contributions by each of these parties – an agenda for almost endless haggling, data collection and research. It was also agreed not to introduce any new commitments for non-Annex I parties, but to continue the implementation of existing commitments in Article 4.1. Australia alone had pressed for the inclusion of developing countries in some form of commitment, but was not supported by any other country and hence accepted their exclusion. Significantly, the Mandate also committed the parties to consider the best available scientific information and relevant technical, social and economic information including IPCC reports, thus putting ever more pressure on the research enterprise to come up with the required consensus both on the problem and its solution (see Chapters 6 and 7).

Negotiations under the Mandate took place in an *ad hoc* group, the Ad Hoc Group on the Berlin Mandate (AGBM), which met eight times between COP-1 and COP-3 in Kyoto in December 1997 and largely represented the now mushrooming climate change related interests inside national bureaucracies. COP-2, in Geneva in July 1996, came at the mid-point in these negotiations, just after the well-timed publication of the IPCC Second Assessment Report (SAR). A joint ministerial declaration at COP-2 endorsed SAR as the most comprehensive and authoritative assessment of climate change science, and included a call for the outcome of the Berlin Mandate negotiations to include legally binding emission reduction targets.

Much of the coverage of the negotiation of the Kyoto Protocol (and thus the popular understanding of the issues) focused on the negotiation of these targets. Other issues were just as significant, however, and we shall canvass those here. Particularly important were the questions of coverage of gases and sources and sinks, targets, flexibility mechanisms (such as provision for emissions trading and joint implementation with developing countries), national policies and measures, and compliance and monitoring.

Coverage

While all the parties to the FCCC notionally agreed that emission targets should ultimately cover 'a basket' of six GHGs and all emission sources and sinks, there was disagreement over what should be included in the Kyoto Protocol. Some were citing large uncertainties over measurement and monitoring as reasons for restricting coverage of gases and sources. The differences which emerged during the deliberations of the AGBM centred on the 'gross' versus 'net' approach and the 'basket' approach versus a 'gas-by-gas' approach. Both issues did indeed involve major problems of measurement and equivalence and as such were research intensive and hence attractive to the IPCC.

Under the gross approach, targets were to apply to actual emissions only, and the protection and enhancement of sinks could not be subtracted, and hence 'stored' or even not yet released carbon would not count towards a country's emission target. The net approach would allow carbon dioxide fixed in sinks which were managed or established for this purpose to be subtracted from gross emissions. In short, sinks would take the pressure off emission reductions in the energy sector, an outcome sought by countries with very high emission reductions costs, like Norway, Japan and Australia.

Under the basket approach, all GHGs were to be included, weighted according to their relative calculated and scientifically contentious Global Warming Potential (GWP) integrated into a single target. The GWP numbers were expressed relative to CO_2 which had a GWP of 1 under the IPCC SAR in 1996. Thus methane had a GWP of 21, nitrous oxide 310 and perfluorocarbons 9,200. As this indicates, CO_2 is the least potent of the GHGs per molecule. Under a gas-by-gas approach, either each GHG would have a separate target, or targets would only apply to a limited set of gases and to sources and sinks where measurement uncertainties were sufficiently small. One approach was for a target to apply only to CO_2 emissions from the energy sector.

The European Union had relatively limited opportunities for sink creation and enhancement, especially compared with countries with a larger land mass relative to population, such as the USA or Australia, and did not express a strong view during AGBM on the question of net versus gross coverage. There was some variation among EU member states on the question of a gas-by-gas versus basket approach, with the UK and the Netherlands consistently supporting a basket approach. Most of the remainder of the EU members, including Austria, Belgium, Denmark and Germany, supported the CO_2-only approach which would have focused the cuts even more on the electricity sector. The EU eventually developed a compromise, and one which naturally reflected its interests. The compromise was a limited basket, which included CO_2, methane and nitrous oxide. It omitted gases such as sulphur hexafluoride where it had no advantage, but included methane, which its national communications reported would be at or below 1990 levels by 2000 in all EU member nations.

Accurate measurement and verification of emissions was an important consideration in the negotiation. Japan wanted a CO_2-only approach because of uncertainties over measurement and verification and over the science of GWP numbers. But it also had negligible domestic potential for sinks. The USA wanted an emission trading regime, and feared this proposal would be undermined by the possibility of unmeasurable or unverifiable emissions that would allow cheating, which might undermine the value of emission permits. This initially inclined the USA towards a CO_2-only, gross approach applied to the energy sector and industry, but most US domestic policies and joint implementation projects in developing countries had focused on sinks and on sectors other than energy and industry. It had initially supported a comprehensive approach, but in January 1997 indicated support for limiting the proposal to those gases and sinks where there were agreed methodologies. Australia, which has significant sink potential as well as significant source activity from land-clearing, favoured a comprehensive approach.

In general, it became increasingly difficult to find consistency between the environmental long-term objective and shorter-term non-environmental interests. While there were concerns over technical uncertainties behind most of these differences, even approaches to those uncertainties reflected differing interests. For example, there are uncertainties of the order of 60–100 per cent over methane emissions, but this did not prevent the EU from proposing to include methane to its advantage. (Methane reduction had occurred with the reduction in coal production, for example, and the end of gas flaring and the use of landfill gas.)

Targets

There was little agreement on targets in the lead-up to Kyoto. If the EU is counted as a single party, the nine OECD parties listed in Annex I to the FCCC submitted seven different proposals on targets, with more coming from economies in transition and developing countries. The main broad proposals were for either uniform targets for Annex I countries or targets which were differentiated between parties according to national circumstances. Little effort was expended on the fundamental difficulty of measuring emissions adequately to ensure later compliance.

There were other minor issues, such as whether targets should be legally binding, but only Australia argued that it was premature to make targets legally binding when the nature and content of commitments was unclear. The USA then favoured legally binding targets as a necessary condition for its emissions trading proposal.

The only specific proposal for individual targets from an Annex I party came from the European Union, which proposed a target of a 15 per cent reduction for a basket of gases – as we have seen, CO_2, methane and nitrous oxide – on 1990 levels by 2010. This target was to apply uniformly to all Annex I parties regardless of national circumstances, with one exception: the target was to be differentiated internally within the European Union 'Bubble' according to the national circumstances of member states. The EU was proposing for the rest of Annex I what it could not secure internally, since agreement on 15 per cent within the EU could only be secured by allowing less stringent targets for some members. These would apply not only to less affluent members such as Spain, Portugal and Greece, but also affluent members which would find mitigation disproportionately more difficult.

Emission reduction would have been more difficult for France, for example, because it had already made a major shift from fossil fuels to nuclear energy, most of this prior to the base year of 1990 for the FCCC. France was therefore given a zero target, as was Finland. Portugal was given a target of +40 per cent, Greece +30 per cent, Spain and Ireland +15 per cent, and the affluent environmental 'vanguard' state Sweden +5 per cent. These increases were to be offset against reductions in members such as Germany (–25 per cent), Austria (–25 per cent), Denmark (-25 per cent) and the United Kingdom (–20 per cent). The UK domestic target is 25 per cent and the government has stated that the UK expects to benefit financially from future global emission trading.

As we saw earlier, these targets did not reflect any great preparedness on the part of the countries concerned to sacrifice national interests for the global good. Rather, they would ensure that the windfall gains resulting from the closure of coal mines in the UK and the collapse of former East German economic activity would be retained within the EU. Also, strong external political pressures for ending the heavy subsidies for German coal mining or continuing Danish government support for its wind turbine industry (where it had world dominance) could be expected.

The USA supported uniform targets, but failed to specify any number. It formally opposed the EU Bubble, but then linked its acceptance to that of emissions trading by the EU and gaining satisfaction of its concerns over compliance. This was an important point for the EU Commission, because it had earlier failed to gain competence for energy policy, an ongoing objective in Europe. The USA was insisting that such a competence should be established so that the Commission could be held accountable for compliance at both the member level and for overall EU emission reductions.

The Alliance of Small Island States (AOSIS) also wanted uniform reductions for Annex I of 20 per cent by 2005, but the other proposals were for various approaches to differentiation. Japan proposed a complex formula that would allow countries with emissions below a specified level to choose either a per capita target or a uniform target. Norway, a major exporter of fossil fuel with little domestic reduction potential, proposed a kind of 'Annex I bubble', with a collective Annex I reduction target of 15 per cent on 1990 levels by 2010, but with targets for Annex I parties differentiated relative to business-as-usual emissions according to the energy intensity of economies, greenhouse gas intensity, and an indicator of GDP per capita. Iceland was broadly in agreement with this proposal.

Switzerland proposed a collective Annex I reduction of 10 per cent on 1990 levels, differentiated so that higher reductions would be made by those with higher per capita emissions, but adjusted to take account of emissions produced in manufacturing exports with high emission levels. In a similar proposal, Australia wanted differentiated targets based on the national circumstances affecting the costs of abatement. It proposed that five economic indicators be factored into the negotiations to produce individual targets. These indicators were to cover population growth, GDP per capita growth, emission intensity of the economy, emission intensity of exports, and dependence on fossil fuel trade. These factors reflected Australia's fears that, because of its energy-intensive, export-orientated economy and its location among non-Annex I parties in the Asia-Pacific, targets not differentiated on these grounds would result in significant 'carbon leakage'. This would be brought about by the relocation of energy utilization activity to countries outside Annex I and thus exempt from requirements to reduce emissions. Australia thus found itself in the Umbrella Group with the USA.

Russia proposed that stabilization rather than reductions apply to economies in transition, plus the ability to choose the base year. Korea wanted GDP per capita to serve as the basis for differentiation, and Brazil wanted differentiation (as we have seen) on the basis of cumulative emissions over the preceding 150 years, which would have given the UK the highest reduction target.

With the exception of proposals from non-Annex I parties, such as AOSIS or Brazil, each of these proposals was heavily infused with the interests of those proposing them – including the European Commission, which would expand its competence in enforcing the European Bubble. Similar factors were at work with the USA. The executive branch of government, especially Vice-President Gore, was strongly in favour of a successful outcome, but it was very much playing 'two-level games', trying to place pressure on the legislative branch. The US constitution requires that all treaties must be ratified by a two-thirds majority of the Senate, which adopted the bipartisan Byrd–Hagel resolution in mid-1997, indicating that it would not ratify a protocol without any commitments by developing countries, by a margin of 95–0.

Australia (which relied upon economic analysis conducted by its Bureau of Agricultural and Resource Economics, ABARE) was the most transparent in pointing out the beneficial or negative impact of the various proposals, perhaps because it had most to lose. It was faced with the prospect of an increase in its population (according to World Bank projections) of over 20 per cent between 1990 and 2010 whereas the EU collectively was looking at around 2 per cent. Australia had an economy which was more energy-intensive than the EU (and the OECD average): the index of energy use per unit of GDP in Australia was 0.45, the EU 0.42, and the OECD average 0.39. But the difference was even more marked in the manufacturing sector, with Australia at 1.50, the EU 0.77, and the OECD average 0.97. (Similar differences were apparent between the EU and the USA.) The EU was also below the OECD average on CO_2 intensity. Similar differences were apparent with respect to both energy and CO_2 intensity of exports.

Emissions Trading

If the issue of targets revealed substantial differences between the EU and other parties, as did the question of emissions trading, it also brought the interests of intergovernmental bodies, such as the UN and World Bank concerned with investment and aid, to the negotiations. Trading would require administrators, bankers and accountants; new sources of income and new markets for knowledge beckoned.

The establishment of tradable emission rights or permits is a policy instrument favoured by economists, since it creates a value attached to rights to pollute and therefore an incentive to reduce emissions at lowest global cost and realize the exchange value of the permit. There is thus in theory always an incentive for those engaging in polluting activity to find ways of reducing emissions and selling permits, always provided a target or ceiling is set for emissions by an outside authority. New industries have to acquire permits, and so a market develops and entrepreneurs can make money by reducing emissions in all kinds of ways, ways often difficult for policy-makers to imagine. On the other hand, permits may be withheld to damage competitors, or trading may simply encourage growth, including of emissions by making it cheaper.

Regulations limiting emissions to particular levels or the imposition of emission taxes impose costs and create incentives to subvert the regime. Tradable permits are usually seen as offering greater flexibility in responses by polluters: those who can mitigate most cheaply have the greatest incentive to do so and to sell the permits thus freed up, while those for whom mitigation is most expensive must possess or acquire permits sufficient to cover their emissions. Such a system therefore tends to be preferable in terms of economic efficiency, because there are incentives to mitigate at least cost. It does not, of course, obviate the need for regulation, for without some means of ensuring that there is compliance there is no incentive to reduce emissions. The big issue remains how to divide the responsibilities, and spoils, between (private) polluters and governments.

Such a system obviously leads to some wealth transfers between those who have permits they do not need and those who need permits they do not have. And the willingness (and ability) to pay to acquire permits is likely to be greater among those who are more affluent, for whom diminishing marginal utility makes the cost less than for those closer to subsistence. These aspects together, however, make tradable permits – and indeed pollution taxes – objectionable to many environmentalists. This is because they consider the act of pollution to be morally wrong, rather than a matter of misallocated resources. (More on this later.) Much would depend on the price of permits, and hence the relationship between supply (Russia) and demand (USA, Japan).

Fearing the costs of emission reduction 'at home' and sceptical about state regulation, the United States was the most prominent advocate of emissions trading in the Kyoto negotiations. It also had experience at the domestic level of emissions trading with sulphur dioxide. Emissions trading came after the acknowledged failure of a regulatory approach which required percentage reductions in pollutants in emissions from power stations and other large industrial sources (Maloney and Brady, 1988). Uniform percentage reduction targets under Kyoto would also have rewarded those who were least energy efficient at the 1990 base year, while disadvantaging those (such as Japan and

France) who had restructured their energy industries before 1990. Emissions trading for sulphur dioxide in the USA was limited to the electricity sector, placed a cap on allowances, and allocated 30 years of permits on a differentiated basis to utilities, which were allowed to bank savings for future use but not borrow from future allocations. Utilities were required to install continuous monitoring equipment and an annual reconciliation was made between recorded emissions and the Environmental Protection Agency (EPA), which also had to be notified of any trades. Penalties for non-compliance were high: over 20 times the market price, to make non-compliance a high-risk activity.

It is germane to list these details of the emissions trading regime for sulphur dioxide because it makes clear what institutional mechanisms were required to put in place such a regime, albeit for a very limited range of large sources. These institutional mechanisms underlie the operation of any market, since governments must provide the rights to property, means of exchange, enforcement of contracts, a system of weights and measures, and so on, for a market to operate. The problem in international politics is that there is no government, so as a minimum a system of governance must be set up which can meet these 'functional prerequisites', as Lowi (1993) has termed them, for a workable and effective system of emissions trading to be established. Without such 'functional prerequisites', trading of CO_2 emission permits would run the risk that those selling them would fail to limit their future emissions to that level for which they had permits, thus free-riding and seriously undermining the regime. Such a policy instrument would involve sizeable transfers of wealth, but it would be ineffective.

Institutional arrangements therefore had to be made as to the scope of any emissions trading scheme, further increasing the complexity and compulsory nature of an implementation regime in the end still based on precaution – that is, poorly understood causality. Targets would have to be legally binding. Rules governing trading would need to be established, including rules governing banking and borrowing, and (fundamentally) methods established for measurement and verification of emissions and for compliance with permitted emissions. Decisions were also required on whether trading should be permitted only between national governments, between individual firms, or (as the USA proposed) a mixture of the two.

This was a substantial agenda, but there were further problems. Even if such a market could be established, some of these problems would remain: those relating to the possible abuse of market dominance, and to the role of government policies in distorting the market. On the first point, Russia would be the dominant seller in the emissions trading market thanks to its substantial windfall gains. The windfall gains of the former East Germany and the UK would be captured by the internal *political* 'trading' of the European bubble, and those of the collapsed 'economies in transition' would go the same way as those states acceded to the EU, thus leaving Russia holding the predominant number of permits, assuming they actually exist, allocated on the basis of 1990 emissions. On the second point, governments had the potential to distort the emissions trading market with their own policy instruments, such as border taxes and subsidies.

The USA proposed a scheme on which it sought broad agreement at Kyoto, with technical details to be developed subsequently. It included legally binding targets, banking and borrowing, establishment of monitoring, reporting and verification mechanisms tighter than in the FCCC, a scope including participation by both governments and individual firms, and trading only between countries with emission targets. Inconsistencies were clearly developing between these various national needs and interests.

Joint Implementation

Article 4.2(a) of the FCCC provided for the implementation of policies and measures by Annex I countries jointly with other parties in order to achieve a return of emissions to the 1990 level by 2000. This allowed for countries without low-cost reduction opportunities to invest in lower-cost abatement in other countries and gain credit towards their own commitments. Article 4.2(d) required COP-1 to determine the criteria for Joint Implementation (JI), but JI turned out to be contentious, especially among developing countries. Despite recognizing the potential advantages, developing country governments feared that Annex I parties would get off lightly by pursuing opportunities elsewhere, and that aid flows would be simply diverted from other areas instead of being 'additional'. Developing countries finally allowed a pilot phase for 'Activities Implemented Jointly' (or AIJ) among Annex I parties and involving any willing developing countries on a voluntary basis. A key issue at Kyoto was what would happen to JI post-2000.

G-77 and China opposed JI credits being permitted after 2000, but some countries such as Costa Rica had adopted the idea with enthusiasm, largely because it was keen to sell credits for forest sink creation, for which it had considerable potential. Economies in transition were also developing JI projects. Nations sponsoring such projects included the US, Norway and Australia. The EU wanted JI restricted to operate between Annex I countries only, and they wanted only limited opportunity to use JI to meet targets. Again, they wanted the effort focused on domestic mitigation measures. Australia, Canada and New Zealand all supported JI between Annex I parties and developing countries.

Joint Implementation would be similar to emissions trading or the exchange of credits and emissions under the European Bubble, and as such it raised similar issues about compliance. Credits allowed to offset emissions elsewhere would have to be genuine; counterfeit credits would undermine the effectiveness of any protocol. But there were other institutional issues which were raised by JI, such as how JI credits would be integrated into an emissions trading regime. Further JI could lead to the entry of non-Annex I parties into emissions trading, so any unreliability or lack of compliance in JI could undermine any trading regime. Growing complexity made the private sector at least increasingly sceptical, while emission accounting, trading and banking were opening up new opportunities, and hence stakeholders, in the success of the Kyoto process.

National Policies and Measures

Three broad positions on policies and measures regarding energy, transport, industry, agriculture, forestry, waste management, economic instruments and mechanisms under the Berlin Mandate emerged during the meetings of AGBM. The EU, Switzerland, Norway and AOSIS favoured the Annex I parties being subjected to mandatory policies and measures. The USA and Australia considered that the parties should have complete freedom in the selection and implementation of policies and measures. Japan and Canada, broadly supported by New Zealand, proposed the establishment of a menu of policies covering mandatory categories from which parties would be free to choose specific policies and measures. The EU worked with Annex I parties other than the USA and Australia to try to find a compromise on mandatory policies and measures.

The EU proposal was for Annex I parties to be bound to one set of policies and measures to be listed in an annex to the protocol (Annex A). In addition there would be a list of policies and measures which Annex I parties would give high priority to adopting and implementing and which should be coordinated (Annex B). Finally, there would be a list of policies and measures for priority inclusion in national programmes as appropriate to national circumstances, again revealing the large intervention potential of the Kyoto Protocol.

Annex A was proposed to include matters such as removing barriers to the development of renewable energy technologies; measures to improve the energy efficiency of products; measures to improve fuel efficiency in the transportation sector; removal of subsidies for fossil fuels and taxes which counteracted energy efficiency; market reform to increase energy efficiency and competition and promote fuel switching; and the development of forest management practices to expand carbon storage. This was a substantial agenda, which would have required the wholesale reform of the energy sector – and much more – in Annex I countries; it went far beyond any existing MEA – indeed beyond any treaty in terms of the scope of its demand on domestic policy actions. The EU position was that matters listed in its Annex A related to energy competitiveness; they were policies they stated could not be implemented unilaterally because competitors should have to face the same disadvantage.

In taking this position, the EU was moving well beyond questions of GHG emissions to try to make Kyoto an agreement which constituted an unprecedented move towards global governance of energy, if only to strengthen the Commission's position inside the EU, where resistance to energy competence moving to Brussels was particularly strong. Most of Europe suffered substantial disadvantage on energy competitiveness when compared with other Annex I parties. Most governments had come to rely for revenues on heavy taxes on fuels and many had adopted policies aimed at reducing reliance upon imported energy, as much as anything because of concerns over the impact of high-priced energy imports on the balance of payments. This was, for example, the rationale behind the French move towards nuclear energy, and Britain's relative advantage during the 1970s and 1980s when it had ample oil and gas, both now declining.

The energy-related rationales went beyond making Kyoto principally a CO_2 regime (rather than a comprehensive approach to GHGs), towards making it into a global regime about energy competitiveness and investment, and a regime fundamentally related to commercial advantages in economic globalization. Many non-European parties considered that the important thing was to reduce GHG levels and leave parties to determine the best way under their circumstances to make a contribution to this. The EU appeared quite willing to exploit the possibilities provided by climate change to remedy its lack of energy competitiveness and advance its investments abroad.

Together with the European Bubble requiring European-level enforcement, this regime would have enhanced considerably the competence of the European Commission in relation to energy policy, but this was a goal that clashed with the other apparent goal of the EU, namely to achieve an outcome at Kyoto for the rest of Annex I which did not substantially reflect the respective interests of these parties. The establishment of competence over energy, and (importantly) on energy taxation, simply required an agreement; establishing a regime which redressed Europe's lack of energy competitiveness required the imposition of costs on competitors which they would resist, lessening the chances of a competence-enhancing agreement being reached.

The other Annex I parties were more likely to subsume their interests and sovereignty in an agreement to limit emissions of all GHGs than they were to support an energy treaty implicitly aimed at exporting European energy competitive disadvantage. At least this is the appearance given by the EU focus on a gross, CO_2-orientated approach and mandatory policies and measures to other Kyoto negotiators. The incorporation of proposals for mandatory policies and measures made Kyoto resemble a trade negotiation, rather than one where science and global interdependency norms would triumph over interests and sovereignty norms. This was made especially transparent in many of these proposals for some kind of supranational monitoring and compliance.

Compliance and Monitoring

The United States was the party most concerned with compliance. Its legalistic culture and fear of losing economic advantage meant that proposals for trading and flexibility mechanisms called for back-up by a strong compliance regime. This would prevent, for example, emissions exceeding the levels for which permits existed. The USA proposed enhanced reporting obligations to enable the performance of parties to be scrutinized closely. They would have required parties to establish national-level enforcement mechanisms to ensure implementation of commitments, and proposed review of parties' performance by expert review teams under the supervision of the Secretariat. Parties that did not comply with these obligations would be disqualified from participating in emissions trading and therefore from cost-effective emission reduction and access to investments. On the basis of these reports, the Meeting of the Parties would then be able to make recommendations or impose penalties on parties, including disqualification from emissions trading. It proposed further development of an implementation regime to address non-compliance, including the establishment of an 'Implementation Committee'.

The European Union also proposed the establishment of an Implementation Committee, but a compliance regime which posed much less of a challenge to sovereignty and was modelled on the Montreal Protocol. This involved the Implementation Committee reviewing compliance with obligations at the initiative of a party in respect of itself, a party in respect of another party, or the Secretariat of its own motion. Again like Montreal, it specified that the procedure should be 'simple, facilitative, cooperative, non-judicial and transparent'. Japan, deeply worried about the political implications of being 'shamed' by inability to comply and deeply distrusting the state's ability to implement what Kyoto might demand (Watson, 2002), proposed an even less obtrusive regime, with performance assessed by expert review teams, after which, if they found a party was 'in difficulty', the Meeting of the Parties would do no more than make recommendations to the party that it review its policies and measures and report the outcome of its review to the Meeting of the Parties within a year.

Positions on monitoring provisions similarly reflected the requirements of the differing proposals of the major Annex I parties, with the EU proposing similar provisions to the FCCC, the USA a more stringent regime as befitting the needs of an emissions trading regime, and so on.

THE KYOTO PROTOCOL

The Berlin Mandate led to the conclusion of a Protocol to the FCCC at the Third Conference of the Parties in Kyoto in late 1997. FCCC Executive Secretary

Michael Zammit Cutajar, at the opening plenary session of COP-3 in Kyoto, drew on what he saw as the consensus-generating power of both science and normative arguments in urging agreement, simultaneously denigrating interests which might stand in the way. In using what the UNFCCC secretariat saw as the drivers of the Kyoto process, he criticized the propaganda from certain industrial sectors that 'unashamedly plays games with the science and statistics of climate change'.[2] And stressing the North–South dimension of the issue, he added that 'in the present constellation of economic and political power, it is those who have already built their strength – often through unsustainable economic growth – who must lead the way towards a sustainable future'.

The EU (through Luxembourg) stated its position at the beginning of Kyoto in the following terms: it rejected differentiation, wanting a guarantee of comparable commitments for major economies at least; it considered 'environmentally detrimental loopholes' unacceptable, and favoured a 'three plus three' approach to coverage (CO_2, methane and nitrous oxide first, HFCs, sulphur hexafluoride and PFCs later); it would accept trading along with strong targets and domestic action, monitoring, sanctions and market safeguards, and JI with rules and safeguards. But it held that mandatory and internationally coordinated policies and measures were indispensable, and rejected any suggestions of any new commitments for developing countries.

Article 2 as adopted described policies and measures that each Annex I party should implement or elaborate in achieving its quantified emission limitation and reduction objectivess (QELROs) in accordance with national circumstances. A subparagraph listed measures 'such as' energy efficiency, sink protection and enhancement, carbon sequestration, phasing out subsidies, and adoption of renewable energy technologies. This Article did not prove particularly contentious and the text was effectively agreed by 5 December and reported to the Committee of the Whole (COW).

Perhaps the most contentious Article to negotiate was Article 3 on QELROs and sinks. Discussions on QELROs were conducted in a negotiating group chaired by COW Chair Raúl Estrada Oyuela (Argentina), who had chaired the AGBM, throughout the first week and in COW sessions on 4, 5, 6, 9 and 10 December (the last session running into 11 December). Discussions on sinks were conducted throughout the first week in a contact group chaired by Antonio La Viña of the Philippines, who had chaired an informal group on sinks in AGBM. Informal negotiations on language to describe commitment periods were conducted under the leadership of Luis Gylvan Meira Filho (Brazil), and contact groups were formed to discuss differentiation and the number of gases to be covered.

The USA had offered to be flexible in its approach to differentiation, an offer repeated by Vice-President Gore when he attended the high-level session in the second week. Gore also reiterated the US commitment to reduce emissions by 30 per cent by 2010, a commitment by the executive branch of government which was barely credible in the light of the Byrd–Hagel Resolution passed by the US Senate by a 95–0 margin.

Extensive discussion of differentiation took place in informal discussions, in both bilateral sessions and sessions guided by Chair Estrada, and by the end of the first week Estrada had reportedly produced a set of differentiated targets for Annex I parties. On 9 December he introduced a new draft text to the COW, and indicated that the proposed text on Article 3 would be treated as a 'take it or leave it' offer. The proposal was for a 'big bubble', which had been suggested by Russia in particular, with a 5 per cent global reduction from 1990 levels of emissions of CO_2, methane and nitrous oxide for a commitment period between 2006 and 2010. After intense negotiations within and between groups, Estrada reported to the COW at 3.20 a.m. on 10 December that the text needed 'refinement' to indicate that each Party would be responsible for its respective QELRO, to be listed in an annex. Several parties indicated they were not yet willing to accept the QELRO commitments in the chair's draft, which had the EU at –8 per cent, the USA, Russia, Canada and Ukraine at –5 per cent, Japan at –4.5 per cent, New Zealand at 0, Australia and Norway at +5 per cent and Iceland at +10 per cent. Australia in particular was criticized for rejecting this figure, with its shadow environment minister stating that +5 per cent was better than could have been hoped for.

On the issue of coverage, on 3 December the negotiating group discussed the 'three-plus-three' coverage proposal with two baskets. In the first, CO_2, methane and nitrous oxide would be subject to QELROs immediately, while the second basket, containing HFCs, PFCs and SF_6, would be decided at COP-4. This was effectively a compromise between those parties which wanted comprehensive coverage and the EU's preference for a basket of three gases which advantaged it, and there was substantial opposition to it. At the COW meeting on 4 December, Chair Estrada indicated that a gas-by-gas approach was still open, but in the COP plenary on 5 December the options were an immediate regulation of six gases or the three-plus-three approach. The Chair's draft presented to the COW on 9 December retained the three-plus-three option, but by early on 10 December support had emerged for immediate inclusion of six gases.

On the issue of sinks, support for a net approach providing for limited inclusion of verifiable changes in forests since 1990 to offest changes emerged from the contact group chaired by Antonio La Viña. La Viña introduced a 'non-paper' during the COW on 6 October providing for limited sink activities to offset emissions. The device of having 'non-papers' discussed by 'non-groups' was a way of excluding NGOs from sensitive consultation, because official papers and contact groups would have had to be open to NGOs enjoying accreditation within the FCCC. This received wide support, but New Zealand, Australia, the USA and Norway called for an earlier text to be kept as an option for consideration by ministers. It was important to get broad consensus on this issue before QELROs were determined, because it would affect the targets that parties would accept. The text introduced to the COW meeting on 9 December included provision for afforestation, reforestation and deforestation as sinks.

By 6.30 p.m. on 10 December, when Chair Estrada reported to the COW on informal discussions, the collective emissions reduction target had increased from 5 per cent to 6 per cent, but commitments were conditional on the satisfactory conclusion of negotiations on a wide range of matters. These included emissions trading, individual Annex I commitments, JI, the establishment of a Clean Development Mechanism, and compliance. Further discussions then occurred and the COW reconvened at 1.15 a.m. on Thursday, 11 December, with the Chair introducing the final draft of the Protocol.

Russia and Ukraine immediately specified targets of 100 per cent for themselves, and Iceland stated that actions taken before 1990 would make its 110 per cent target unattainable. Australia put an amendment that: 'Parties in Annex B for whom land use change and forestry constituted a net source of emissions in 1990 shall include in their 1990 emissions base the aggregate anthropogenic CO_2 equivalent emissions minus removals in 1990 from land use change.' This amendment had been notified in advance and accepted by the chair on assurances that it had been agreed to by all major parties, but the chair neglected to include it, requiring the Australian Minister for the Environment, Robert Hill, to move the amendment from the floor. Some observers saw this as some kind of sharp practice on the part of Australia, taking advantage of the near-exhausted state of delegates to dupe them into accepting a clause to Australia's advantage, but this appearance resulted only from the Chair's procedural slip in failing to introduce the previously agreed text.

Agreement among Annex I parties on QELROs was secured only after acceptance of the need for differentiation outside the European Bubble. Russia offered to trade its windfall emission reductions, and the US negotiators fashioned a negotiating bloc based loosely around Annex I members of APEC (the Asia-Pacific Economic Cooperation forum, which Russia had joined only the previous week), crafting an 'umbrella' of differentiated responses to counter the EU Bubble. Previously, the group had been JUSCANZ (Japan, the United States, Canada, Australia and New Zealand – effectively the non-European members of the OECD before its membership was expanded). This group later became known as the 'Umbrella Group'. At the end of the day, the negotiation took on all the appearances of a trade negotiation, with the USA conducting a series of private bilateral negotiations with parties in the Umbrella Group until a set of targets was agreed which provided a reasonable result overall. (This approach closely paralleled that used by the USA in trade negotiations, although it is more difficult under the expanded membership of the WTO than was the case with the GATT.) This agreement was conditional on both the acceptance of a comprehensive, six-gas, net approach including sinks and the possibility of emissions trading, since the USA wanted to be able to buy, and Russia wanted to be able to sell, emission reduction credits resulting from the collapse of the former Soviet Union economy post-1990.

The overall target agreed to was for a 5.2 per cent reduction on 1990 levels by Annex I parties collectively by a first commitment period of between 2008 and 2012. The EU Bubble was to have a target of –8%, the United States –7 per cent, Japan –6 per cent, Russia and New Zealand 0, Australia +8 per cent and Iceland +10 per cent. Demonstrable progress was required by 2005. This represented a 10 per cent reduction in emissions of all six gases from projected 2000 levels and a 30 per cent cut on 'business as usual' projections for 2010. Provision was made for transfer of certified emissions reduction credits between parties as a means of meeting QELROs, and the banking of credits to subsequent commitment periods was allowed. The 'Australia clause' was to apply to including land use changes in 1990 base emissions estimates, and forestry sinks were included, but a decision was to be made at the first Meeting of the Parties or as soon as practicable thereafter on 'modalities, rules and guidelines as to how and which human-induced activities related to changes in GHG emissions and removals in the agricultural soil and land use change and forestry categories, shall be added to or subtracted from assigned amounts for Annex I Parties' (Article 3 (4)). A decision on this aspect was to apply only from the second commitment period.

There was some remaining concern, particularly on the part of AOSIS, that 'hot air' trading of credits such as those accruing to Russia would be permitted; AOSIS wanted this to be permitted only within the EU. Parties did, however, prevent further credits being gained by the EU upon the accession to the EU of additional members which were economies in transition, because Article 4(4) stipulated that any alteration in the composition of the economic integration organization (EU) would not affect existing commitments under the Protocol.

The Protocol as adopted also included provision for, but no details of, emissions trading. Annex I parties were to be permitted to engage in emissions trading to meet their commitments under Article 3, but Article 17 provided for the Conference of the Parties to 'define the relevant principles, modalities, rules and guidelines, in particular for verification, reporting and accountability for emissions trading'. Emissions trading was also to be 'supplemental to domestic actions for the purpose of meeting quantified emission limitation and reduction commitments under that Article'.

This effectively established a work programme for subsequent COPs, which also included further work to establish a multilateral consultative process (Article 16) and compliance mechanisms (Article 18). But emissions trading was perhaps the most contentious measure aside from the setting of QELROs, and perhaps even including QELROs. It had been proposed by the USA at

COP-2 as part of its preparedness to accept legally binding commitments, and was therefore central to the participation of the USA, without whom any Protocol would be rather meaningless. But it was opposed not only by the EU, but by G-77 and China throughout the negotiation: G-77 even threatened to block paragraphs 3.10, 3.11 and 3.12 allowing some trading in response to a compromise suggestion from the USA (supported by Canada, Argentina and New Zealand) that the details be deferred until COP-4.

Chair Estrada at one stage suggested that the lack of flexibility on the part of G-77 and China might 'blow up' the possibility of reaching an agreement, and noted that flexibility on one side of the debate was not being matched on the other. Eventually the compromise of deferring consideration until the subsequent COP was reached but, together with the deferred questions related to non-forest sinks, this meant that there were substantial issues which had not been resolved, and that ratification of the Protocol by the USA was highly unlikely until these elements were settled in a manner acceptable to it. And because the USA was unlikely to ratify, few other parties would be prepared to do so. This meant that the Kyoto Protocol was only a first step (reductions of 60 per cent were thought to be needed for stabilization of atmospheric CO_2 levels). It was an *incomplete* first step, because key elements essential to a workable agreement to which all significant parties would commit were lacking.

The other substantial stumbling block to US ratification, given the Byrd–Hagel Resolution, was the lack of any commitments by developing countries in the Protocol. The problem was that the Berlin Mandate excluded any such commitments. Nevertheless, on 5 December New Zealand stated that Annex I parties' constituencies needed assurances that developing countries would adopt binding emission limitation commitments in a third commitment period (that is, beyond 2014), and called for 'progressive engagement' of developing countries in accordance with relative levels of development, with exemptions for least developed countries (LDCs). A draft text to this effect was introduced and supported by the USA, Canada, Poland, Slovenia, Australia, Switzerland and Japan. The EU cited the fact that the Berlin Mandate precluded any new commitments and G-77 rejected any such suggestion. The USA stated that it wanted no more than commitments by all except the LDCs to slow the growth of their emissions. Japan and Canada suggested that a sequencing of commitments could work, as it had under other agreements, but G-77 and China rejected any such notion and stated that they would not participate in a contact group as a matter of principle. The matter was dropped, and with it any realistic chance that the US Senate would ratify Kyoto.

The significance of this rejection was that the Berlin Mandate (and thus the Kyoto Protocol), under the rhetoric of global justice, exempted countries such as Malaysia and Brazil, with GDP per capita levels in the same ballpark as those of Portugal or Greece, from any commitment even to slow the growth of future emissions. But it also exempted countries such as Singapore and Brunei, which are considerably *more affluent,* and are among the highest GHG emitters, especially Singapore, with its substantial petrochemicals industry. Many of these countries, several 'Asian tigers' among them, stood to be advantaged considerably by a Protocol which would make fossil fuel consumption more difficult and costly in countries in the region such as Australia without any restrictions within their borders.

G-77 and China managed to defer emissions trading until a later date and rejected any suggestion of even voluntary commitments by developing countries. They also exacted a price for supporting the compromises the Umbrella Group wanted in the form of the Clean Development Mechanism (CDM) brokered by Brazil and supported by the USA. The CDM brought together JI and trading with developing country participation and held out considerable promise of development assistance. It was responsible for bringing many developing countries on board, despite the continuing opposition of India and China.

The EU was the champion of NGO concerns over flexibility, sinks and trading at Kyoto, but it was first and foremost pushing for features which advantaged itself and exported its lack of energy competitiveness to its trading competitors. It was able none the less to play to the green gallery, even though it conceded significant ground on almost all measures except securing the European Bubble. It had succeeded in having some policies and measures specified, but with flexibility according to national circumstances, and it relented on coverage, sinks, trading and differentiation. It was able to secure a target which was acceptable within Europe, but it was unable to impose as much disadvantage on other Annex I parties as it had set out to do.

The mechanism for entry into force was ratification by 55 parties accounting for 55 per cent of Annex I 1990 emissions, in order to prevent the two largest emitters stopping the Protocol entering into force by their failure to ratify, but ensuring it could not enter into force without substantial Annex I support.

FROM COP-4 TO COP-6

At the end of the day, Kyoto resembled a trade negotiation, right down to the nomination of targets by Annex I parties, the USA running a series of bilaterals in a GATT-like 'Green Room', the assumption on the part of parties that surveillance would be attempted to discover negotiating positions – right down to the thirteenth-hour conclusion when agreement was reached in a state of exhaustion. But it left unspecified significant details that would need to be enunciated if the achievements at Kyoto were to amount to anything, and all the signs were there in the meetings of AGBM and at Kyoto that success could not be assumed to come easily.

As it happened, little progress on filling in the blanks left at Kyoto was achieved at COP-4 in Buenos Aires, held 2–13 November 1998. Rather a 'Buenos Aires Plan of Action' was adopted, reflecting a determination to achieve 'demonstrable progress' on the mechanisms of the Kyoto Protocol and several other issues, with a view to strengthening the implementation of FCCC and preparing for the entry into force of the Kyoto Protocol. COP-4 was marked by a set piece by hosts Argentina and the USA over voluntary commitments by non-Annex I parties, which divided further G-77 and China and the Umbrella Group (Russia plus JUSSCANNZ – Switzerland and Norway had been added to JUSCANZ).

At the High-level Segment on 12 November, Argentina President Carlos Menem announced that at COP-5 Argentina (a US ally) would make a commitment to lower emissions in the first commitment period, 2008–2012. This brought condemnation from G-77 plus China, but (as if on cue) prompted the USA to sign the Kyoto Protocol within 24 hours, hailing the Argentinian move as 'historic' and the kind of 'meaningful participation' that was a pre-condition for ratification by the US Senate. This prospect was immediately quashed by Senator Chuck Hagel, co-sponsor of the Byrd–Hagel Resolution, who pointed out that the Resolution stated the USA should not become a *signatory* to any agreement which excluded developing countries from legally binding commitments or caused serious harm to the US economy.

The key point under the Buenos Aires Plan of Action was to be COP-6 in The Hague, where delegates were to attempt to reach agreement on a number of issues critical to the Protocol and the FCCC. These included rules for the mechanisms of the Kyoto Protocol, a monitoring regime, accounting methods for national emissions and emission reductions, and rules for carbon credits through sinks. At COP-5 in Bonn (25 October–5 November 1999), the dates for COP-6 were set as 13–24 November 2000 in The Hague, a timing supported by G-77 and China, against the wishes of the USA, supported by Canada, Australia and New Zealand, which preferred early 2001. Significantly, this set up the possibility – given the timing of the US presidential election on the first Tuesday in November, that the USA would be represented by a 'lame duck' administration, even if it proved to be succeeded by one of the same party. As it happened, not only did Republican George W. Bush (and not pro-environment Vice-President Al Gore) succeed President Bill Clinton, but on-going confusion over the result of the election cast a shadow of uncertainty across COP-6. In pressing for a November date, G-77 plus China demonstrated a lack of appreciation of the political risks which might, and did, arise from the electoral process in a significant party.

COP-5 completed its work programme on time, but was always merely a stepping stone to COP-6. At COP-5 Bonn, however, there was continuing opposition from the environment NGOs in the Climate Action Network (CAN) and the EU to sinks on the grounds that they would provide loopholes for Annex I parties to 'avoid their responsibilities'. But, while there were uncertainties over sink activities, vegetation clearance had always been reported as a source of GHGs, so all the Umbrella Group was proposing was partial avoidance of the requirement to achieve reductions primarily in their energy sectors. NGOs also worked hard to encourage parties to exclude nuclear energy from consideration under the JI and CDM mechanisms. (The nuclear industry had emerged again in strength at Buenos Aires.)

COP-6 was therefore to be the significant meeting at which the gaps in Kyoto were to be filled in. In the event, COP-6 ended in failure, with the EU rejecting an eleventh-hour compromise negotiated by UK Deputy Prime Minister John Prescott, who thought he had a deal with the USA, only to be undermined by the French and German environment ministers – both Green Party minority members of their governments. Then, after George W. Bush had been inaugurated as US President, he announced the US withdrawal from the process in March 2001. It was fair to say that by this stage Kyoto was, if not dead, then at least mortally wounded, and that Bush merely drove a stake through its heart. Certainly, had Gore won the White House and the USA not signalled its rejection, it is difficult to see that the effective position would have been any different post-COP-6 or that Kyoto stood any realistic prospect of being ratified by the US Senate – had Gore indeed had the political courage to submit it for ratification. But the signals being sent out after The Hague were that the USA could have almost 'named its number', so keen was the EU to keep it in the Protocol, but in the substantial transition which occurs with a change of government in Washington that message was lost, underscoring the questionable wisdom of those who insisted that COP-6 be held immediately after a US presidential election.

Irreconcilable differences also emerged between the EU and the Umbrella Group over sinks or 'land use, land use changes and forestry' (LULUCF), which again the CAN, G-77 and China and the EU saw as providing loopholes. The issue of whether provision for sinks should be made in the CDM divided not only the Umbrella Group and the EU, but also caused divisions among the G-77 and China. Costa Rica, Bolivia, Senegal and Guatemala all supported the inclusion of sinks in the CDM because they had much potential for sink creation. Prescott's last-minute deal came close to overcoming these differences before being undermined within the EU.

COP-6 fell apart over the refusal of the EU to grant the Umbrella Group very much at all by way of flexibility on sinks. The USA reportedly made a substantial concession by accepting that only a small part of its target could be reached by using sinks (*The Daily Telegraph*, 26 November 2000), and this encouraged Prescott to believe he had secured a deal. UK Environment Minister Michael Meacher even announced on BBC radio that a deal had been struck, and that the USA would now have to cut GHG emissions by 'something approaching 40 per cent' (*Independent*, 25 November 2000). But Prescott was to be humiliated by his EU colleagues, particularly France, Germany and Denmark, who were not satisfied even with this burden being accepted by the USA. France held the EU presidency, and France and Germany were reportedly furious with Britain for reaching a deal they saw as giving the USA too many concessions and which lacked 'environmental integrity'. French Environment Minister, Green Party member Dominique Voynet, stated bluntly: 'The British made too many concessions' (*The Daily Telegraph*, 26 November 2000). The Saudis also played their role, putting up about 200 amendments aimed at scuttling the talks, so there was little time left for negotiation, but Mme Voynet described the US concessions as 'so unacceptable as not even worth discussing' (*Guardian*, 27 November 2000), so it is unlikely that more time would have helped.

Mme Voynet's performance in The Hague was popular domestically, where, as the sole Green member of the Socialist-led government, she had struggled to be heard, leading to criticism from her party members; she had been held responsible for a number of gaffes, including a slow response to the sinking of the tanker *Erika* off the French Atlantic coast in 1999.

Technically, COP-6 was suspended until July 2001 and was saved, apparently, at least for the EU, though without the USA. It had collapsed primarily over the failure to agree on mechanisms, particularly on so-called supplementarity, or the notion, pushed by the EU, that the various flexibility mechanisms would have allowed targets to be met by anything other than domestic emission reductions – ground which suited the EU. The Umbrella Group wanted simple procedures that would facilitate the use of a wide range of mechanisms (including nuclear energy and sinks) to enable cost-effective attainment of Protocol targets. (The International Atomic Energy Agency (IAEA) urged parties at the COP to consider nuclear energy.) Any economist would regard favourably measures which allowed mitigation to occur at the least cost, but this was to regard emission as 'wrong in its consequences'. For the environment NGOs, pollution was 'wrong in itself' and was not to be permitted; it was to be discouraged at all times. (We shall take up this point later.) The CAN and the EU saw flexibility measures as providing loopholes to allow targets to be met without the desired 'pain' of domestic reduction.

The EU was insistent that there should be a quantitative limit placed on the use of flexibility mechanisms. This position was softened during the COP to a qualitative limit, but Chair Jan Pronk's compromise that targets should be met 'primarily through domestic action' did not go far enough for the Umbrella

Group. Pronk was Minister of Housing, Spatial Planning and the Environment of the Netherlands, and assessments of his performance as Chair of the COP were mixed. It was perhaps not helpful that he was a high-level official from an EU member nation which had been prominent in the Kyoto negotiations.

US WITHDRAWAL AND COP-6 PART II

Bush first announced on 13 March 2001 that he would back away from requiring domestic regulation of CO_2 emissions from power plants, on the grounds that CO_2 was not a pollutant under the Clean Air Act. In a letter to Senators Hagel, Helms, Craig and Roberts on 15 March, he stated that he opposed the Kyoto protocol because it exempted '80 per cent of the world, including major population centres such as China and India, from compliance and would cause serious harm to the US economy'. He also referred to 'the incomplete state of scientific knowledge of the causes of, and solutions to, global climate change and the lack of commercially available technologies for removing and storing carbon dioxide'. Bush was responding to a letter from these Senators which explicitly mentioned the paper by Hansen *et al.* (2000), which suggested that other, non-CO_2 options might be preferable to Kyoto.

The German Environment Ministry at this time was threatening to proceed with ratification without the USA (*Reuters*, 15 March 2001) and soon had that opportunity. On 28 March, Bush stated his opposition to Kyoto, stating that it was not in the United States' 'economic best interest', and pointing to the lack of commitments by developing countries. The US Administration did not, however, seek to withdraw its signature from Kyoto, but rather did what the Clinton Administration had refused to do: it stated that it would not submit the Protocol to the Senate for ratification. Politically, it would have been easier to submit the Protocol for ratification and allow the Senate to kill it, but by not submitting Bush has actually left open the option of doing so at some future date. Bush was to meet in Washington the next day with German Chancellor Schroeder, who only a week earlier had urged the USA to abide by the agreement (*Reuters*, 28 March 2001). In addition to Schroeder, European Commission President Romano Prodi and the Prime Minister of Sweden (which then held the EU presidency), Goran Persson, also wrote to Bush, going so far as to state that the issue was an integral part of EU–US relations (*Reuters*, 23 March 2001). (France had held the EU presidency in the second half of 2000, which meant that Green minister Dominique Voynet had carriage of the issue. In the first half of 2001, the presidency rotated to environmental vanguard state Sweden, but by the time of COP-6 Part II in Bonn, the presidency had passed to the more moderate Belgium.)

This unusual step of elevating Kyoto to a level usually reserved for trade or defence issues was clearly ineffective, if not counterproductive, although British Prime Minister Tony Blair subtly linked climate change to EU support in the battle against terrorism after the World Trade Center attack on 11 September. It remained to be seen whether the USA would take the hint and what any concessions might be. Canadian Environment Minister David Anderson laid the blame for the US decision at the door of the EU: 'The problem was the rigid position of the Europeans who thought they could force the Americans to do something they knew the Americans couldn't do' (*Reuters*, 31 March 2001). The EU very quickly ruled out any possibility of trade sanctions against the USA as a result, as environmental groups organized boycotts against US oil companies, which were widely seen as having orchestrated the decision, a $1.2 million contribution to the Bush campaign from Exxon-Mobil frequently being cited as significant.

The withdrawal of the USA diminished the prospects for the entry into force of Kyoto, but also elevated Japan to a key role, thanks to the trigger being not just ratification by 55 parties, but also that ratification by Annex I parties should account for 55 per cent of 1990 emissions. This measure had been crafted so as to prevent any two Annex I parties from blocking entry into force. The USA accounted for 36 per cent of 1990 Annex I emissions, the EU 24.2 per cent and Japan 8.5 per cent. If Russia joined the EU, Switzerland, Estonia, Latvia and Norway in ratifying, this group would account for 49.7 per cent of 1990 emissions, Japan's ratification would raise it to 58.25 per cent and the Protocol would enter into force.

By early April, the EU was indicating that Kyoto could be renegotiated to suit the USA (*Reuters*, 7 April 2001). But despite high-level talks on the issue in May, the EU and USA could find no compromise (*Reuters*, 23 May 2001). The EU then began to court Japan heavily, knowing that its support was crucial to rescuing Kyoto without the USA, especially as Italy under new Premier Silvio Berlusconi was beginning to weaken EU unity on the issue. It also sent delegations to Australia and Canada. Japan, which was under potential domestic political pressure because it had parliamentary elections on 29 July, was initially offered (in April) a deal which would allow only 0.8 per cent of its 6 per cent Kyoto target to be met by sinks, whereas it wanted 3.7 per cent. The USA was given a generous provision, which would have required only 2.8 per cent of its 7 per cent target to be met through non-sink measures in Pronk's proposal, which the Worldwide Fund for Nature (WWF) estimated would reduce the cuts required by Annex I parties to only 2 per cent (*Kyodo News*, 18 April 2001). By the end of June Russia, too, wanted a more generous provision for sinks in line with the concession extended to Japan by Pronk (*Reuters*, 28 June 2001).

The EU attempted to split the Umbrella Group (USA, Japan, Canada, Australia, New Zealand, Iceland, Norway, Russia, Ukraine and Kazakhstan), taking advantage of differences between it members. Japan had some 'face' invested in the Kyoto outcome, but while it was chastising the USA for its withdrawal, it did little pending a lead from the USA. Russia and Ukraine both had the prospect of large economic gains (theoretically perhaps as much as $5 billion per annum for Russia) through emissions trading disappear if Kyoto failed, so they were open to suggestions that ratification go ahead in 2002 even without the USA. The problem was whether, without the USA in the system, there would be a buyer for Russian credits (*Moscow Times*, 16 May and 18 May 2001). In October 2001, this prospect clearly worried negotiators preparing for COP-7 in Marrakesh, for supply remained high, and without the USA prices would fall – an advantage for Europe perhaps, but would Russia sell or hold awaiting a possible US return and higher prices? In the end, at Marrakesh Russia and Japan were able to extract substantial concessions in return for likely ratification, with Russia able to double its allowances for the use of sinks.

CONCLUSION: THE FAILURE OF THE KYOTO PROCESS

The Kyoto process consisted of a formula which had been employed successfully with other MEAs: an emphasis on science and strong moral arguments to ensure that interdependency norms prevailed over sovereignty norms; the use of 'iterative functionalism', or vague non-binding agreements in the FCCC which were then to be tightened and made more specific. Whereas this process worked with ozone, for example, it resulted in failure or at best a partial rescue with climate change. This raises the question of why this occurred. We argue here that the explanation is complex. It lies not just in the strength of the interests at stake, in the weakness of the science, despite the best efforts to create a scientific consensus to drive a political consensus, but also in the failure of normative arguments in that the actors employing them were not seen to rise above the interests we have described here.

The negotiations in the Kyoto process were at times almost surreal to the outside observer. There were meetings of Friends of the Chair, of Contact Groups on various issues, of non-groups (which thus excluded NGOs) which discussed non-papers, of informal groups and 'informal informals'. These activities frequently took place in all-night sessions, with delegates snatching sleep when and where they could. The delegates in attendance were all highly skilled and dedicated, and relied on armies of well-paid experts. And yet the process failed.

We suggest that this occurred because the key protagonists were essentially operating within different paradigms. The negotiations can be understood as a clash between those for whom interests were important (even though norms are acknowledged as a significant component of institutions) and should be negotiated explicitly, and those who considered that a radical idealism – either derived from or reinforced by science – would be sufficient to deliver desired outcomes. This idealism not only ran counter to the interest-based politics dominant at the domestic level (outside the EU at least), it usually presented itself as a radical rejection of interests which drew much power from that very rejection. Those opposed to the EU position, which was strongly supported by selected green NGOs, were seen as 'merely' acting out of self-interest. Dissenting scientists were portrayed as corrupted by fossil fuel interests.

Yet, as we have seen, this position was based just as much on interests as those of developing countries and the Umbrella Group, and a negotiation which acknowledged this and proceeded to try to equalize costs and benefits is likely to have been ultimately much more productive. The result would probably have been an agreement which involved less compulsion and greater provision for countries to focus on differentiated responses to achieve long-term reductions in a variety of GHGs – via either emission reductions or sequestration in sinks – plus provision for JI in developing countries and compensation for them for impacts. Ultimately, something like this will probably replace the Kyoto require- ments *de facto*, assuming the science firms up the risks. Less immediate advantage would result for nuclear, gas and renewables interests and for countries that suffer existing energy disadvantage. The cost for the Umbrella Group would also be less, but any Protocol of this more permissive nature is more likely to be accepted and implemented and thus serve as the 'insurance institution' which the 'world community' seems to be seeking. (It will certainly provide cheaper insurance than Kyoto.)

In the Kyoto process, the protagonists have spent much time talking past each other, at least in the public discourse between NGOs, governments and intergovernmental bodies. Government negotiators knew exactly what the interests were, but as good diplomats seeking allies, they disguised them and politely did not speak of them. They were, quite literally, operating in different paradigms – or to put it in contemporary parlance, were engaged in different discourses. The Umbrella Group was operating in a liberal discourse, where costs and benefits were trumps; the EU appeared to be operating in a radical discourse, where moral rectitude and consensus science provided a cloak for the interests which were just as significant. Such coalitions between morals- based and interest-based positions are powerful and frequently decisive at the level of domestic politics, where outcomes can be imposed on citizens. But when sovereign states are involved, we suggest, such a result is not possible

and both the apparent strength of the coalition and the sense of self-right-
eousness it encourages is likely only to produce an impasse of the kind seen
in the Kyoto process.

NOTES

1. We have relied for this account on two major sources, unless otherwise indicated. First, the
   Earth Negotiations Bulletin, published by the International Institute for Sustainable Development, and widely regarded as an authoritative and balanced account of events. It is published
   on a daily basis during negotiation meetings, with a summary at the conclusion of these
   sessions. Second, we have relied upon the excellent analysis of the key negotiating issues
   produced just before Kyoto by the Australian Department of Foreign Affairs and Trade
   (Australia, 1997).
2. 'Report of the Third Conference of the Parties to the United Nations Framework Convention
   on Climate Change: 1–11 December 1997', *Earth Negotiations Bulletin* 12 (76): 3.

5.   The failure of principled discourse

In 1991 there was conflict between experts at the US-based World Resources Institute (WRI) and non-Western scientists at India's Centre for Science and Environment (CSE). WRI research focused on current GHG emissions, which, if they were to be cut, would place a higher burden on developing countries than would have been the case with a ranking based on cumulative emissions over a longer time. The burdens would have been different again if calculated as per unit area or per capita, or even per income group. The troublesome issue of 'equity' had been raised. The CSE group went so far as to argue that WRI's methodology was flawed. It disregarded not only the West's higher per capita emissions, but also placed the 'essential' agricultural emissions of the world's poor ('subsistence emissions') on a par with 'non-essential' emissions from the world's wealthy ('luxury emissions') (Jasanoff, 1998, 179–80; see also Hammond *et al.*, 1991; Subak, 1991; Agarwal and Narain, 1991). It was not that a significant group of wealthy Indian citizens did not also emit at high levels per capita, but the general point was made: the reasons for emitting had been ignored and therefore given equal value.

The ethical debates surrounding the climate change issue are more complex than this distinction allows, of course. The middle classes in industrializing countries are growing, so the distribution (not just the average per capita) of emissions among income groups inside countries should be part of any genuine ethical debate; anything else becomes a mere intergovernmental debating point, where ethics are used for blackmail, or rather greenmail.

And ethics may change with what we believe about the causation of climate change. If natural, no blame can be attached and the utility of the issue for political purposes would be much reduced. However, if we assume that climate change is caused by man-made emissions, then the idea of responsibility and even liability is introduced at the very start, and hence the quantities emitted and their distributions in time and space matter very much for policy based on the principle of 'fairness' or justice. The appeal of such value or principle-based arguments to those interests that hope to benefit from emission regulation is obvious.

At a more fundamental level, such normative questions pervade even the interpretation of the science of climate change and thus the definition of the problem. Are the 'subsistence emissions' of methane from a rice paddy to be given equal weight with respect to abatement action to emissions resulting from the construction of a Mercedes Benz or a Rolls Royce? And should responsibility attach to states or to their citizens whose actions produce emissions? By making states responsible, undeliverable burdens may well be placed on a majority of them; by making citizens responsible, who is to monitor and enforce if the state is too weak? New religious taboos might be needed, and there are clearly groups ready to provide these on the assumption that the planet rather than souls needs 'saving'.

Ideally, the costs of pollution should be paid by polluters and thus by consumers, but many of these remain outside the money economy, and many others have votes through which they might reject new taxes or mobility restrictions; competitiveness arguments on the other hand call for 'equal' burdens. So a problem such as climate change can only be addressed through negotiation between sovereign states, despite idealistic views which increasingly see states as redundant. Historian Paul Kennedy (1993, 341) has suggested that we are now all members of a 'world citizenry', an argument which finds enthusiastic endorsement by those such as participants in the Pugwash Conferences on Science and World Affairs (Rotblat, 1997) as well as among some environmental groups, such as Greenpeace. But, regardless of whether we do increasingly owe a planetary allegiance, we are first and foremost citizens of nation-states that may lawfully control our behaviour and raise taxes and that represent us in international politics and negotiations.

These arrangements, developed over many centuries of strife and negotiation, give rise to some less than ideal outcomes. Nation-states are legal constructions of greatly unequal power (and emissions and climates). And GHG emissions, their sources, consequences, and the costs (and benefits) of their abatement all relate to citizens or corporate actors including politicians and officials whom governments, in turn representing states, may or may not be able to regulate in practice. The most one can expect from governments might be that they assist 'natural' technological change, for example by subsidizing R&D, and encourage 'better behaviour' by citizens, perhaps by making undesired behaviour and goods more expensive. But such interventions should be at minimum cost. The reluctance of some states to accept intergovernmental compulsion has one of its roots in this reality.

Pre-existing arrangements also bias the future. Negotiating groups already active within the international system (or seeking participation) will seek prominent roles in negotiations, even if they do not coincide neatly with meaningful categories in terms of either affluence or effluents. The Group of 77 (G-77) 'non-aligned' nations, for example, represents the developing world, but its members include both very poor nations, very prosperous places like Singapore and Saudi-Arabia, emerging economic powers such as Malaysia,

China and Brazil, as well as those with an immediate interest in blocking emission cuts, such as oil and coal exporting states.

The national level of analysis obscures further difficulties at the level of individual human beings. One estimate puts at 500 million the number of people in developing countries with per capita GHG emissions above the Swiss average, and they are by no means all poor (Sandbrook, 1997, 650). The discourse of global justice at the level of the nation-state would result in a street kid in New York being required to bear the costs of the USA abating GHGs, while exempting the Sultan of Brunei. Climate itself is a factor in how much heating and cooling people seek, irrespective of what they can afford. Indeed, we consider the non-uniformity of climate itself, together with highly uneven population densities and settlement patterns – that is the geography of the planet itself, a fundamental barrier to the very idea of equating uniformity with respect to emissions (be these national or even individual) with environmental justice. However, this is a popular idea in some environmentalist circles, and has even been promoted by the UK Royal Commission on Environmental Pollution under the idea of 'convergence'. The idea is that in future the emissions of all should converge to a single global number, a sort of emission 'communism', which can be approached, in the meantime, by emission trading moving wealth from rich to poor countries.

While we do not argue that more equality with respect to health, wealth and income should be discouraged by policy, on the contrary, we do want to stress that making emissions a proxy for these much more complex and important aspects of 'quality of life' is likely to create even more conflict between human groups than it is likely to resolve. Being simple to measure, however, makes emissions attractive to global modellers as well as visionaries and some economists. The idea is undoubtedly a part of the Kyoto negotiations at the fringes, and is promoted under the ethical agenda.

More realistically, norms of interdependency are also advanced as ethical. They are often seen as both causes and products of international cooperation to address global issues such as climate change. As cause, they are seen as one of the important factors which can overcome 'sovereignty norms' – or the reluctance or even inability of nation-states to commit to actions agreed at the international level. As product, the development of norms of cooperation and interdependency is seen as a crucial part of any successful international environmental regime. The development of shared norms within a regime adds legitimacy to the regime (Stokke and Vidas, 1996) and may help to exert what Franck (1990) has called 'a pull towards compliance'.

The appeal to 'one world' ('pollution knows no borders') ideas inherent in much of the environmental discourse is therefore an important factor in any environmental negotiation. It resonates powerfully with norms of global justice and global citizenship – indeed, since the UN Conference on the Human Environment (UNCHE) in Stockholm in 1972 it has *had* to, for the commitment to address simultaneously global justice and 'saving the planet' is the grand compromise which was necessary to secure the agreement of developing countries. It evolved eventually into the concept of sustainable development and is reflected in provisions in most MEAs for double standards, capacity building, technology transfer and other forms of development assistance which have replaced the failed 'North–South dialogue' of the 1970s. We repeat, global climate change, whatever its causes, does not create uniform local or regional impacts, and winners as well as losers must be expected.

For these reasons, it is important that we examine both the nature of the 'principled discourse' brought to bear during the Kyoto negotiation and the agents employing this discourse, environmental NGOs. As we shall show, while NGOs employed powerful values, these did not transcend the differences of interests which divided parties, and worked instead to advantage some parties – the same ones from which NGOs drew their support.

CIVIL SOCIETY AND ITS REPRESENTATIVES

Non-governmental organizations (NGOs) that see themselves as the principal agents dispensing this international morality do not restrict themselves to human rights or development assistance, but almost routinely include global environmental protection as well. Claiming to represent ordinary people in 'civil society' they thus stake a claim to be acting outside and beyond the world of states, though often they act and are sought as tacit allies, or even partners, by governments, or sections of governments. As Henry Shue (1995, 458) has put it, an important element of the international politics of the environment has been the rise of 'politically active forces who are acting in defence of what they take to be the interests of the environment itself or of elements of the environment, such as endangered species and endangered ecosystems'. Being single minded, they also make easy coalition 'fodder' for groups who may seek similar ends for non-environmental reasons. Political naiveté is therefore a charge one could level at green NGOs, as well as their failure either to obtain support for their policies from 'civil society', or to be accountable to the mass public. Future generations here make the easiest group to represent.

A discourse claiming to be about saving the planet from 'degradation' and for future generations cannot but be powerful, and can substantially disempower those whose interests are, or are asserted to be, opposed to it. It also raises a set of issues that is increasingly complicated by the role of visions, predictions and expectations of the future in such discourses. As Shue (1995, 455) puts it: 'powerful norms make liars of everyone who is afraid to challenge them head-on'. Business interests are often a casualty of such 'truth' because they frequently find themselves and their economic interests standing in the way of such moral crusades – although, as we shall see, some business interests are advantaged by them. Also, as a persuasive tool ethics are particularly powerful in negotiations that *a priori* pay little attention to 'who pays' and other cost issues, as is the tradition in intergovernmental negotiations where the 'state' is expected to pay in the first instance.

Richard Sandbrook (1997, 646) has noted that in the Commission for Sustainable Development, 'attendance is made up of environment ministries or the UN representatives who play out the same games in every forum. There is very little evidence of the finance or big economic players.' Sandbrook is critical of much populist 'leftish' writing which sees corporate players as villains almost by defnition (see, for example, Korten, 1996). Business might be part of the problem (as are of course all consumers and taxpayers) but it is also part of the solution, and rather than excluding business, Sandbrook (1997, 649) sees a need to 'bring the private sector into the discourse'. But business tends to hand costs on to people and, if pressed, 'excludes' those it does not need and hands the problem back to the state; also business is never keen to pay higher taxes so that the state can better look after those not included in the 'economy'. As we noted in Chapter 2, Hanf and Underdal (1998) have pointed out that a discourse which can help initiate negotiations in a framework agreement, if continued into the negotiation of a protocol, can marginalize those very interests whose expertise is central to the development of practicable policy responses.

To illustrate our view of the role played by ethics in MEAs more fully, we assume in this chapter, for the sake of argument, that the mainstream hypothesis about global warming is correct. We shall then examine the way in which the moral discourse employed by NGOs active on this issue not only has failed to produce interdependency norms of sufficient weight to counterbalance sovereignty norms and the significance of interests, but has probably worsened the prospects for reaching agreement. The discourse adopted limited the possibilities for negotiating a practical response by not just marginalizing some interests by labelling them unethical, but by advantaging others and thereby widening the distance any compromise would have to bridge. Further, the sheer claim to moral rectitude helped to maintain a regulatory approach to the issue rather than to facilitate 'management' approaches which were not only more conducive to the achievement of results in a flexible, effective and efficient manner, but also promised a less state-centred and potentially less bureaucractic regime.

Our focus will be on examining the moral discourse employed by the Climate Action Network (CAN), an umbrella group for all climate NGOs, including the main NGOs, during the negotiation of the Kyoto Protocol and after. First, however, we discuss some conceptual issues related to NGOs and 'civil society', a discussion which will help illuminate reasons why normative concerns, despite their obvious appeal, were unlikely to prevail.

Speaking for Global Society?

While some welcome the emergence of 'global civil society' (Lipschutz, 1992; Wapner, 1995, 1996), not all scholars are as sanguine about the role played by non-state actors. While Shue is correct in pointing to the emergence of those claiming to act on behalf of interests of the environment itself or endangered species and endangered ecosystems, Walker (1994, 675) raises some sceptical questions:

> To act in relation to 'the environment' . . . is to act explicitly in the name of allegedly 'natural' forces and interests that refuse to acknowledge the merely historical boundaries of states; nevertheless, exactly what it means to speak of the environment, or to act in the name of nature, or how the relationship between the supposedly historical should now be mediated, or who has the authority to act in the name of rainforests and dolphins, is more difficult to specify.

Such moral authority is usually claimed by green groups by means of a biocentric or ecocentric ethical system, because this raises their claims above the level of reflecting mere human preferences and escapes the inconvenient fact that not all people share such preferences. The idea that ecology can provide a set of ethical principles sufficient to unify the world (Laferrière, 1996) is highly contentious and politically dangerous. There are serious doubts that this is the case in a practical sense at the domestic level, and there are conceptual difficulties associated with the fact that the interests of 'nature' can be read in a variety of ways – a point to which we shall return below.

It has been argued that a cosmopolitan global culture is emerging (Beitz, 1983), and that this includes norms of citizenship, racial equality, human rights, progress, and so on. Some would respond that these norms sound very much like those of Western middle-class culture, but (regardless) it is problematic whether shared environmental norms can be identified. Hence, we suspect, green groups place considerable emphasis on 'scientific' justification for their claims, thereby escaping the need for democratic testing in favour of 'scientific' authority. Also ignored by green ideologies tends to be the variety, resilience and variability of nature. There is no 'single' environment, just as there cannot be a single ethic.

Whether or not universal environmental norms can be claimed to exist is an important point, because sociological institutionalists, like constructivists, predict they generate similarities in behaviour induced by a common global culture, whereas realists or liberal theorists would expect differences in behaviour among differently situated actors with different interests. Finnemore (1996, 328) claims that the work of sociological institutionalists 'provides powerful evidence of global cultural homogenization'. They see actors as a product, not a producer, of society and culture (ibid., 333). They argue that, for realists, liberals and others, different actors with different interests are expected to behave differently, and similar behaviour by dissimilar actors or actors with dissimilar interests would be anomalous. But sociological institutionalists in turn claim that such behaviour is easily explained: 'Global cultural norms may make similar behavioural claims on dissimilar actors' (ibid., 334). We maintain that the Kyoto process might have been based upon such hopes, but that the strength of those similar moral claims on interests remained far too weak to be effective for policy. Indeed, some of these 'claims' have had positive as well as negative impacts on interests.

Ethical claims can also serve as a mask for interests, and thus protect them. For example, in climate change politics the case for exempting developing countries from undertaking mitigation of greenhouse gas emissions on the grounds that they have not had the opportunity to develop and have not contributed to the problem to the same degree as industrialized countries, is a strong one (Grubb, 1995, 478). Shue (1992) has posed this question as one of whether the poor nations should have to sell their blankets so that the rich nations can keep their jewellery. But this argument masks interests at both the national and individual levels. The beneficiaries of actions to mitigate GHG emissions (the nuclear, gas and photovoltaic industries, for example, as well as energy efficiency innovators in general) and the countries for whom these commercial interests are important, benefit along with the non-Annex I countries, which include some which are relatively affluent. (Why should Portugal abate, but Singapore – the largest per capita emitter and with higher GDP per capita – not do so?) We return to this point later.

Norms are not the exclusive domain of NGOs, and we not seek to deny that norms, independent of material considerations, are an important factor in determining states' policies. For example, a global norm of racial equality played a crucial role in reconstituting US interests, allowing it to favour sanctions against South Africa in the mid-1980s, despite these going against its material structural interests (Klotz, 1995). Yet the key to this change was the passage of the Comprehensive Anti-Apartheid Act of 1986 and its defence against presidential veto, a domestic event which reflected the coming of age of African-American politics and its long-standing linkages (dating back to the civil rights era) with liberation politics in South Africa. Nevertheless, this was the triumph of a *domestic* norm which was shared internationally, but by no means globally, reconstituting US national interests so that they moved beyond mere defence of access to minerals. (Klotz also fails to distinguish short-run and long-run interests: acceding to a norms-based decision to introduce sanctions can also be seen to serve the longer-run interest of securing on-going access to minerals in the face of the prospect of a new majority regime.)

Interests can include material expectations about future costs and benefits, and actors frequently invoke claims about the lack of representation of future generations in calculations of interests – even elevating such claims to the level of principled discourse. Thus, some actors in environmental politics claim to be acting on behalf of future generations. As with claims to be acting on behalf of nature or some non-human species, this can create rhetorical power, but, since there is no sure way of verifying whether future generations *really* would prefer any particular outcomes, such claims are usually contested. The future *is* represented: in the preferences and expectations of *present* actors about what the future should look like (see Kirsch, 1986). Dressing up such preferences and expectations in moral language has some rhetorical value, but it is often low precisely because it is seen as an attempt to privilege particular views about the future.

Our position here is that the relationship between norms, interests and behaviour is more complex than the sociological institutionalists claim. They are profoundly cultural and integrated in human behaviour. We tend to follow Nadelmann (1990, 524), who holds that norms emerge and are promoted because they reflect both the economic and security interests and the moral interests and emotional dispositions of dominant members of international society. Consistency is not essential, and they also reflect historical factors. They are promoted by both states and transnational moral entrepreneurs who lobby governments and mobilize popular opinion and political support at home and abroad. The norms promoted in this manner are usually cosmopolitan in nature. That is, they relate not to the ways states treat each other but to the ways individuals are treated by both states and one another.

Nadelmann writes of prohibition regimes, but many of his observations apply equally well to any regulatory regime. He notes that global prohibition regimes have usually represented the desire and capacity of European nations or the USA to impose their norms on the rest of the world. The most successful regimes *reflect* widely shared norms, rather than seek to impose new norms, but the temptation to impose norms is strong because global prohibition regimes are driven by a sense of evil and are likely to pay little heed to costs and consequences: 'like crusades, they are instigated and pursued even when alternative approaches appear less costly and more effective' (Nadelmann, 1990, 511). There is something in the nature of a moral crusade, we suggest, with climate change, and we elaborate this point later.

NORMS AND INTERESTS: NGOs AS MORAL AGENTS?

NGOs seek to perform significant roles in international politics as moral agents (Keck and Sikkink, 1998), often acting across national borders in what Kathryn Sikkink (1993) termed 'principled issue networks'. We are sceptical of whether such activity is often capable of 'trumping' interests and are concerned about the political implications of such universalist claims. Rather, we suggest that norms-based campaigns can advantage one set of interests relative to others instead of simply failing to override interests. This can make a successful resolution of an issue more problematic than if a transparent negotiation of interests were undertaken. Institutionalized NGOs such as Greenpeace, WWF and Friends of the Earth also have resource requirements (so-called system-maintenance goals) and thus their own sets of interests. This need to secure resources and generate public support is thus also part of the equation.

NGOs such as Greenpeace and CAN (and their perhaps major ally today, UNEP) do not transcend the interplay of interests between industrial sectors and sovereign states. This can be shown by examining the pattern of financial support for Greenpeace (arguably the most cosmopolitan environment NGO) on the climate change issue (arguably the most global environmental issue). The distribution of support in the form of funds for Greenpeace, especially the 'balance of trade' for individual national branches, reflects the nature of national interests on the climate change issue in the period before the Third Conference of the Parties of the Framework Convention on Climate Change in Kyoto in December 1997 (see Kellow, 2000). There is also a considerable coincidence between support for Greenpeace within nations and provision by nations of extrabudgetary funding within the FCCC process: an indicator of which nations are seeking to drive the negotiating process.

Where Greenpeace support comes from is significant not only because budgets reveal so much about support and priorities in general, but because decision-making power within the organization is quite explicitly determined by fundraising performance (see Kellow, 2000). The piper most definitely calls the tune. It is possible to examine the extent to which support for a campaigning group mirrors the interests and positions of the national government in question. These national policies, of course, are the result of the interplay of domestic political factors that include both bodies like Greenpeace and other interest groups *and* the voting behaviour and support for political parties which may also be supportive of Greenpeace.

Greenpeace funding reflects support in a very narrow range of nations: Germany, USA, UK, Canada and Sweden contributed almost two-thirds of global revenue (64 per cent) in 1996, with Germany alone providing slightly more than half (53 per cent) of the revenue for the international operation head-quartered in Amsterdam. These funds were then used to subsidize operations in the many countries where Greenpeace cannot generate sufficient funds to support its operations. These included not just China and all developing nations, but the USA (a very slight deficit), France and Japan.

Ignoring tranfers to the international office and focusing on revenue-raising success globally, Europe provided 76 per cent of global funds in 1996, a figure which is even more significant when funding for the operations of the international arm are considered, since these are financed from national surpluses remitted to Amsterdam. Just six nations – Germany, the Netherlands, Switzerland, the United Kingdom, Sweden and Austria – provided 88 per cent of the funds for Greenpeace International.

Since voting strength inside Greenpeace is determined according to financial and campaign performance, Greenpeace represents a means by which an agenda reflecting Northern European values is prosecuted in international politics, even to the extent of being progressed in developing countries and other nations, in a way which would not be open to the northern European nations themselves. For example, the government of Germany is unable to engage in campaigns to shame national governments into supporting positions which favour German interests, but Greenpeace can do so. Greenpeace can be seen as acting so as to affect German policy and then assist with the export of that policy (see below).

The differences in support for Greenpeace between Northern Europe and Southern Europe are stark and perhaps even greater than an analysis of Greenpeace alone would suggest, since (in addition to Greenpeace) there is a well-developed domestic environment movement in Scandinavia which competes with Greenpeace for support (Lester and Loftsson, 1993). It would appear that the relative affluence of the two regions is not sufficient to explain these differences, since the low level of support is not confined to the less affluent southern European states such as Greece, Spain and Portugal, but also extends to France and Italy. It would appear that a more complete explanation must be found in some deeper cultural analysis, probably reflecting different cultural dispositions to risk (Douglas, 1992; Wildavsky and Douglas, 1981). German environmental language frequently not only increases the threat image (*Klimakatastrophe*) but also promises more control and salvation via state action (*Klimaschutz* cf. *Grenzschutz, Rassenschutz*) (Boehmer-Christiansen, 1988, 1992b).

The above reference to the provision by Germany of extrabudgetary funds is an important indicator of the extent to which international organizations reflect national interests rather than genuine cosmopolitanism values. In the United Nations system the provision of extrabudgetary funds or voluntary contributions is an important means by which nations exert influence. Projects that otherwise might not be undertaken are made possible, assistance is provided to developing countries so that they can participate in the dozens of meetings in different arenas, and so on. The importance of such funding derives from the budgetary constraints under which the UN must operate. The UN budget is less than 1 per cent of that of the US federal government, and only about a fifth of that is contained in the regular budget; the rest are extrabudgetary funds (Jacobson, 1984, 79). As Jacobson (ibid., 80) has put it: 'What international organizations can do is sharply restricted because of the limited resources at their disposal.'

With voluntarily financed programmes, governments which do not agree with the direction of the programme may reduce their contributions at the so-called pledging conferences for the announcement of voluntary contributions, so that these programmes depend on the confidence of the principal contributing governments (Kaufmann, 1988, 64). While the USA fell behind on its general commitments to the UN and took exception to the activities of agencies such as UNESCO, it continued to support UNEP with voluntary contributions. But UNEP remains heavily dependent upon extrabudgetary funds, with a core budget a little over $20 million, or less than a third of its total budget. Activities which are most heavily dependent upon this type of funding are clearly more likely to reflect the national agendas of their beneficiaries.

There is now strong German support for UNEP, with former German environment minister Klaus Töpfer succeeding to the position of Secretary-General. German support is especially strong on climate change, the German government providing funding to assist with the location of the FCCC secretariat in Bonn. Germany has also suggested the establishment of a 'World Environment Organization' to be headquartered in Bonn (and UNEP is now calling for IPCC-type panels to be set up in other environmental areas).

This lack of budgetary autonomy also makes UNEP dependent upon the assistance of other actors (see Gosovic, 1992). Unlike WHO, for example, it lacks independent scientific capacity and so is open to influence and thus problem definition by NGOs and other actors who can provide this function for them. NGOs can also lobby at the national level in support of UNEP initiatives, which the UN Charter prevents its agencies from doing, so NGOs can also gain influence by redressing this lack of capacity, as well as resource limitations. In contrast UNEP has been trying, fairly unsuccessfully, to obtain money for research and projects from the Global Environmental Fund (GEF), established at Rio and administered by the World Bank. At the World Bank, the climate change related research is being funded by eight Northern states, led by Norway, which wants emissions trading.

Extrabudgetary sources are important in the FCCC: they accounted for two-thirds of the FCCC Secretariat budget for 1995, for example. Examination of the Special Voluntary Fund for Participation reveals that almost 60 per cent of these funds were being provided by five nations: Germany (20 per cent), the United Kingdom (10 per cent), Switzerland (10 per cent), the Netherlands (9 per cent) and the USA (9 per cent). We find a similar pattern with 1995 contributions to the Trust Fund for the Negotiating Process, from which travel and subsistence was provided for delegates from 92 parties to attend meetings in 1996. Two-thirds of the 1995 contributions to this fund came from just four nations: Switzerland (20 per cent), the USA (20 per cent), Denmark (19 per cent), and Germany (7 per cent).

What is particularly significant here is that the provision of extrabudgetary funds for the climate change process reflects closely the national pattern of support which is evident in funding for Greenpeace, the most important NGO on the climate change issue. Northern European financial support was also provided to assist Greenpeace and other climate change NGOs in their task. For example, *Eco*, the newsletter of the Climate Action Network (of which Greenpeace, FOE and WWF are members), was produced during the negotiation of the Kyoto Protocol with funds provided by the Environment Ministries of Germany, Denmark and the Netherlands. As we shall see, *Eco* used strong shaming tactics, such as referring to fossil fuel lobbyists as 'reptiles' during the Kyoto negotiations. Germany, Denmark or the Netherlands could not use this kind of language, but their funding facilitated its use by these NGOs. The language was often that of a morally sanctioned 'carbon war' combating climate change, combining militarist language and strong normative statements in a kind of crusade (see Leggett, 1999).

In addition to this direct funding from national governments and differential support from citizens, several of the NGOs most active on climate change were in receipt of substantial funds from the Commission of the European Union. It is thus hardly surprising that their criticisms of trading did not extend to the European Bubble, the creation of which helped enhance the energy competence of the Commission. The Commission encourages the formation and maintenance of NGOs that are helpful to it. This includes the overarching European Environmental Bureau, which received funding of about €500,000 in 1999, as well as the Brussels agencies of Friends of the Earth (€250,000) and WWF (€250,000), both of which were active members of the Climate Action Network. But the European branch of CAN itself, the European Climate Network, also received funding directly, receiving around €140,000 for 'Capacity building, through the NGO network, on the problems of and the solutions to climate change and the co-ordination of European NGO policy on climate change.'[1]

NGOs might not act as direct agents of national interests, but this analysis suggests that their activities – even those of the most avowedly cosmopolitan of them – appear to reflect the interests of the same nations which provide the basis of their support. This applies even on an issue such as climate change which appears to provide the best opportunity for sovereign realities to be 'trumped' by the norm of planetary loyalty justified with reference to 'objective' scientific consensus.

Greenpeace staged protest action in Australia in the lead-up to COP-3, in which it brandished posters labelling members of the Australian government 'Climate Criminals' for resisting the proposal being advanced by the European Union in the Ad Hoc Group on the Berlin Mandate. In so doing, it no doubt considered it was acting on the basis of a global morality aimed at 'saving the planet'. Whatever its motives, however, it was also using resources provided by citizens of the German nation state – without their explicit approval – to progress an agenda being prosecuted by this state which, if adopted, would be to the advantage of, if not all of its citizens, then certainly of its bureaucracy and significant political coalitions.

Moreover, as we shall see, the CAN overwhelmingly directs its moral discourse at those parties whose interests differ from those of the EU, upon which they are financially dependent. The inconsistency of the CAN arguments is most apparent with their toleration of 'hot air trading' within the European Bubble by means of political bargaining while condemning it on a market basis among the Umbrella Group. While this 'principled issue network' undoubtedly created moral pressure on governments in the Umbrella Group (especially because many journalists accept their claims, moral status and press releases uncritically), the respective governments and especially their negotiators are well aware of this coincidence of norms with interests. If anything, this made them more determined to resist the normative arguments. Further, domestic groups outside Europe which are part of CAN may lose substantial legitimacy in the eyes of governments at the national level, because they can be dismissed as running arguments to the advantage of the EU.

The device of an 'action network' also allowed NGOs active in single states to circumvent the rules for UN accreditation of NGOs (now relaxed: see Willetts, 2000) which required them to have branches in at least two nations. The Australian Conservation Foundation and the Australia Institute (a think-tank producing material critical of the Australian government) were members of CAN. There is something ironic in members of a network that receives funds from a national government which seeks to use climate change to justify its nuclear programme attacking the extent of the influence of the coal industry in the constitution of the national interest of the nation in which they are based.

It is one of the great myths that environmentalists struggle for resources and are readily outspent by industry, and it is a myth which misunderstands the nature of corporate influence. The latter, as we have seen, comes primarily from structural power (the importance of corporate profitability to the state's revenue base and the electoral prospects of governments) rather than from PR campaigns and contributions to electoral campaigns. Greenpeace spends about $140 million annually world-wide. In the USA private foundations are estimated to give more than $700 million a year to causes related to the environment (*New York Times*, 28 June 2001). By way of contrast, the chemical industry made an exceptional commitment of $60 million over five years to counter Greenpeace's Chlorine Campaign, a measure which required the personal commitment of CEOs and which even then only matched Greenpeace's previously established campaign chest.

This suggests that our understanding of NGOs and their role in the development of MEAs must admit the possibility that issues of sovereignty and national interests continue to be important in ways that are not obvious at the rhetorical level avowed by such actors, for whom the claim to moral cosmopolitanism is an important tool by which influence is exerted and resources are attracted. This suggests to us that NGOs and the role they play do not exist in some independently existing global civil society totally outside the operations of sovereign states. Rather, we see claims to universality and global solidarity (*inter alia*) as important tools by which political influence is exerted *by* sovereign states, and frequently following the pattern of 'concertation' observed in neo-corporatist patterns of intermediation at the level of the nation-state. This is not to say that nations pursuing national interests precludes the possibility of such action adding to the international public interest, as liberal institutionalists would be quick to point out, but it does require us to be very open-minded as to the interactions between power, interests and morals.

CASE STUDY: THE MORAL DISCOURSE AFTER KYOTO

We illustrate these points by means of a brief case study of the moral discourse employed by CAN after Kyoto while details were being negotiated, in its newsletter, *Eco*.

Eco is a newsletter produced by NGOs at international negotiating meetings since the 1972 Stockholm conference. For climate change negotiations it is the work of the Climate Action Network, a loose grouping of NGOs active on the climate issue, and it is circulated on a daily basis to delegates to meetings. It thus not only reflects the views of CAN, but forms part of the means by which CAN seeks to promulgate those views during negotiations. While the *Earth Negotiations Bulletin* produced by the Canadian-based International Institute of Sustainable Development provides a much less value-laden and more comprehensive record of deliberations, *Eco* constitutes a good record of the moral arguments which are mustered by CAN.

CAN saw provisions for trading by Annex I parties outside the EU ('buying hot air') and 'reliance on land-use change and forestry accounting tricks' as 'loopholes' (*Eco,* 2 November 1998). Citing scientific evidence for the latter generated in the UK, they saw the need as being for *domestic* action on CO_2, which effectively meant energy-related action, thus delivering, potentially at least, success to supporters at home. CAN also wished that the negotiations focused on science rather than on interests. On the eve of COP-4 in Buenos Aires, it stated: 'Historically in the negotiations, science has, correctly, driven the process, a principle that was abandoned when setting the targets of the

Protocol. Science must again be center stage of the negotiations' (*Eco*, 2 November 1998).

And yet in the very same issue, CAN was perfectly content to misuse science. Despite the IPCC consensus not supporting any claims that warming thus far had resulted in an increase in extreme weather events, CAN exploited a recent natural disaster to try to force the pace of the negotiations. It stated:

> Last year, floods left 50,000 people homeless and caused losses of 320 million dollars and 80 per cent of cultivated land in one Argentine province alone. This shows what can happen when the climate turns nasty. . . . It is clear therefore that Argentina, our hosts for COP-4, cannot fail to be aware of the threats posed by undue human interference with the climate. (*Eco,* 2 November 1998)

Delegates were also offered fresh evidence of pending virtual catastrophe: a new report from the UK Hadley Centre for Climate Change on new modelling showed a 'runaway' greenhouse effect in 50 years; a briefing sponsored by the University of California's Institute on Global Conflict and Cooperation gave a similar story of non-linear change; and there were several other examples of extreme weather (all within the range of natural variability). Among these last was Hurricane Mitch, a severe Caribbean hurricane (by no means unusual), which had killed 10,000. CAN disingenuously stated:

> Although it has to be said that not all weather-related catastrophes may be directly due to climate change, they do demonstrate how extreme weather events can have profound impacts, primarily on developing countries, with their low resilience due to poverty and lack of resources, as well as an already threatened ecosystems [*sic*]. One thing is sure: we can expect continually increasing numbers of events of this kind in the future. (*Eco*, 4 November 1998)

Aside from its sense of surety, this passage captures nicely CAN's bringing together of 'science' and normative arguments related to distributive justice. This 'discourse' was central to cementing the coalition between, on the one hand, the NGOs of the North and the EU which was advantaged by the position supported by the NGOs, and the developing countries represented by G-77 and China on the other. It also points to an implicit coalition between the IPCC (see Chapter 6) and climate NGOs, which can provide political support for the advancement of the interests of science itself, that are supported by the IPCC. While groups like Greenpeace frequently make statements which cannot be supported by the scientific evidence, one can search long and hard for any correction of such statements by IPCC spokesmen.

CAN was also active in employing rhetorical arguments which attempted to weaken the legitimacy of those who might be arguing against the position favoured by CAN/EU/G-77 plus China. It customarily did so in satirical 'gossip columns' with clever titles ('El Tango' in Buenos Aires, 'Ludwig' in Bonn, 'Skunk' in The Hague). For example:

> has anyone wondered about the so-called 'principled' stand the Australians are taking in support of Iceland's attempt to claim special rights to pollute? El Tango has learned that not only does an Australian company intend to build an enormous magnesium plant in Iceland, but also Iceland already imports large quantities of Australian aluminium ore, and seems set to import more for its new smelters. Seems like the 'principles' in question might be those core Australian values summed up in that quaint old proverb: 'Bugger off mate, I'm alright Jack!' (*Eco*, 11 November 1998)

Aside from pointing out that no such 'proverb' exists, the attempt to make something remarkable out of the mundane (Australia is the world's largest bauxite exporter, after all), and the supposition that the Australian government would 'sell' its position on an issue to advantage a company intending to deliver economic benefits to Icelanders, this passage shows an attempt – albeit unsubtle – to try to dismiss proposals of others as merely reflecting crass materialistic motives.

Another device was seen in captions to photographs. Many of these employed unrelated illustrations to make humorous comments which had a kind of under-graduate charm, but others were more personal and pointed.[2] For example: 'The Carbon Mafia: Washington lawyer and fossil fuel lobbyist Don Pearlman yesterday instructing Mohammed Al-Saban (Saudia Arabia) on further obstruc-tion of the process' (*Eco*, 11 November 1998). Again, the discourse is one of delegitimizing the position of those who might have legitimate interests to defend at odds with those of the EU and others advantaged by the dominant moral discourse.

At Buenos Aires and again at Bonn in 2001, however, the fossil fuel industry was not the only industry group CAN had to worry about, because already COP-4 was marked by the re-emergence of the nuclear industry, with 150 lobbyists – about half the industry lobbyists present – being from the nuclear industry. CAN was therefore now caught at the international level in the pincers Helmut Kohl had sought to create for the German Greens at the domestic level. Because it represented a constituency opposed to nuclear energy, it had now to oppose *both* the fossil fuel interests *and* the nuclear lobby, by arguing for the exclusion of nuclear from the Clean Development Mechanism, an issue to come to the fore in Bonn in 2001. Here Japan (with China) pleaded for, and lost (for the time being at least), the inclusion of nuclear power. CAN did not stop at nuclear, however, and argued against the inclusion of hydro-electricity from large dams in the CDM along with any fossil fuel development (even if it would produce greater energy efficiency) (*Eco*, 13 November 1998).

The acknowledged resources for this effort in *Eco* in Buenos Aires and Bonn came primarily from like-minded groups such as WWF, Greenpeace International, the National Environmental Trust, Environmental Defense Fund, Union of Concerned Scientists, the David Suzuki Foundation and the Swedish NGO Secretariat for Acid Rain, raising the interesting question of their funding sources. Possibly for tax deductability reasons, support was also provided by the Glastonbury Festival of Contemporary Performing Arts. In The Hague, however, support was also forthcoming from Climate Network Europe – significant because this body is (as we have seen) directly funded by the Commission of the European Union.

The re-emergence of nuclear power caused problems for CAN. On the eve of COP-5 in Bonn CAN focused on various attempts to have nuclear energy included in the CDM, criticizing Canada, for example, for seeking carbon credits for exporting CANDU technology, and claiming that a number of other Annex I parties (Japan, Australia, the USA, France) were also supportive of a role for nuclear energy in meeting Kyoto targets (*Eco*, 25 October 1999). Particularly worrisome was the resolution adopted at the General Conference of the International Atomic Energy Agency on 30 September, which had stressed the importance of the transfer of atomic technology to developing countries and the need for its inclusion under the CDM. While Austria, Denmark, Ireland, Luxembourg, Norway and Sweden questioned this resolution, it was fully backed by Belgium, Germany, Finland, Switzerland and the Netherlands. As it happened, Germany did oppose the inclusion of nuclear energy in the CDM at Bonn in 1998 but the EU was blocked from adopting this position because of the opposition of the United Kingdom. At COP-6 Part II in Bonn in 2001 nuclear energy was not allowed to be funded via the CDM.

Nuclear energy aside, CAN was also strenuously opposed to the inclusion of substantial provisions for crediting sinks, either at the domestic level in Annex I countries or in developing countries under JI. Their discourse, despite the adoption of a net rather than gross approach at Kyoto, was that the parties should be required to take the hard steps of reducing gross emissions of GHGs at home whatever their domestic energy endowments, rather than be permitted to lessen the burden of such measures by using sink credits.

They were also strongly opposed to the trading of emissions, which similarly would have lessened the burden for non-European Annex I parties. Consistently, they found no difficulty with allowing other European states to 'trade' the windfall emissions of Germany and the United Kingdom within the European Bubble, while condemning Umbrella Group members for seeking to minimize their costs of compliance, attempting to use 'blame and shame' tactics to force concessions from these countries. For example, CAN stated on the eve of COP-6 in The Hague:

> The heart and soul of the [Kyoto] Protocol were the targets for industrialized countries. That heart and soul is now very much at risk. Due to the positions of the US, Japan,

Canada and Australia, the Protocol may not even result in the reduction it set out to do in Kyoto. This would place the world's people and creatures under severe threat – a train wreck for the planet. The loopholes of the Kyoto Protocol could be the noose around nature's neck. Countries must stop this madness, finalize what they agreed in Kyoto – a strong downward trend in industrialized country emissions – and move forward. The planet cannot wait. (*Eco*, 13 November 2000)

Of course, what the Parties had agreed in Kyoto was a *net* approach with provision for trading and sinks, and the post-Kyoto process was to establish the modalities for such measures. CAN was seeking to revisit issues it did not agree with, seeking to overturn decisions by effectively limiting provision for sinks and trading to such an extent that the Kyoto targets would bite on Umbrella Group energy activities. For example: 'It was rash to allow forests to be used as sinks by Annex I countries' (*Eco*, 14 November 2000). The same kind of approach was evident in relation to the 'Australia clause' (Article 3.7) which CAN claimed was 'proposed to bleary eyes early in the last morning of the 1997 Kyoto negotiations' (*Eco*, 16 November 2000). This was an attempt to delegitimize this clause, notified to the Chair after it had been agreed by all negotiating groups, simply because it lessened the burden for Australia by including changes to activities which had formed part of its baseline 1990 activities. CAN was reading qualifications into and out of the text of Kyoto.

It is true that there remain considerable uncertainties over the science of sinks, as well as concerns over their transience, since they provided a one-off opportunity to fix carbon and would return that carbon to the atmosphere unless managed in perpetuity. This is the basis of the critique of Kyoto by Victor (2001). But there were considerable uncertainties over methane accounting, and CAN was unperturbed by these (which happened to favour the EU). Further, even a one-off sequestration of CO_2 could conceivably play a valuable role in any transitional phase, and the atmosphere was indifferent as to whether reductions in CO_2 levels resulted from emission mitigation or sequestration in sinks. (Burning a tonne of coal is similarly a 'one-off' action.) But one further problem was just how sizable were the reductions the USA (for example) could attribute to sink creation and maintenance: a WWF estimate was that this could account for 84 per cent of the US Kyoto target reductions under the US negotiating proposal (63 per cent in a CAN estimate). This was so large it seemed to the Europeans and G-77 plus China that the USA would get off lightly; the EU would not impose inefficiency on the US energy sector, and G-77 would receive less assistance under the CDM if the USA could meet more of its commitments at home. But both, of course, were ignoring just how advantageous Kyoto had been to the EU. (Note that the EU has very little chance of gaining credits from sinks, so CAN is pushing not just science but its funders' policy.)

CAN estimated that 'hot air' trading under Article 17 (buying emissions not yet made) would allow the Annex I parties (that is, the Umbrella Group, since they were not at all critical of the EU Bubble) to make emissions 5 per cent higher than their targets, allowing them to 'back out of their responsibility to make real cuts in emissions' (*Eco*, 13 November 2000). Further, CAN was concerned that credits for coal, gas, oil, nuclear and large hydro projects under the CDM could remove entirely the need for any action to meet Kyoto targets, with a further 8 per cent allowed there. But sinks were their greatest concern, probably because establishing plantations or maintaining natural areas which were fixing carbon sounded so environmentally attractive. So, in addition to exploiting the uncertainty in the science, they attacked them as a threat to bio-diversity (depicting sink forests as monocultures) or threats to the land rights of native peoples, the latter by a somewhat tortured piece of reasoning: 'By giving a carbon value to the natural vegetation amongst which they live, there is an unacceptable risk that their rights will be taken away again' (*Eco*, 14 November 2000). Whereas forest clearing was once such a threat (and is still regarded as such by the Rainforest Action Network), now forest preservation was a risk which solar energy schemes or windfarms presumably were not.

CAN considered that 'bad definitions' of 'afforestation, reforestation and deforestation' under Article 3.3 would allow further increases of 5 per cent by way of additional sink activities under Article 3.4. These definitions were those developed over many years by the UN agency responsible for forestry, the Food and Agriculture Organisation (FAO), so it must be presumed that they were 'bad' precisely because they allowed this result. Further, if Annex I parties were allowed credit for all the reported Article 3.4 sinks, they would be allowed a further 10 per cent increase on 1990 emissions. The CDM provided for a further 19 per cent, according to CAN: 5 per cent through conservation; 10 per cent through additional sinks; and 4 per cent through afforestation and reforestation.

In total, therefore, these activities could account for almost 50 per cent of Annex I parties' 1990 emissions. This might have been regarded as good news and as pointing in a promising direction for the further evolution of the regime, but it was condemned. From the perspective of economic efficiency alone, this constituted a significant block of emissions from which parties (or, more accurately, entrepreneurs acting within the borders of parties) could have identified least-cost means of mitigation. Such potential could have been seen as providing a basis for significant reductions in developing countries (paid for by Annex I parties) through the CDM. Some of this capacity could have been traded off to allow developing countries to increase their emissions, while the CDM provided the means for slowing this emissions growth below BAU, as all the while energy utilization plant in Annex I countries underwent inevitable 'churning': with the turnover of capital plant with time, conservation, renewables, gas, nuclear and even higher efficiency coal plant (with or without CO_2 removal and disposal) could replace less efficient plant as it became obsolete. The possibilities, if the CAN analysis were valid, promised the selection of a basket of measures which could have brought about substantial reductions in future growth of emissions, and possibly stabilization at somewhere less than double 1990 levels.

Such a possibility was anathema to CAN. Rather than welcoming the possibility that time might be bought and trading of sinks and sources might reduce the overall burden, CAN condemned any possibility of such 'loopholes' being permitted. It would let Annex I parties (and especially the Umbrella Group) 'off the hook'. CAN revealed that its concern was not so much with measures to limit atmospheric levels of GHGs by whatever means were most efficient, but with attacking the fossil fuel industry. It stated that such measures 'could invalidate the already small incentives that the Kyoto Protocol could have to reduce the consumption of fossil fuels' (*Eco*, 13 November 2000). The war against climate change had become a war against the evil of carbon.

ENVIRONMENTALISM AS MORAL CRUSADE

It was not just that an attack on a particular means constituted the end for the CAN, but that any suggestion that parties should be able to 'buy their way out' should be morally condemned. The objection here was, as philosopher Robert Goodin (1992, 102–3) has pointed out, to the very notion of 'buying' a right to pollute. We often forget that the notion of 'pollution' is first and foremost a moral or at least judgemental category. We were reminded of this by the anthropologist Mary Douglas (1966), before the emergence of modern environmentalism and since. 'Purity' and 'pollution' are moral categories, usually applied regardless of whether they are also associated with the presence or absence of risks or dangers, as in the German use of the word *Schmutz* (dirt), for pollution. The *emission* of GHGs such as CO_2 thus represents the *commission* of a sin for morals-based environmentalists. As Goodin has argued, environmentalists object to the selling of 'licences to pollute' through either tradable permits or payment of fees and taxes for the same reason that Martin Luther objected to the selling of papal indulgences at the dawn of the Reformation: that what is morally wrong cannot be made right by the payment of a price. But whereas indulgences, we now have reason to suspect, are ineffective, emissions trading might be. Emissions trading tends to be morally repugnant to environmentalists, while being a mere matter of interest to the EU policy-makers.

This is an important point, because this difference between a utilitarian approach to environmental problems and a morality-based one has consequences for politics, and ultimately for policy development. To anticipate the discussion of this point, the distinction between those things which are wrong in their consequences and wrong in themselves distinguishes the political mainstream from radical politics. Much environmental politics is radical for this reason, and such radicalism is indeed useful in getting issues on agendas. It is of more dubious value in developing policies of any complexity. But most policy issues of this kind also involve interests, and those interests which coincide with or are reinforced by strong moral arguments are advantaged, particularly in comparison to those which are opposed by the moral argument. More on this later.

Not all environmentalists are strongly ethics-based, but most of the prominent NGOs such as Greenpeace and Friends of the Earth demonstrate a considerable element of such a basis for their ideologies, and use 'blame and shame' rhetoric both to bring pressure to bear on their targets and to 'affirm the faith' with their adherents. Such morality is usually linked quite strongly to science, in a set of ecocentric or biocentric ethical beliefs. Greenpeace, for example, professes allegiance to the 'laws of nature' which are higher than the laws of man. We do not wish to engage in a detailed critique of such ethical approaches, but it does seem to us that there are substantial difficulties associated with this, not least of which are attempts to derive ethical principles from factual statements (the naturalistic fallacy). Even leaving aside the epistemology of ethics, there seem to be substantial difficulties with the science from which such ethics claim to be derived (see Chapter 6). Most such sets of ethics are based upon assumptions that nature is stable, benign and harmonious, and should be left to find its own balance in the absence of human agency. And it is held to have intrinsic value without human appreciation. Such ethical positions contain a substantial element of teleology, and see nature as involving a purposive progression towards the balanced, climax community. Unfortunately, such a myth of nature is no longer supported even by ecological science, though its 'poetry', as Budiansky (1995) has put it, retains a political appeal especially to a generation of younger people clearly disenchanted with humanity and frightened by the prophets of man-made ecological doom.

Nature, contemporary science tells us, is chaotic. It is marked by perturbation, disturbance and ecological succession, 'non-linearity' and unpredictability, where small changes can have large consequences. A decision for humanity to leave nature alone, were it possible, would be a decision, for example, to allow a particular ecological succession to proceed, and might result in the loss of the ecosystem for which protection is sought. For example, the American prairies and much of Australia's 'natural vegetation' are the products of fire – much of it initiated by indigenous people. To suppress fire in the prairies is to create the very conditions which will allow it to return to forest. Much of modern environmentalism both is out of tune with this science *and* ignores the substantial role of indigenous people and farming in modifying their environments. This rather patronizing view of indigenous peoples, reflected in the frequent description of forest cover, for example, at the time of European contact (1492 in the USA, 1788 in Australia, and so on) derives from a sentimental romanticism which still runs through much environmentalism. There is a yearning for a past golden (pre-Enlightenment) age, or even the Garden of Eden, when people lived in a more harmonious relationship with nature, ignoring the point that life for most people was, compared with today, nasty, brutish and short.

Environmentalism is often described as a new social movement; like the social movements of the past, it emerged in a period of rapid social change (as during the Industrial Revolution). It reflects a yearning for stability, including the certitude of moral rectitude. It involves a radical politics, which (as Theodore Lowi, 1987, has put it) concerns itself with things which are 'wrong in themselves' rather than 'harmful in their consequences', which is the basis of the mainstream politics of post-Enlightenment liberalism within which most mainstream political parties and interest groups operate. In liberalism, the concern is with the minimization of inevitable harm; in radical politics, the concern is with putting an end to sin. In liberal politics, most things are fungible; in radical politics, almost nothing is, and economic motives are considered base. What makes some environmentalism here more persuasive, and from our perspective more dangerous, is that the consequences of the sin of GHG emission are not observable today or even in the past, but rely on predictions from rather dubious 'earth systems' models that can be 'tweaked' to predict doom or nirvana, once these states are defined by the modeller or his funders.

Much of the way in which climate change science has been employed reflects this erroneous view of nature as being stable if left alone, but subject to enormous perturbation through human interference. Ironically, chaos theory informs much of climate science, but is usually accommodated in representations of the results of human agency rather than in depictions of nature itself. Most graphic representations of mean global temperatures, for example, tend to depict the available surface record since about the middle of the nineteenth century; this neatly coincides with the beginning of the Industrial Revolution and the commencement of widespread fossil fuel combustion. It is a fundamental part of the definition of the 'Climate Change Problem' as one resulting not just from burning coal and oil, but from the folly of post-Enlightenment Man and this is enshrined as given in the FCCC, with the IPCC (see Chapter 5) not asked to discover whether this assumption was true, but to quantify it and work out how to prevent it.

If the frame of analysis is taken out to accommodate geological timescales (as John Adams, 1995, for example, has done), the observed changes of the past 150 years are but a minor bump on the course of time. Temperatures and major GHGs such as CO_2 and methane have danced about in chaotically choreographed fashion for as long as geologists can tell. (The apparent connections between temperatures and GHGs in the absence of significant anthropogenic sources is one reason why many sceptics consider the causality might be the opposite to that in the IPCC consensus: that global warming might lead to rises in GHGs; see, for example, Mudelsee, 2001).

Data for the past 150 years do show a rise, but zoom out to a frame of analysis which covers the past millennium, and the 'stability' view of nature runs into perhaps even more serious difficulty. Not only does the post-1850 rise in mean global temperatures seem to be associated with the long, slow climb out of an unusually cold era (which caused widespread famine), but our best existing knowledge (scientific and historical) suggests that in the early Middle Ages the climate was substantially warmer than it is now. Not only does this 'Medieval Climate Optimum' followed by the 'Little Ice Age' suggest substantial natural variability, but these are also reports of enhanced agricultural productivity during the former. Much of Greenland was farmed and grapes were grown in Britain, suggesting that future warming might be at worst benign and at best beneficial, rather than the catastrophe predicted.

For the above reasons, the 'hockey stick' research picked up so enthusiastically by the IPCC and used as the basis to announce that the 1990s were the warmest decade of the millennium resonates perfectly with the marriage of morals and science inherent in green political thought (see Chapter 6). This argument not only attempts to do away with the inconvenience of the Medieval Climate Optimum and the Little Ice Age, but it produces a picture of a relatively stable climate, with a long, slow decline in temperatures before the rapid rise post-1850. It is perfectly suited to the green view of nature. Ironically, much of the 'chaos' recorded by historians is removed from the 'handle' of the hockey stick, yet chaos theory is relied upon to produce the sharp upturn, since only positive feedback loops in General Circulation models can turn even a doubling in concentrations of a minor GHG like CO_2 (responsible for less than 2 per cent of natural forcing) into a warming which is so rapid as to be catastrophic. The climate before anthropogenic contributions of CO_2 is viewed as relatively harmonious; afterwards, chaos leading to catastrophe. Perfect!

Many other aspects of the climate catastrophe discourse suffer a similar distortion. For example, malaria is absent from Europe and the USA, so it is assumed that the *status quo* is stable and benign. As we shall see in Chapter 6, the reality that malaria was endemic on both continents and conquered only recently in human history even in Europe *by human agency* is ignored. 'Climate change from anthropogenic causes will bring malaria', goes the warning cry. Floods, famine, pestilence (and possibly even death of the first-born) lie ahead. All are bound to happen regardless, and each occurrence will be (and already is being) marshalled as evidence of the perils which result from the 'sin' of emitting CO_2. Like all claims of miracles and witchcraft, such bringing of evidence to the 'morally ordained' theory will ultimately be undone one way or the other by science, which restores scepticism to its rightful, central place. But to the extent that sceptics can be dismissed as practising the 'witchcraft' sponsored by economic interests such as the fossil fuel industry, the defence of the discourse will be robust.

If talk of witchcraft sounds a little like 'old time religion' it is probably because this strand of environmentalism is closer to religion than its devotees would care to acknowledge. Besides alerting us to the cultural and moral significance of pollution, Mary Douglas (1992, 15) has also suggested that risk (like witchcraft) is often used as a blaming device to attack disliked elements in society, including multinational corporations such as oil companies and coal producers. Here we note a link with left-wing infantilism, a simple Marxist faith that equated profits with corporations and now with emissions. We all fear the power of large corporations – often with very good reason – so implicating them in the cause of some looming catastrophe serves as a ready means of attacking them and causing them harm. The fact that the catastrophe is unlikely to be disproved in our lifetimes makes it ideally suited to the task. Anti-corporate rhetoric has replaced Marxism since the fall of communism, so many sceptics are found on the political right.

But, as with all risks, there is a serious danger related to man-made global warming that we need to consider. To assess the size and likelihood of this we need the best possible (sceptical) science, rather than 'incomplete science' which has made itself too closely relevant to a particular 'problem' and thus moral discourse. As Douglas (1992, 33) has noted: 'When science is used to arbitrate in these conditions, it eventually loses its independent status, and like other high priests who mix politics with ritual, finally disqualifies itself.' This danger is inherent in the dominance of the IPCC in climate change science, with the marginalization of sceptics from the process by various means, ranging from the rhetorical to the institutional. Douglas also notes that the likely result, when 'objective' science is used to mask evaluative questions, is that the different sides to any dispute will simply engage their own experts, and science will be debased and its all-important integrity, its function of speaking truth to power, will be lost (Wildavsky, 1987).

There is ample evidence that this has occurred with the science of climate change (see Chapter 7). Those with interests reinforced by the IPCC pronouncements on the supportive scientific consensus enthusiastically endorse especially its summaries for policy-makers, and seek every new piece of published research which supports the theory they prefer on principled grounds. All the while, they have developed a new scepticism in the science of sinks, a subject previously of little interest to them. On the other side, those with interests disadvantaged by the IPCC science bring every contrary finding to support their position. This extends not so much to a disagreement over the raw, ungarnished science, but over what it means. Most sceptics acknowledge that we are experiencing some warming, but remain sceptical about causes, about whether it is a bad thing globally, and whether the proposed abatement costs are worth it, given so many other competing global and not so global problems. They also point to the undoubted progress of technology towards reduced carbon intensity. It extends to how the problem is defined: is it just a fossil fuel/technological innovation problem, or should other GHGs be tackled first if that can be done more cheaply?

There is nothing unusual in the various parties to a disagreement seeking their own expertise to assist their argument, but it does mean that we should not be particularly sanguine about the extent to which complex science still engaged in active research (prior to 'closure') can be a force for consensus in international politics, even when linked to strong moral discourse (see Skolnikoff, 1993). As we noted in Chapter 2, Ernst Haas sees more potential than Peter Haas for science to redefine interests, but it is fair to say that this is likely to be a slow process and one which will be limited by the relative importance of existing and nascent interests. While a consensus over science is not insignificant in international environmental politics, it is probably best seen as a necessary rather than a sufficient condition for political agreement. This was of course recognized by the pro-warming interests, who therefore strongly supported the idea of IPCC consensus rather than the once mooted idea of allowing minority reports. Moreover, where that consensus has been 'manufactured' by institutional means (as with climate change) rather than allowed to evolve (as with acid rain and ozone depletion), the more likely it is that its practitioners will be seen by those with contrary interests as 'high priests mixing science with politics', and the less likely that science will produce agreement beyond the initial stage of agreement on the need for more research and undefined action in a framework convention or similar device.

BAPTISTS AND BOOTLEGGERS

The marriage of principled and causal discourses would therefore appear to be problematic. It remains highly unlikely that science can be of much assistance to those wishing to progress purely principled arguments, because science is not a reliable ally for it may (indeed, should) always change its mind with new evidence. While the relationships between science and interests and that between morals and science are of significance, it is that between morality and interests which is of perhaps greater significance.

As we noted at the beginning of this chapter, Henry Shue has argued that powerful norms can make liars of those afraid to challenge them head-on. But Shue (1995, 455) argues that any sharp dichotomy between 'interests' and 'ethics' is misleading, and that 'Ethical judgments are inextricably embedded in international affairs.' Ethical claims are routinely smuggled into what are advanced as explanations, and they sometimes 'change the outcome of the calculus from what it would have been if only one's own interests, such as national interest, were considered'. But, Shue (ibid., 456) warns, we should not assume that interests and ethics always (or even usually) clash. 'When they clash and when they converge upon the same answer, are precisely the questions.'

One problem with climate change would seem to be that there is a markedly uneven distribution of what we might term 'ethical resources' on the issue and the failure of the opponents to marshall their own set. Here the Left might have made a stronger sceptical argument but was probably prevented from doing so, in the North, by its anti-capitalist green sympathies and hence by the 'moral blackmail' of the Greens.

The 'powerful norm' with climate change is the need to ensure the 'salvation of the planet' rather than salvation of the poor and weak alive today. This is indicative of a turn away from humanism, and thus from the perceived consequences of the economic activity of primarily the modern industrial states. The developing world collectively has contributed little to historical GHG emissions and contributes much less on a per capita basis now than the Annex I parties – a most useful normative argument for intergovernmental bureaucracies terribly in need of money. There are risks that it will disproportionately suffer the consequences of catastrophic climate change and (regardless of whether this is the case in terms of science) the most vulnerable of such countries lack the resources with which to adapt to climate change. These characteristics make it an ideal issue for global politics and efforts at developing 'global governance' structures via the Bretton Woods institutions: the affluent North is responsible for the causes, while the costs threaten to fall disproportionately on the developing world.

The climate change issue therefore resonates strongly with the agenda for global redistribution, and G-77 plus China are presented with considerable potential influence by using a discourse which lays blame on the North for the problem and demanding action which exempts themselves, while seeking development assistance through the CDM. The restrictions on fossil fuel energy utilization in Annex I countries that Kyoto proposes further creates advantage for them in the possibility of carbon leakage, thanks to the double standard nature of the commitments. To oppose the Kyoto Protocol is to oppose this development agenda while simultaneously laying oneself open to accusations that one is indifferent to the fate of the global environment. This is enough to make any country afraid to tackle these norms head on, because no country could or would wish explicitly to oppose such norms. Such strong linkage makes the importance of climate change undeniable in any practical sense – at least for democratic governments.

This linkage with the development agenda is significant because it is such a positive one, rather than just a negative complication which must be dealt with by providing a double standard exemption for developing countries as the price of the agreement. While the Montreal Protocol made some undertakings (largely unfulfilled) in terms of technology transfer, it is doubtful whether any other environment issue holds so much positive promise for the South in terms of potential for global redistribution. For the green NGOs in the North, this linkage is crucial precisely because its norms are not shared globally and are held in suspicion by many in the South (see Lal, 1995).

Indeed, while climate protection might be a global public good (see Chichilnisky and Heal, 1994), like any public good, some might have a net interest in opposing measures to advance it (Barry, 1967). An oil-rich state such as Saudi Arabia, Kuwait or Brunei, for example, might be better off maximizing oil consumption and spending part of the proceeds on mitigating the effects. But, as Shue notes, it is erroneous to assume that norms are always opposed to interests, and it is the coincidence between the strongly coupled normative arguments of climate change, global redistribution and the advantage for the nuclear, gas, hydro and other renewables and energy efficiency industries (at the level of industrial sectors) and Europe (at a geopolitical level) which is significant.

A coincidence between a strong ethical principle and an appeal to the common good is a common feature of many regulatory regimes. And any regulation creates not just losers, but winners – in either relative or absolute terms – among those whose goods and services are advantaged by the restrictions on the use of others. In the classic theory of regulation, the more narrowly focused are these benefits, the stronger are the incentives for the beneficiaries to seek them through political activity. But seeking benefits for special interests is not a particularly persuasive discourse; and this is where a public interest or strong normative argument is important, because it can not only add allies to a coalition in favour of regulation, it can also provide a moral cloak to mask the economic interests seeking regulation. Thus, tariff protection is usually justified not in terms of the benefits for manufacturers and their employees, for whom consumers would be reluctant to pay this tax on imports, but in terms of the favourable impact on the balance of payments or the strategic advantages of protecting an industry.

This is the basis for Lindblom's (1959) point that winning political coalitions are comprised of both those concerned for the ends of a policy and those interested in the means employed, and it suggests that there is frequently interaction between Lowi's radical and mainstream dimensions of politics. But, as foreshadowed above, normative considerations do more than just add numbers to the supporters of a cause; they make possible coalitions and a level of support that would not be possible for purely self-interested actors. The cloak of morality enhances the influence of the interest-based actor by legitimating the provision of support to a cause which would otherwise be viewed with extreme suspicion. So the funding of Ralph Nader's Public Citizen Trade Watch by cotton magnate

Roger Milliken to try to oppose trade liberalization at the 1999 World Trade Orgainization (WTO) Ministerial in Seattle was more effective than his openly campaigning for import protection against cheap imports from developing countries such as Bangladesh would have been. And Helmut Kohl's and Margaret Thatcher's early support for action on climate change provided structural advantage for the nuclear industry they both supported in a way that was more effective than any amount of pro-nuclear campaigning.

Bruce Yandle (1989) has referred to these (usually tacit) coalitions between moral agents and economic interests as 'Baptist and Bootlegger' coalitions: Baptists oppose the sale of liquor on Sunday because it is morally wrong, while bootleggers do so because they cannot make money unless there is prohibition. The Baptists would vehemently deny that they were assisting the bootleggers, just as Greenpeace and its partners in the Climate Action Network would bristle at the suggestion that they were assisting the nuclear industry and the oil companies with their holdings of natural gas, or even the expansionist instincts of states. Yet this is the effect of their campaigns.

CONCLUSION

The moral discourse provided by CAN and its members reveals the general failures of an approach to complex MEAs which relies heavily on principled discourse. Its members have so far failed to drive enough of the parties together in the Kyoto process to achieve a truly global agreement that would impose substantial costs for the sake, as they claim, of saving the planet for posterity. Instead, we have a coalition of potential winners with, once again, much to be resolved, or postponed, or ignored. Indeed, because it supported so many of the interests of the European states, whose citizens were the most numerous subscribers to the cause through support for groups such as Greenpeace, CAN hardened the resolve of the European governments to dismiss the USA and the Umbrella Group as merely self-interested because the fate of the planet hung in the balance.

An approach which allowed parties to accept responsibilities and then find the way best suited to their circumstances to meet them, with provision for trading, flexibility, sinks, investments in energy efficiency and renewable – or even nuclear – energy as they saw fit, would undoubtedly have been signed, ratified and entered into force much earlier. Kyoto required a degree of regulation – and thus global governance – heretofore unseen with an MEA or perhaps *any* international treaty instrument, including that on the Law of the Sea, which also lacks US ratification. It did not affect relatively minor ozone-depleting chemicals, as did the Montreal Protocol. Moreover, even Montreal saw interests as central to the successful outcome. Kyoto involved the energy and agricultural competitiveness of industrialized nations, and did so, thanks to the inclusion of some structural features at an early stage, in a way which fractured interests roughly along the lines of major trading blocs: Europe vs. Annex I APEC, roughly speaking.

The prospects for moral discourse to bring about unity largely on European terms were always remote given the ambivalence of science, to which we turn next. In adddition, the strength of the resonance between the moral discourse and the European position meant that these blocs were even *less* able to negotiate because they were speaking different languages: the EU and CAN were in a moralistic discourse typical of radical politics (in Lowi's terms); the Umbrella Group was largely operating within an interest-based discourse typical of liberal or 'mainstream politics'. They were effectively in parallel universes, and the strong moral discourse helped sustain the separation rather than permit the finding of a common language of compromise.

This outcome, while viewed by environmentalists with disappointment, might in fact be just as functional for European politicians as those in Umbrella Group countries, since they can continue to appeal to strong green constituencies, garner support for energy taxes and other measures and so on, while having to do very little. It is important to remember that politicians, not countries, participate in negotiations such as Kyoto. As such, they are playing multiple level games (as Putnam pointed out), though not necessarily only at two levels.

The executive branch of the US government certainly plays principally at two levels: at the international 'board' and at the 'board' of domestic politics (including the politics of ratification in the Senate). But the effective constitutional makeup of different parties varies according to both formal and informal constitutional requirements and also to matters related to a state's location in international politics. Australia, for example, is only a medium power, and its overriding interest lies in the existence of a rules-based international system, so it takes international agreements seriously, because it wants others (especially hegemons) to do the same. It must (since the conclusion of the Intergovernmental Agreement on the Environment in 1992) refer new treaties to the states prior to ratification, because new MEAs alter the relative competences of state and federal governments. Canada faces even more stringent requirements, with the support of the provinces *required* before ratification. Australia (like the UK) therefore takes MEAs and other treaties very seriously, and generally honours what it accedes to (and accedes to only what it intends to honour). Its delegations include both industry and environment NGO representation, and reflect a 'whole-of-government' approach, with all agencies contributing to the development of the negotiating position. For the UK as a unitary state (despite some devolution) the situation in relation to domestic politics is simpler and, in this particular case only, reinforces the interests of EU institutions. Hence, a simpler game is being played, and probably will be partially lost should the expected benefits of a tough Kyoto Protocol fail to come about.

Such simplicity is not always the case, and some parties to international negotiations do not involve industry in MEA negotiations: one of the reasons why they are more honoured in the breach than the observance, since industry is likely to oppose domestic implementation. The European Union represents a more complex case, and its own environmental directives and regulations suffer from considerable compliance problems. It has been remarked that those members most willing to agree to decisions are the least likely to implement them. Environment ministers are typically among the least influential members of their governments, and for them a new European or international commitment provides a means of creating influence *vis-à-vis* their colleagues in economic ministries – who frequently ignore them as best they can. The EU Commission is also notorious for avoiding whole-of-government approaches to issues, with separate directorates-general often pursuing inconsistent policy directions: it is considered environmentally progressive (reflecting the preferences of northern European green states), yet EU fishing policies (reflecting the interests of states such as Spain) are supportive of practices which are far from sustainable. Even on climate change, the Commissioner for Energy, Loyola de Palacio, was arguing the need to continue coal subsidies even while Environment Commissioner Margot Wallström was trying to save Kyoto (*Reuters*, 27 June 2001). Germany was simultaneously subsidizing coal and renewable energy such as wind power.

Decomposition of tasks to different agencies is one of the classic means governments use to try to avoid having to make difficult choices between incompatible options. Normative arguments add to the mix, not only masking and advantaging interests, but also providing the possibility of inaction or contrary actions while symbolically appeasing difficult constituencies. Where commitments are made to undertake actions which are remote in time, even better. The differences between the economic ministries and the environment ministry in Germany are illustrative here, as is the proposed nuclear phase-out in that country, which strains its credibility to outside observers who wonder how this might be achieved while meeting its Kyoto commitments. The phaseout (between 2003 and 2021) is central to the coalition between the SDP and the Greens, but the logic of Kohl's commitment to climate change might still have the effect he intended in driving a wedge between them.

The focus on the principle-based dimensions of climate change, the claim to be occupying the high moral ground for all of humanity and the planet, and the deflection of blame on to those allegedly driven by the base motives of economic interests, permits German domestic politics to be played out at a symbolic level where the incompatible can co-exist, as if the world imposed no opportunity costs. Meantime, those with interests can bide their time. As the Chairman of the German electric utility E.On stated after signing the deal to phase out his company's nuclear reactors: 'Nothing in life is irreversible.' He went on to add: 'I'm sure that nuclear energy will still play an important role in the future' (*Associated Press*, 11 June 2001).

NOTES

1. 'List of organizations having received Community funding for environmental purposes,' *Europa* (http://www.europa.eu.int/comm/environment/funding/finansup.htm, accessed 27 November 2000). The Commission allocates €3.1m annually for the period 1998–2001 in line with Council Decision 872/97/EC of 16/12/97.
2. A good example of this genre – though a somewhat offensive one – showed a web-surfing nun, hand on mouse, licking her lips. Caption: 'Holy See delegate discovers FCCC website's "hidden" section' (*Eco*, 1 November 1999).

6. Institutionalizing scientific advice: designing consensus as a policy driver?

The negotiation of the Kyoto Protocol and the decisions afterwards to give it effect, as we have seen, largely amount to an attempt to resolve conflicts of interests. Strong normative or rhetorical discourse not only did not help the process but, we suggest above, actually made agreement more difficult. Differences between significant parties were hardened, keeping them in 'different discourses' for so long that the quality of what was agreed suffered considerably.

But what of the unifying power of science? After all, as Skolnikoff (1999) pointed out, the importance of science to the climate change issue made the Intergovernmental Panel on Climate Change (IPCC), set up as an advisory body to UN bodies and governments on the science, impacts and responses on climate change in the mid 1980s, a key institution in the process. The Panel did generate a scientific consensus; or rather in its most recent claim 'an authoritative, international consensus of scientific opinion',[1] and disseminated this widely to researchers, governments and the public. Why did that not suffice to 'underpin' a political consensus?

We address this question in this chapter. We suggest the answer lies in the inherently inconclusive nature of climate science, but also in the limited potential of science to resolve issues deeply affected by conflicting interests. The danger, which was realized in our case, is that this 'constructed' consensus, like moral suasion, will be used to support one side against the other and will therefore make agreement more difficult while also biasing research to generate results consistent with policy. It is now likely that the USA and a few others will not ratify the Kyoto Protocol while remaining loyal supporters of the less specific, commitment-free or even opportunity-creating treaty itself. We suggest that the prospect of a scientific consensus driving parties together to secure a global convention despite their substantial differences of interests, while anticipated as likely by key actors, had to remain a chimera. The natural sciences, even when aided by 'social scientific' scenarios of future technological and economic as well as population developments, could not deliver, even in combination with 'precaution', the credible intellectual foundations upon which other types of expertise, especially economics and engineering, could build convincingly. Perhaps more appropriately, it was a quest which involved much tilting at windmills.

In this chapter we examine critically the process of institutionalization of the science of climate change in the IPCC, a role some had clearly intended for it. This involves examining the origins of the IPCC as well as its functioning, drawing attention to the role of science as an interest and the manner in which other interests interrelate with the IPCC and its science. We conclude that the case shows that the ability of science to reconstruct interests cannot but be highly limited; indeed, there is evidence that interests (including the interests of science) have also in part reconstructed science, especially as it is presented to the public and 'stakeholders' for political effect. In the next chapter, we shall examine the way in which the IPCC constructs climate change science by examining some examples of contested evidence and theory, as well as the use made of ambivalent science by NGOs and the media.

We shall begin the present chapter by discussing what we mean by 'science' and how scientific information can be misused by those wishing to harness knowledge to advantage particular causes. We demonstrate that several motives are apparent in climate change research, including among the leading figures in the IPCC, which are consistent with the particular construction placed on the science by environmentalists and EU institutions. As we shall show in the following chapter, this construction includes minimizing the uncertainty of climate science in its most widely disseminated pronouncements, accentuating the negative aspects of possible change relative to beneficial consequences, and ascribing greater than justified causation to the emissions of radiating gases from fossil fuel combustion. In addition, we note the absence of public arguments by IPCC officials against simplification and exaggeration, for both these political processes would serve 'ethics' against 'interests'. In brief, this biased construction of science by the IPCC would advantage its main funders, that is governments with more rather than less interest in actions promising a 'carbon constrained' world, or rather energy sector, for their countries.

THE NATURE OF SCIENCE

There is a natural tension between an institution designed to yield a consensus on the basis of the latest scientific research (as was the IPCC) and the usual conception of science. Science is inherently both conservative and conflictual, and is a kind of game of 'last man standing': the explanation which has survived numerous attempts to falsify it and which has been supported by numerous subsequent studies is to be preferred to that which is based upon a single study. Conflicts between explanations or theories may take a long time to resolve, and may only happen when a new paradigm or instrument of measurement decides the issue in favour of one side. Policy-relevant science may not be given this chance to develop 'naturally' towards agreement; policy relevance may push it too early towards 'closure', with the subsequent danger of loss of credibility for science or of ineffectiveness for policy.

And science thrives on controversy. Scepticism is an essential element in this process of discovery, since scepticism drives attempts at falsification. Both attributes conflict with the desire of science politicians and their clients to capture the imagination (and support) of the public and the media by high-lighting new and significant research results. Findings which replicate or counter earlier findings are not as newsworthy as an initial finding, despite the fact that they are perhaps more important to the advance of science.

Michael Fumento (1993) has listed some common logical fallacies often committed by those abusing science. Several of these apply to the IPCC consensus on climate change science. For example, as we shall see, there is strong reliance on the fact that recent warming has come *after* the Industrial Revolution, and there is a strong danger of reasoning of the *post hoc ergo propter hoc* kind (after this, therefore because of it) in attributing warming to anthropogenic activity. There is more than a touch of circular reasoning about the use of General Circulation Models which are developed and validated against understandings of current climate and are then used to 'predict' future scenarios on the basis of assumptions about future key inputs such as emissions, technology, land-use, economic growth and population. The whole IPCC process relies heavily upon *argumentum ad populum* (arguing by popularity), since the call is always that the assessment reports represent the consensus of 2,500 or so scientists. As Fumento (ibid., 283) notes: 'Democracy is a very nice thing, but it doesn't determine truth.' Or, as Galileo put it much earlier: 'In questions of science the authority of a thousand is not worth the humble reasoning of a single individual.' A consensus on the state of knowledge can surely be negotiated among researchers, but this is informed politics, not science.

And there is ample evidence of the genetic fallacy, which involves bypassing the argument and going after its origin, usually assigning motives to the actor providing the argument. The motives of sceptics are always subjected to scrutiny, with the common implication (or outright accusation) that they are in the pay of fossil fuel producers, and their views can therefore be dismissed (see Gelbspan, 1997; Leggett, 1990). This tactic is not just confined to journalists or NGOs, and former IPCC Chair Bert Bolin is not averse to a touch of guilt by association, once stating (1999, 152):

> Relatively few researchers have questioned the IPCC's conclusions. Their views have, however, for instance received support of a number of industries that have an interest in the continued use of fossil fuels as well as of countries that have large reserves of oil and coal.

There is also much 'either–or thinking'; most sceptics are depicted as being in denial of the 'reality' of anthropogenic climate change. In fact, they over-whelmingly accept the basic elements, but question, for example, whether: the role of solar variability is given sufficient prominence; GHGs are as important as the IPCC assumes in the earth's energy balance and hence the 'forcing' of climate; warming will be as rapid and large as 'predicted';[2] the socio-economic scenarios used to generate a doubling of CO_2 at different dates are realistic (given our poor record with shorter-term forecasting); and whether the warming most likely might be benign or beneficial rather than catastrophic. Sceptics may reject the IPCC consensus, but they do not and are not required to reject all climate change science. What they have not been able to generate, however, is a single testable counter-hypothesis, nor funding to develop one.

We find other pitfalls among at least the 'users' of climate science which can be seen as possible sources of distortion: the corrupting effects of a quest for relevance to the needs of society in the face of the coming ecocatastrophe; collection of data to support the warming theory rather than attempting to falsify the theory by seeking data which would counter it; and attempted marginal-ization of dissenters as 'mavericks'. Stephen Schneider (author of *The Genesis Strategy* (1976) and one of the most quoted authorities on global warming) once stated that scientists should stretch the truth 'to get some broad-based support, to capture the public's imagination'. He added: 'That, of course, entails getting loads of media coverage. So we have to offer up scary scenarios, make simplified, dramatic statements, and make little mention of any doubts we have' (quoted by Schell, 1989). This stretching of the truth is justified for some because it would force the adoption of the kind of technologically simple society popularized by those such as E.E. Schumacher to which clean, cheap, abundant energy is a threat. For others (such as Wolf Häfele), using knowledge selec-tively is convenient to justify fast-breeder reactors, while others see in conservation a kind of Christian asceticism. Several technophobes, including Amory Lovins and Paul Ehrlich, once argued that an abundant, clean energy source (such as fusion) would be undesirable even if it were technologically possible. Various ends can find it convenient to employ the means of this kind of 'science'. This threat is not a new phenomenon but has concerned students of science policy at least since the mid 1980s (Gibbons and Wittrock, 1985).

Key figures in the IPCC and its progenitor institutions are on record as supporting energy technologies which are advantaged by the thrust of their climate science. Bert Bolin (anti-nuclear but pro-renewables and conservation), Herman Flohn, Wolf Häfele, John Houghton and Robert Watson have all made very specific statements on energy policy. Bert Bolin and John Houghton have addressed the energy community and spoken in support of rises in energy prices and ending subsidies to coal (WEC, 1993, 43, 47). Bolin published on energy policy and climate change as early as 1971, and Flohn and Häfele did so in

1981. This combination of stating problems together with promoting specific technical solutions has disturbed governments and some industries. It lends support to the point we are emphasizing: that environmental protection policy can be as much a complex reflection of available solutions and research agendas that require government support to succeed in the market place as a response to real problems – and often it is both of these. This resembles closely Cohen *et al.*'s (1972) 'garbage can' model of organizational choice, which describes how problems and policies 'find each other'.

While Bolin, Flohn, Häfele, and Houghton spoke as well-known scientists and leaders of research institutes and programmes, it was their task to ensure that research fields to which they had devoted their active research lives were adequately funded and continued to have their respective governments' ear. The claim to policy relevance is a well-known aspect of the politics of research funding. These men were eminent researchers but made their impacts as opinionated bureaucrats who may have predispositions which, if they influence any judgements they make, are likely to accentuate their interpretations in such as way as to strengthen the apparent evidence for climate change. Bolin was particularly close to Swedish energy policy and Houghton himself gave 'teach-ins' to Margaret Thatcher and senior UK bureaucrats, many of whom were unable to be critical of the science presented to them (they had the archetypal civil service classical education without any science) but saw the world view presented to them as close to their personal beliefs, while those who could follow the debate foresaw major opportunities for themselves and their departments.

Häfele, once closely associated with energy modelling at the International Institute of Applied Systems Analysis (IIASA) had a predisposition which was decidedly pro-nuclear, and while the conservation and alternative energy theme is more commonly voiced in climate change politics, the nuclear theme is still present. For example, Robert Watson, who replaced Bert Bolin as the chair of the IPCC and is also a senior environment official at the World Bank – and who started his professional life as an atmospheric research scientist in the UK before moving to NASA, began his keynote address to the Uranium Institute, London 1998, with the following words:

> I would like to present the case of why climate change is a serious environmental issue, which presents the nuclear industry with a major opportunity to meet the growing energy demands of the world. There is absolutely no question we need to increase the amount of energy in the world. Today there are two billion people who do not have electricity. . . . I do believe climate change is an argument your industry can use, that we need to move away from the fossil era, to produce and use energy in very different ways from the ways we do it today. (Watson, 1998, 19)

Resonances such as these between renewable energy technologies and nuclear energy are usually overlooked, even though they have just as much potential to corrupt the scientific process as industry funding for research. (Similarly, BP is not just an oil company, but a gas company and a major producer of photovoltaic cells.) This is especially so when we consider the effect of directed funding by governments in structuring the priorities of research institutions, and creating a 'grant-dense' environment in which scientists must operate and in which they are increasingly asked to do policy-relevant or strategic research, research which serves predetermined ends.

The nuclear industry gains most structural advantage in the climate change debate because it is already well-integrated into prevailing infrastructure and is well able to replace fossil fuel technology on the necessary scale. Indeed, we have already cited much evidence that the industry now hopes for a major revival even in Europe and North America, but energy prices must be 'right'. Renewables come up short on technical and economic grounds. Even more highly favoured, even if as a one-off step, is the switch to gas, because it can occur without significant government assistance, if the price is right. Fuel shifting from coal to gas and nuclear capacity are well-tried emission reduction strategies, especially in the EU where they have the additional (or even, perhaps, primary) advantage of reducing dependence on imported fuels. The advocates of renewables, energy-efficient housing, cars and appliances, as well as the usually neglected advocates of conservation, accept nevertheless the IPCC consensus because many of the scenarios fed into the GCMs do not assume nuclear energy as an option. Ironically, the results of these modelling exercises drive policy-makers to the conclusion (as Watson notes above) that nuclear energy is very much a viable option, so model results which assume nuclear phase-out in order to drive up assumptions of future emissions of CO_2 ultimately provide political support for the opposite effect.

A BRIEF HISTORY OF CLIMATE CHANGE RESEARCH

Curiosity over the effects of anthropogenic emissions are almost as venerable as the Industrial Revolution which was marked by a shift from largely renewable energy sources to fossil fuels. The possibility that emissions of carbon dioxide might produce an enhanced greenhouse effect was first raised in 1827 by Joseph Fourier. In 1896 Svente Arrhenius predicted an increase in air temperature of between 4 and 6°C and in 1938 a British steam technologist, Guy Callendar, also concluded that the planet was getting warmer because of carbon dioxide emissions. This prospect was usually regarded positively, Callendar concluding that there was no need for concern as this would prevent another ice age or be resolved by the advent of nuclear power. Callendar's views influenced Herman Flohn in the 1940s in Germany, and Flohn was an important figure in the rise of interest in climate change in the 1970s and 1980s in both Germany and the

USA. Many scientists did not see global warming as a serious problem because they considered nuclear power the solution to any problem that might arise. The climate change research debate began in earnest in the late 1950s with reference to *weather modification* and military activities, with the USA, Germany and Sweden most deeply involved. In 1957 American scientists pointed out that human beings were carrying out a large scale geophysical experiment that might yield far-reaching insights into the processes determining weather and climate. This was a theme later picked up by British Prime Minister Margaret Thatcher in 1987, when she propelled the United Kingdom to the forefront of the battle against global warming, first on the research front and later by encouraging 'the market' to switch from coal to gas for electricity generation. Long before such drastic action came to pass, by 1961 Charles Keeling had proved that the carbon dioxide concentration in the atmosphere was indeed increasing. Occasional warnings in the media began a bit later for, in the early 1970s, there was scientific concern over global cooling, a threat of apparently little interest to political communities.

At the First International Conference on Environmental Futures held in 1971 in Finland, the climatologist R.A. Bryson gave a keynote paper on 'Climatic modification by air pollution' which considered the cooling role of aerosols in climate, as well as threats to the ozone layer (Polunin, 1972, 167).[3] Atmospheric dust was feared to be the causal agent of global *cooling*, though Bryson in discussion admitted to a 'sneaking suspicion' that the loud demands for more monitoring were 'mostly for the care and feeding of big computers' rather than the welfare of man (Bryson, 1972, 165–7). In the subsequent discussion, a research scientist from Finland, E. Halopainen stated that the development of numerical general circulation models to simulate the present climate and the behaviour of the atmosphere in long time scales was 'a natural first step in attempts to predict what happens to the atmosphere as a result of man's activities.' He claimed that this was the ultimate goal of the Global Atmospheric Research Programme (GARP), a joint effort of the International Council of Scientific Unions (ICSU) and the World Meteorological Organization (WMO), which was considered to be the predecessor of a later major research effort, the International Geosphere Biosphere Program (IGBP).

The research director of GARP during the 1960s was the Swedish meteorologist Bert Bolin, who was later to become the first chairman of the Intergovernmental Panel on Climate Change (IPCC) after its establishment in 1988.[4] Bolin had come to international prominence for his work in bringing Sweden's concern over acid rain to international attention in 1972, at a time when Sweden was at the beginning of a transition from imported heating oil to nuclear power (Lundgren, 1998).

Concern about warming would not become prominent on the world political agenda until the mid 1980s, when the price of fossil fuels began to drop sharply, thus ending the 'oil crises' of the 1970s and the easy market access of 'clean' fuels and technologies which had been developed in response to high energy prices. The IPCC had its origins in events between 1986 and 1987.

Until this opportune moment, the study of man's potential influence on climate had advanced but slowly with the development of computing power and satellite data collection, but the pace accelerated when research institutions learnt to link their interests to fundable human concerns and political opportunities (Hart and Victor, 1993). From the 1970s the 'limits to growth' debate and later predictions of 'nuclear winter' each acted as strong stimulants, with each advancing computer modelling capacity in the institutions capable of participating in this development of earth systems science. As early as 1965, the US President's Science Advisory Council argued that useful climate change predictions down to the regional level would be possible within two or three years, given sufficient computing power and funding. Ironically, more than 30 years later, no such detail was possible and some doubt that it ever will be (McCracken, 1992, 13). In 1970 the Massachusetts Institute of Technology, always at the forefront of research planning, convened a 'Study of Critical Environmental Problems' which concluded nevertheless that global warming was a serious possibility and advocated the aggressive expansion of climate research, combined with population control and protection of the food system. Large research agendas had become 'policy relevant'.

ACID RAIN PRECEDES GLOBAL WARMING

The issue of global warming was discussed at some length at the 1972 Stockholm Conference on the Human Environment when climate change was accepted as a research issue and a UN institute for planetary survival was proposed by the USA after a considerable domestic debate which brought German and American scientists together (Kellogg and Schware, 1981). However, the political climate, supported by energy policy concerns, was ready only for concerns about acid rain rather than for global warming (Boehmer-Christiansen and Skea, 1993).

As the concerns of Bryson (above) indicate, in the mid 1970s some began to worry about global cooling, in response to the observed decline in average global temperatures which had occurred from about 1940 (see Ponte, 1976; Schneider, 1976). All the evidence then pointed towards the fact that we were nearing the end of an interglacial period and scientists were warning us that the onset of the next ice age could be sudden. By the early to mid 1980s a similar research-generating threat came from the possibility of a nuclear winter, due to the masking effect of atmospheric dust kicked up by numerous nuclear explosions. Some otherwise quite detailed accounts of the history of climate politics manage to ignore completely the global cooling scare in the 1970s and the nuclear winter scare of the 1980s (for example, Soroos and Nikitina, 1995).

Following the US example, the executive of the WMO soon afterwards included climate change in its research portfolio. By the end of the 1970s the United Nations Environment Programme (UNEP) had made climate both a research and a development issue. UNEP director, Mustafa Tolba, mentioned energy and the need for better climate forecasting in 1974 without any reference to global warming; but when he addressed the First World Climate Conference in 1979, he referred to climate change as the process of carrying out an uncontrolled experiment in the earth's atmosphere and assured his audience that UNEP was ready to assess the environmental impacts of increased levels of carbon dioxide (Tolba, 1982). The idea was soon to find its way into the Brundtland Report, written by an anonymous group of environmental experts for senior politicians who saw potential in bringing developing and developed countries together under a green umbrella. Its energy chapter concluded with the well-known assertion: 'a low energy path is the best way towards a sustainable future. . . . nations have the opportunity to produce the same level of energy services with as little as half the primary supply currently consumed' (WCED, 1987, 201). A powerful plea for renewables was made, already then backed up with the claims of Irving Mintzer of the World Resources Institute that: 'The ultimate potential impacts of a greenhouse warming could be catastrophic' but also that that 'the greenhouse issue is an opportunity . . . it provides another important reason to implement sustainable development strategies' (ibid., 175). The cited source for the threat was Bolin *et al.*'s *The Greenhouse Effect, Climate Change and Ecosystems* (1986).

The rhetoric has changed but little, but moved from research to bureaucracy, and hence into R&D. But technology, oil prices, energy demand and global politics have moved on.

THE WARMING THREAT PREVAILS

The WMO executive itself began to attract climate change research to its research portfolio by the late 1970s. Efforts to draw attention to the subject with reference to energy demand forecasting can also be traced to this period when American, Canadian, Swedish and British research groups began to collaborate on integrating energy forecasting and environmental futures.[5] From then on, the more specific threat of global warming, rather than simply climatic change and above all the immediately useful forecasting of climate variability, became linked with the already described strong advocacy of certain energy policies, be these fast-breeder nuclear reactors, 'soft' renewables or energy conservation. A politically influential alliance was emerging as the rapid rise of energy prices experienced during the 1970s, which had pushed 'clean' energy technologies in the 'right' direction without government intervention, came to an end.

With the two OPEC-inspired energy shocks of the 1970s receding and environmental concerns in general on the rise, particularly fears about nuclear energy, energy demand forecasters became increasingly interested in the environment. In particular, they became attracted to the possibility that the prospect of a warming earth might be 'mitigated' by burning less fossil fuel. American, German, Canadian, Swedish and British research groups began to collaborate on energy forecasting and environmental futures, including projects such as those at the International Institute for Applied Systems Analysis (IIASA) in Austria where East could meet West on non-ideological matters. The designers of fast-breeder reactors in particular were attracted to the subject of climate change, as only a vast nuclear programme was thought to be able to cope both with the enormous predicted growth of energy demand and global warming. In Germany this led to the previously mentioned collaboration between climatologist Herman Flohn and Wolf Häfele, the father of the fast-breeder reactor, at IIASA in the 1970s (Cavender and Jager, 1993; see also Flohn, 1981; Häfele, 1981). Estimated temperature changes put forward in the late 1970s for a doubling of carbon dioxide concentration were lower than those put forward in the nineteenth century (Kellogg and Schware, 1981) but differed little from those proposed a decade later by the IPCC. Häfele is said to have influenced the 20 per cent target adopted by the organizers of the 1988 Toronto Conference, when a 60 per cent reduction had been proposed as the necessary target, a figure also resurrected by the IPCC and later the UK Royal Commission on Environmental Pollution. When the 60 per cent target was suggested, Häfele argued for a more modest target because the fast-breeder reactor, which would recycle plutonium from conventional reactors, would not be ready in time.

This resonance between nuclear energy and climate change science was complicated by the minor nuclear accident at Three Mile Island, Harrisburg, Pennsylvania in 1979. While Three Mile Island involved only a negligible release of radioactivity to the environment, it galvanized public opposition to nuclear energy at the precise time policy-makers were looking for an alternative to dependency on oil. It had a severe dampening effect on further nuclear construction in the United States. European nations such as France and Germany had made major technocratic commitments to nuclear construction programmes that were opposed by vigorous social movements. While the issue was largely decided in France in favour of nuclear power and weapons by the end of the 1970s, it came to dominate German politics in the 1980s and initiated the rise of the Green Party to political power as a coalition partner in the 1990s. Climate change was a convenient issue for nuclear advocates, because it seemed to compromise their environmentalist opponents, forcing them to confront directly the choice between the risks of climate change and the risks of nuclear energy. The green lobby has, however, proven remarkably adept at avoiding having to make the choice by exaggerating the technical promise of renewables and energy efficiency, as well as the acceptability and painlessness of energy saving.

The accident at Three Mile Island threatened to stall German efforts to implement its nuclear power programme, as it did in the USA, and the German government explicitly used climate change to counter this opposition. To recall, Chancellor Schmidt, when opening the European Nuclear Conference in Hamburg in May 1979 had already stated that he believed that GHG emissions might soon evoke discussions 'equally as emotional as those about the exact consequences of Harrisburg' (cited by Hatch, 1995, 415). Chancellor Schmidt's prescience in the aftermath of Three Mile Island was followed by the publication of a report in 1983 warning of global warming which could be avoided only by switching from fossil fuels to non-fossil fuels, with nuclear and solar power being seen as the only viable alternatives (ibid., 420). Significantly, this report came not from the German Meteorological Society (DMG), but from a society whose members would benefit from an expansion in both solar and nuclear research, the German Physics Society (*Deutsche Physikalische Gesellschaft* or DGP), which had established an 'energy working group' (AKE) in 1979. This first press release made dire predictions of sea level rises of 5–10 metres and was largely ignored, but a second report published in 1985 in which DMG cooperated was more moderate and was accorded more credibility.

German responses to the oil price shocks, however, had not included just a commitment to nuclear energy, but an investment in energy efficiency and alternative energy, especially solar power combined with the idea of the hydrogen economy. This, together with action to implement the principle of 'preventative action' (or *Vorsorgeprinzip*) was the beginning in Germany of what became known as 'ecological modernization' or 'Green Keynesianism': that is, technological progress through state guidance towards ecological efficiency. In response to these measures (and higher energy prices) West German CO_2 emissions fell by 1.2 per cent per annum in the period 1980–9 (Brenton, 1994, 174). The German investment in energy efficiency was, however (like its nuclear programme), predicated on high energy prices, and two dramatic events in 1986 jeopardized both. First, the price of energy collapsed, oil falling from \$25 per barrel in 1985 to \$15 in 1986. Second, the Chernobyl accident in Ukraine in April 1986 spread radioactive fall-out across much of Europe and accentuated opposition to nuclear energy.

In the 1987 German election, the Social Democrats supported by the Greens proposed massive expansion in coal-fired capacity as the basis of their commitment to nuclear phase-out (or *Ausstieg*). This accorded with the interests of the coal mining unions affiliated with the SDP, and provided justification for continuing subsidies to coal mining. Chancellor Helmut Kohl, his Christian

Democrats and above all the Bavarian CSU (still guided by the firm hand of Franz Joseph Strong and long supporters of nuclear power) seized the opportunity provided by the second AKE report, which had been published in December 1985, to compromise opponents. Continued investments in nuclear power, energy efficiency and renewables needed justification, for what was needed was an increase in the price of fossil fuels and hence a reduction, worldwide, in the demand for coal and oil (Boehmer-Christiansen, 1993). Global warming, like acid rain, promised to improve the competitiveness not only of nuclear power but also of renewables and save a fledgling energy efficiency industry which was jeopardized by the collapse in oil prices.

The nuclear science lobby, also closely associated with climate research in the USA since the 1960s, now became particularly active in Germany, where the state had invested much in this power source and Green opposition was strongest (Rüdig, 1993). A politically very influential alliance of industrial R&D and commercial interests formed as the rise of energy prices experienced during the 1970s came to an end. Countries with pro-nuclear, if disputed energy policies were among the first to recognize the opportunity 'global warming' presented to them. The AKE report of December 1985 (mentioned above) had already warned the public of a climate catastrophe. It called upon German politicians, the science and business communities and all citizens to reconsider energy policy and support international action to conserve energy and develop new energy technologies. These physicists seemed quite certain about the causation of global warming: they blamed the burning of fossil fuels, including gas (an argument heard much less in the UK, Norway or the USA, where gas came to be seen as the solution in the immediate term), as well as deforestation and various industrial activities. A mean rise in sea level of between 5 and 10 meters in less than a hundred years was predicted, though quantitatively certain predictions about extent and timing would not be available in the foreseeable future. Industry was called upon to supply low-emission solutions which were optimal for the national economy (DPG, 1985). This agenda, to be successful and secure the support of industry, needed internationalization so that German industry would remain competitive, therefore Germany would need to find allies.

A similar logic applied in other nations where nuclear construction programmes were by now problematic. Sweden, for example, had in 1979 voted in a referendum to phase out its reliance on nuclear energy (shortly after having seen it as a solution to acid rain). Climate change became a serious political question in Sweden in 1988 when the Social Democrat government proposed to decommission two nuclear reactors. The Conservative Party opposed this move, using climate change as a rationale. Parliament approved a Conservative proposal to limit emissions, supported by the Centre Party and the Greens, who considered such a limit would lead to support for renewable energy. The Ministry of Finance used the opportunity to raise revenue through the imposition of a carbon tax ten times that later rejected by the EU (Edin, 1999, 140). It is fair to say, however, that the resonance between the climate threat and energy politics was loudest in Germany, where there were also strong concerns over coal for two other reasons: high costs and sulphur content. Any scientific findings suggesting that carboniferous fuel sources were likely to produce catastrophe on a global scale were thus welcome politically as they would reinforce attempts to reduce subsidies against the wishes of industry and unions. France, the USSR and Japan, which were still pursuing largely unchallenged nuclear programmes, remained largely outside the debate, though a joint US–USSR research programme on global warming revealed the first signs of a rift, with the USSR favourably disposed to the prospect of some warming.

INSTITUTIONALISING INTERNATIONAL CLIMATE RESEARCH

The political mood for climate science opting for the warming over the cooling hypothesis was therefore most propitious in the mid-1980s. The time was ripe for a 'knowledge base' that would provide justifications for reducing the use of fossil fuels and increasing use of both nuclear and alternative energy and for supporting struggling energy conservation efforts. If the circumstances were propitious in several key industrial nations, this was also the case internationally provided the possible opposition of the USSR could be overcome, and the Third World, especially China and India, could be assuaged over their hopes for rapid industrialization largely predicated on cheap domestic coal.

However, the 'North–South dialogue' of the 1970s soon proved to be spectacularly unsuccessful in securing significant wealth transfers between rich nations and the developing world. Climate change would then dovetail neatly with this stalled agenda of global redistribution. By definition, the problem had been caused by nations which had burned the largest amounts of fossil fuels – those which had undergone an industrial revolution – while the consequences (such as the projected sea level rise) would harm developing nations. As mentioned, the Brundtland Report published in 1987 made much of this opportunity. Even beforehand, and in association with it, research institutions had begun to till this fertile soil. A small group of environmental scientists and research managers who had been working on energy and climate (including nuclear winter) since the late 1970s met again at Villach, a small village in Austria, in 1985 at a conference sponsored by UNEP, WMO and ICSU. At this meeting an Advisory Group on Greenhouse Gases (AGGG) was established. It was to hold its first meeting in 1986, and it successfully launched global warming into world politics the very year oil prices collapsed and Chernobyl exploded, and it remained active and influential until 1990. In 1988, however, AGGG was replaced by the IPCC as the recognized advisory body on climate change.

The Villach Conference had been organized by the Swedish International Meteorological Institute (IMI), the home of Bert Bolin, and the Beijer Institute (now the Stockholm Environment Institute, SEI), which had close research links to British and US institutions. It concluded that it was now believed that in the first half of the twenty-first century a rise of global mean temperature could occur which was greater than any in mankind's history, and recommended that science-based emission or concentration targets should be worked out to limit the rate of change in global mean temperature to a maximum of 0.1°C (WMO, 1986). Even at this stage, therefore, before much was known of the impacts of climate change (certainly compared with the present) emission reduction rather than adaptation was being advocated. This selection of response strategies had occurred without any substantial evaluation of economics and other factors such as its political implications. Rather, these response strategies were relying on technical options already seeking safer markets as the period of very low fossil fuel was coming to an end (1986).

The organizers had already commissioned a book from SCOPE, ICSU's Scientific Committee on Problems of the Environment. Many subsequent IPCC participants made major contributions to the book, which one major IPCC coordinator has called the Panel's bible (Bolin *et al.*, 1986). The scientific papers read at Villach, commissioned and peer-reviewed by its organizers, were published jointly by WMO/ICSU and UNEP (Bolin *et al.*, 1986). However, the conference was attended mainly by non-governmental researchers. For example, only one scientist from the US Department of Energy's Carbon Dioxide Research Division was present whereas US government scientists and delegation members dominated the subsequent IPCC by their numbers alone.

There was, therefore, no need for consensus-generating procedures at Villach, as only those in agreement with the aims of the group had been invited, but there were apparently worries that government science might be excluded. Instead, participants from Harvard University, SEI and the nearby International Institute for Applied Systems Analysis (IIASA, Vienna) dominated the meeting and had already defined desirable responses to the climate threat as part of a 'sustainable development' strategy. It was considered that another 10–20 years of observation would be needed before the detection of global warming was likely, and ecologist William Clark from Harvard stated that uncertainties, from emission rates through environmental consequences to socio-economic impacts, dominated the greenhouse gas question (WMO, 1986, 24). The Conference felt that refining estimates was 'a matter of urgency' and recommended a list of actions. These remained vague with respect to response policy, but not at all for research. The IGBP and the World Climate Research Program of WMO were recommended to governments. The analysis of decision-making rules under specific kinds of risks, the determination of damage costs from greenhouse warming as well as the behaviour of policy-makers were to be researched. An action plan for technocracy was in the making, one might argue, and has now been handsomely funded by an international funding network for over 15 years. Its latest offerings include 'sustainability science', Earth systems modelling and global environmental governance based on scientific principles.

Yet it remains significant that, at the time of Villach, there was a marked absence of evidence of global warming. The records indicated a slight cooling trend since about 1940, a trend which had given rise to fears of cooling and a possible descent into a new ice age. This concern over an enhanced greenhouse effect as a result of GHG emissions was an entirely theoretical affair at this stage, based on the assumption that rising carbon dioxide levels (which had been observed) would lead to enhanced warming that might be dangerous. Evidence in support of the theory was quickly and enthusiastically mustered by James Hansen at a now famous appearance before a US congressional committee during the heat wave of 1988, where he pronounced that the greenhouse effect was now a reality.

Absence of observational evidence of warming notwithstanding (and despite Russian scientific opposition to the whole idea of warming being a threat), Villach also recommended that a global convention against warming should be considered. The Conference largely approved the broader, political brief urged by Tolba for UNEP under an 'agenda of action'. A proposed non-governmental International Greenhouse Gas Coordinating Committee was to:

• promote and coordinate research, monitoring and assessment;
• promote the exchange of information related to climate warming;
• prepare and disseminate educational material;
• approve the possible advantages of an intergovernmental agreement or global convention.

It was also agreed that a small task force would be set up jointly by ICSU, UNEP and WMO to ensure that periodic assessments were undertaken of the state of scientific understanding and its practical applications. The core of the small group already existed; it had organized Villach and became the AGGG. But AGGG was seen as too independent of governments. The IPCC was established to perform this role, but with governments, the funders, and not scientific institutions in charge of the processes of report writing and consensus creation.

A subtle change from 'climate variation' (in the title of the Villach conference) to 'climate warming' had been made on the basis of a specially requested modelling exercise. The link with energy policy was not explicitly stated, but emerged during discussions and from the research interests of the participants. Professor Gordon Goodman, chairman of the policy group and one of the organizers of the conference, had written the previously mentioned energy chapter of the Brundtland Report. AGGG members subsequently organized the 1988 Toronto Conference on the Changing Atmosphere: Implications for Global Security, it had no official status but called for the 20 per cent reduction of CO_2 emissions that caused much unease among governments, industry and other scientists. AGGG also organized the Second World Climate Conference in Geneva in 1990 and disseminated its results (Jäger and Ferguson, 1991). AGGG also prepared the Meeting of Legal and Policy Experts held in February 1989 in Ottawa; it recommended an 'umbrella' consortium to protect the atmosphere which was to be implemented through subsequent protocols. It also proposed a World Atmosphere Trust Fund and a Convention that should be served by a panel of independent experts.

AGGG recommendations reflected a degree of ambition that added to the pressures in several countries for the setting up of an intergovernmental group. There was therefore considerable bitterness when the AGGG was replaced by the IPCC under pressure from the US State Department on the Executive Committee of WMO. Presumably, with the support of the US Department of Energy, a major sponsor of carbon dioxide research, it wanted scientific assessment to stay in governmental hands, not in that of 'free-wheeling academics'. It would not even trust its own Environmental Protection Agency with a strong role in the negotiations, very much in contrast to the situation in the UK (Boehmer-Christiansen, 1995a).

By 1985, therefore, a network of science leaders (the managers of the research enterprise) had formed that included people deeply involved in energy and policy research and determined to initiate a dialogue with 'policy-makers', a select few of whom they invited to a 1986 meeting in Italy. The AGGG succeeded in taking the research and policy debate into the world of politics, but its institutional base proved too weak to keep the issue out of the hands of big, accountable institutions: governments and the WMO, which had the ability to fund the global change experiment. The IPCC is therefore best understood as resulting from *status quo* forces seeking to control AGGG and its advocacy. The overlap of individuals and institutions attending the Villach conference, and later supporting the IPCC and IGBP, provides the evidence for the ability of the research enterprise to attract attention to its programmes by defining its research problems as global. Informal links between IPCC and IGBP have remained strong.

The positive responses of some governments to the global warming idea, especially from the United Kingdom, surprised many. Australian scientists, for example, were surprised that 'almost overnight, greenhouse-induced climate change moved from being the business of specialised bodies . . . to become the centrepiece of a major political happening' (McTegart and Zillman, 1990). At Geneva, and even more so at subsequent conferences, the specific threat of global warming rather than simply climatic change became linked with the strong advocacy of certain energy policies. In the UK, a sudden and large decline in CO_2 emissions could at this stage be safely predicted, thanks largely to the closure of British coal mines and the switch to natural gas, deindustrialization and recession. Britain was about to emerge, under Margaret Thatcher's prime ministership, as a world leader in the battle against carbon. What elsewhere became a party-political battle remained in the UK, at least until 2001, a bipartisan issue that would serve to justify much more than the wish to become more energy efficient and less reliant on coal. It would provide a much sought after role on the world stage and in the European Union, and help particularly with the urgent task shared by governments of both complexions in raising revenue when increases in income taxes had become taboo.

THE FORMATION OF THE IPCC

The IPCC was set up jointly by WMO and a very youthful and poorly endowed UNEP and was repeatedly called upon by the UN General Assembly to provide 'scientific' advice (Churchill and Freestone, 1992). The Panel was now dominated by scientists from government scientific research institutions using the good offices and machinery of the World Meteorological Organization (WMO) to reach the heart of governments via meteorological offices and eagerly assisted by environmental bureaucracies engaged in flexing their growing muscles. By absorption and rejection of the AGGG network, IPCC lead authors were assembled by science leaders meeting through the WMO, and set to work to write carefully planned but (initially at least) hurriedly reviewed chapters for reports to its sponsors and the UN.

At its first meeting the Panel defined its brief, apparently after considerable debate about the rights and wrongs of giving governments policy advice as distinct from scientific guidance. It was decided to set up three working groups (WGs) meeting concurrently but without any procedural links: on scientific assessment (WG I, UK based), impacts (WG II, USSR/Australia based) and response strategies (WG III, USA based). A fourth group had been proposed to deal with problems faced by developing countries, but it never eventuated. The Working Groups were guided by a Bureau consisting of the chairmen of the groups and located in Geneva, home of the WMO.

The IPCC would be paid for by voluntary contributions, and the funding of the underlying research efforts would remain primarily national responsibilities and as such part of Met Office funding or the general research budget. In the UK, much of climate research was actually funded by the ministry in charge, *inter alia*, of environmental policy, with Sir John Houghton directly advising the bureaucracy and senior politicians. Formally, the IPCC would not sponsor, much less conduct, research. Its task was to gather and assess the findings of research underway, yet virtually all its chairmen were well-known research managers. Each of its many future reports would henceforth require line-by-line approval, not only by the Bureau, apparently representing hundreds of independent scientists, but by individual governments, in the form of a small number of civil servants responsible for research relevant to policy. In practice, this would mean that a handful of governments with the capacity to run model-based climate research: the USA, Germany, the United Kingdom, Australia, and later France, China and Japan, and a strong civil service, perhaps even ministerial interest, would give the final form to IPCC reports.

The Dutch and American environmental bureaucracies in particular collaborated in creating a strong global warming threat (since 1990) by prescribing emission scenarios for IPCC WG I (science)[6] which assumed a rapid doubling of CO_2 and rapid global economic growth. IPCC scientific research, on the other hand, became closely integrated in UK environmental policy formulation in order to advance British science policy. WG I gathered and assessed available scientific information on climate change science, a branch of meteorology and atmospheric physics. Its co-chairman was to be Sir John Houghton, a British meteorologist and research manager (head of the Meteorological Office at the time), with strong religious views and a long career as government adviser on climate and space science.[7] He is reported as seeing climate change as a moral issue, and as having stated that reducing GHG emissions will 'contribute powerfully to the material salvation of the planet from mankind's greed and indifference'.[8] His group was able to base itself, in 1987, on a well-established research network and close links with large climate research institutions in North America and the then USSR.[9] The threat of global warming was disseminated by the IPCC in a highly condensed form through its summaries for policy-makers (SPM), not, initially at least, subjected to full scientific scrutiny and development. The results of WG I would feed into WG II for its assessment of the impacts of climate change, a subject close to the heart of UNEP which had been active to create North–South links with reference to the 'common' threat of climatic catastrophe.

These two groups were, in logic at least, meant to supply data and ideas for the formulation of 'realistic' policy response options from which governments were free to select (old WG III). In practice, there was very little contact, except that WG III would provide the emission scenarios through which WG I would achieve the doubling of CO_2 required by the models. In 1993 the IPCC was reorganized by combining working groups II and III into a vast but fragmented group coordinated from NASA. It was co-chaired by a British atmospheric physicist known for his previous involvement with WG I and ozone research, Robert Watson, who would later replace Bert Bolin as chair of the IPCC.

Watson is also an environmental manager and research director at the World Bank and advised a previous US president on climate change science.

The old WG I was altered little and left to get on with its central task of assessing the outcomes of modelling experiments without 'political interference', as originally intended by WMO. Such interference would only surface when the summaries for policy-makers drew policy advice from the findings, apparently at hotly contested and largely secret meetings between the Bureau and lead authors of the many chapters that made up the full reports.

The new WG III largely became the home of economic modellers who deal with sanitized, that is, value-free, matters loosely described as 'socio-economic' and 'cross-cutting'. The new WG III was given a Canadian chairman with impeccable WMO credentials. It considered efficiency and equity issues as separable.[10] The old WG III was attended by 'policy-makers' who at most would be junior advisers in environment and foreign affairs ministries, and attracted not only governments, but also representatives from industry and assorted invited NGOs. It was the most volatile, unstable and hence least productive group academically, but presented governments (and participants) with a most useful learning exercise about the kind of conflicts that the Inter-governmental Negotiating Committee (INC) and the FCCC would have to face as work progressed on negotiating a treaty and a chance to influence outcomes through the work on providing scenarios for WG I. If the first two groups were seen to supply the rationale for action (causation and negative impacts), the old WG III became a forum for those advocating changes, *inter alia*, in national energy systems. WG III was home to energy policy specialists and, because it produced the scenarios which drove the climate modelling exercises, it effectively determined projections of climate change. The solutions were effectively driving the definition of the problem.

The IPCC began as a 'rich nations' club'. Only 11 nations of the G-77 group of developing countries were represented at the first meeting of the IPCC, with only 15 delegates and advisers between them, thanks to both their inability to cover delegates' expenses and the shortage of scientists working in the area of climate change. The second session was attended by 41 representatives of developing countries, but there were concerns on their part about their lack of representation in the IPCC, and they took their concerns to the General Assembly of the UN, an arena in which their influence was greatest. Here they used this influence to increase their role in IPCC and to advance the issue of technology transfer. The influence of developing countries was to increase dramatically over time, however, as political considerations would have had no difficulty in overriding the scientific basis for action. More individuals participating in the IPCC does not necessarily increase influence or create genuine new science input. The climate modelling and scientific research capacity of many developing countries in general, especially of the smaller ones, remains extremely low even though the IPCC has since used GEF funds to improve this situation.

The efforts of working groups were vaguely coordinated and their meetings enabled by small secretariats provided by a few interested national governments, with (unsurprisingly) Germany and the UK and also Australia showing considerable commitment. Many thousands of pages of scientific research, already compressed into hundreds of summaries, were reduced by these small teams into several tens of pages called 'Summaries for Policy-makers' and subjected, like the report chapters, to a review process. Reviewers were selected by the working groups, again with approval of government officials. Small drafting teams would have the choice of accepting or rejecting any amendments that were received (Skodvin and Underdal, 1994). The politically most important policy-makers' summaries were negotiated among lead authors guided by the working group chairmen, whose personality would define how any conflicts would be resolved. Richard Courtney (2001), who observed the IPCC meeting when the TAR Synthesis Report was agreed, has stated:

> The purpose was to provide a Report that integrates information from the summaries of the recent reports from the three IPCC Working Groups. The Lead Authors had provided a Draft Text for the Synthesis Report and governments had provided comments on it. The Lead Authors had then revised the Draft in an attempt to incorporate those comments. The Meeting ploughed through the revised Draft and approved – or amended before approving – each sentence of it. In the event of disagreement the Chairman convened a small informal meeting called a Contact Group. Any government representatives could attend a Contact Group that would hopefully decide a sentence the Plenary would accept. Only governments were permitted to input any information or comment to the Plenary and Contact Groups ...[11] Only sentences that were agreed by every government were included in the Report. Objection by any one government was sufficient to have a sentence excluded or modified – often, other phrasings would be sought. I would also comment here that given this rule, it is somewhat hard to understand how IPCC can be seen as a cutting edge organization in saying anything. . . . National interests clearly motivated inputs to the meeting. . . .
>
> The IPCC Synthesis Report is a very political document. The UK, US, Germany and Saudi Arabia made about half of all contributions to the Plenary between them. . . . In this sea level debate, as in several others, it was repeatedly stated that the 'message' must be helpful to policy makers. But, in my opinion, the method for achieving this desire was very wrong. The 'message' was clearly a single, one-sided view of the issues that was agreed by all the governments. Absence of complete agreement prevented inclusion of any statement. This resulted in, for example, exclusion of the complexity of sea level change mechanisms from the text. Hence, the Synthesis Report is a document of agreed governmental policy and not a complete assessment of the science. Scientists are not one handed.

As we have seen, John Zillman (then chair of the WMO) has lamented the extent to which political lobbying intruded into IPCC processes (Zillman, 1997).

IPCC Assessment Reports and the Research Base

The IPCC connected research network has grown over the years and now involves several thousands of researchers who, initially at least, worked in the natural sciences and engineering. They were joined after 1992 by a growing number of social scientists and technologists, especially economists, geographers and political scientists, but also epidemiologists, who have added 'global data sets' on emissions, economic impacts of carbon taxes, population growth, health and agricultural statistics and speculative impacts of temperature changes, as well as equity data and strategies, all centred on emission abatement. They were all expected to present their results in 'value-free' form, though this has to some extent been relaxed in TAR (WG III) which now considers various forms of equity between countries and has adopted efficiency, market-based instruments and value for money as basic decision criteria, and includes 'visions' of possible futures. While it is still too early to evaluate fully this global experiment in interdisciplinarity, genuine collaboration appears to have proven difficult and is often resisted.[12] Single research institutes in the social sciences may account for producing proposals that then lay claim to universality, but they have by no stretch of the imagination undergone the global 'peer review' process which is at least attempted for WG I. One observation which can be made, however, is that while interdisciplinarity in the IPCC has been concerned with assisting decision-making and the institutional underpinnings of the issue, it has strictly avoided political analysis of the research community as a political actor in its own right, and of the political impacts of climate strategies. Technology transfer and development related issues, however, have strongly attached themselves and report through WG III.

The First Assessment Report (FAR) was produced in 1990, and helped drive the establishment of an Intergovernmental Negotiating Committee (INC) to prepare the FCCC. An update of the 1990 IPCC report was produced for UNCED in 1992 (Houghton *et al.*, 1992). A shorter version of this report was published by WMO and UNEP and concluded with five key uncertainties: sources and sinks of GHGs; clouds; oceans; polar ice sheets; and land surfaces. These uncertainties were to be reduced by improved model experiments, improved observation, better understanding of processes (climate related, socio-economic and technological), national inventories, more knowledge of past climate changes and improved exchange of data. The Reports were, therefore, not just intended to drive the international politics of climate change, but primarily to set and support the climate change research agenda evolving under WMO and ICSU supervision. The Third Assessment Report appeared in 2001, after The Hague meeting, but there was copious leaking of its contents and Robert Watson addressed the plenary meeting at the beginning of the negotiations, creating a strong threat image.

Since between 1990 and 1992 (that is, when the FCCC was being drafted) there had been a strong perception inside the IPCC and elsewhere that policymakers needed a 'consensus' view, a position typical of the UK civil service where only consensus reports by experts or select committees have a chance of influencing government policy, there was much effort to create this consensus by careful drafting and rewriting under the guidance of government officials. It was noted that model results were reported to be 'in broad agreement', when scientists themselves were most interested in their differences. Given the nature of the knowledge that was being condensed, consensus was most readily achieved on subjects that were least well understood; ambiguity became a virtue and even natural scientists came to appreciate the importance and value of vague language.

Once agreed by small groups of lead authors who had full discretion to take note of (or ignore) 'peer review' comments, these reports were published by a small number of governments, with Britain probably being most generous to 'its' group, the science group, WG I. IPCC products are glossily produced by Cambridge University Press and widely disseminated by interested governments and UNEP/WMO in the name of 'the scientific community', usually accompanied by claims about how many scientists from how many countries had contributed to the effort. The reports were in fact finalized by a handful of people on the basis of drafts provided, selected and evaluated by 'lead authors' who were appointed by WG chairmen in consultation with national scientific elites – that is, research bodies. Each chair would be responsible for the prompt delivery of the report of his/her working group, which was drafted by ten or so lead authors meeting occasionally, often begging for money to allow their third world colleagues to attend. Mexico once complained that it required more meteorologists to participate in the IPCC than it was able to afford to employ to produce its weather forecasts.

Under the IPCC, research, which remains largely government funded, indeed flourished, especially in North America and Europe, but Australia, New Zealand, Japan, India and China were also increasingly drawn into research networks. Knowledge was to be collected and assessed to suit political needs and timetables, a task which was becoming frustrating if not impossible to comply with honestly. In particular, scientists repeatedly argued that policymakers wanted them to deliver quickly on two issues which would make policy-making so much easier: these were to provide a definition of a single global warming potential (GWP) which would include all greenhouse gases into a single index, and to predict climate change at the regional and subregional levels. Because it attempts to express other GHGs in terms of equivalence to CO_2, GWP helped establish the hegemony of CO_2 in the discourses surrounding Kyoto.

A single GWP would allow trade-offs between the various gases and sinks and permit the implementation of the comprehensive approach favoured by the USA because of its profound difficulties with reducing carbon dioxide. This instrument became enshrined in the FCCC and has required further research effort for its 'objective' definition. Regional prediction would allow governments and regional bodies actually to 'plan' for expected changes in various climatic indicators, thus providing for activities which need not, ever, lead to implementation. However, neither of these two issues was of immediate interest to earth systems science. Policy-relevant science thus required to be funded, and policy became increasingly entrenched in the science, with the result that criticisms began to constitute a political challenge which would be increasingly resented. The IPCC has been criticized, but only a few scientists have published their reservations and limited organized opposition was only observed in the USA, from within the world coal industry and most interestingly in Europe.

Unsurprisingly, scientific opposition in the USA has tended to come from the political right within universities and from individuals concerned about academic freedom. For the USA it needs to be remembered how many scientists work in government laboratories where such freedom may be curtailed, and that the right distrusted less the science than the regulatory agenda quickly apparent as part of the IPCC/FCCC process. Also, the National Science Foundation, a major funder of climate science, must sell its products to government as relevant and supportive of national priorities. The George C. Marshall Institute could argue, already in 1992, that 'the fact that the expected "greenhouse signal" is missing from the records suggests that the computer models have considerably exaggerated the size of the greenhouse effect', refer to solar activity as an important factor and suggest that warming of half a degree spread over many decades would have but a small effect 'lost in the noise of natural climatic fluctuations' (Marshall Institute, 1992, 25–6). These views have not changed, and the Institute influenced Bush's decision to withdraw in 2001. There would be enough time to wait for better results before taking action, argued the scientists associated with this body, influential during the Reagan and Bush Senior and Junior Administrations.

Perhaps the most outspoken and well-known critic of the IPCC consensus and an associate of the Marshall Institute is Professor Richard Lindzen of MIT. He has argued that university representation from the USA on WG I was relatively small since funds and the time needed for participation are not available to most university scientists, and that the (first assessment) report was too deeply committed to reliance on large models which were largely verified by comparison with other models. He argued that, given that models are known to agree more with each other rather than with nature (even after 'tuning'), this approach for creating consensus did not seem promising (Lindzen, 1992, 126). He further alleged that pressure had been brought to bear 'to emphasise results supportive of the current scenario and to suppress other results', a conclusion which has been confirmed to some extent by a survey of scientists (Boehmer-Christiansen and Skea, 1993). Lindzen recently became a participant in the IPCC process, but remains highly critical of the research and the procedures.

As IPCC scenarios that receive most political attention remain invariably those most damaging to the prospects of fossil fuels, some see the hand of the nuclear lobby behind their adoption, others the green 'soft' energy lobby, or more generally, from within government that of those desiring more regulation, for example to advance energy efficiency and new technologies. The direction and nature of the pressure varied between countries depending on national energy situations and policies. The combined political pressure on WG I not to make 'neutral' policy pronouncements was therefore considerable and coincided with its own interests, though not necessarily with the views of individual scientists. Scepticism has by no means disappeared, especially as far as the products of very costly model experiments are concerned. Yet the need for accurate forecasting is now enshrined in the FCCC. Its implementation has been made dependent on warming being 'true', dangerous and anthropogenic.

Another problem with the IPCC is that the driver for the whole process has effectively become WG III, since WG III produces the socio-economic scenarios which are in turn fed into the climate models to generate the feared doubling of CO_2 in the atmosphere sometime in the future. WG III is comprised largely of energy policy and technology advocates who are generally supportive of policies for energy conservation and renewable energy technologies that they think governments will be 'forced' to adopt as responses to the prospect of dangerous anthropogenic climate change. Scenarios of economic structure and energy use 100 years into the future should be regarded with considerable scepticism, however, especially since most forecasts of such trends even 20 years into the future have proven remarkably inaccurate. For example, the highest temperature scenario in the Third Assessment Report resulted from a scenario involving high levels of carbon combustion with high levels of particulate removal.[13] That global society would do nothing about CO_2 emissions in the face of warnings of climate change while vigorously reducing particulate emission control seems fanciful. The IPCC therefore prefers to describe its forecasts as projections rather than predictions, but will this alter the usage of its pronouncements in the political process? Baptists and bootleggers will remain attracted to the worst-case scenarios presented as predictions.

SYSTEMIC BIAS IN THE IPCC

This linking of the IPCC to the FCCC created a strong pull on the kind of conclusions it was likely to produce and, because the IPCC exerts a similar pull on the conduct of climate science, in turn on the conduct of research. But there would seem to be a number of systemic factors which have also been a source of bias in the consensus produced by the IPCC.

The problems with the IPCC go right to its foundations. As with most political issues with a high scientific content, a consensus emerges from the conduct of scientific research into the nature of a problem, and this then tends to structure the possible policy responses to it, as was the case with the depletion of the ozone layer by CFCs. The first scientific paper to indicate a problem appeared in the early 1970s, and subsequent research confirmed the existence of the problem. There was no unanimity over the science, but sufficient agreement for international cooperation to develop policy instruments in response. The number of actors was much smaller, substitutes were available and there would be no major losers. Climate change has been very different in all respects. If the science continued to be contested at the end of the twentieth century, it was even less settled in the mid-1980s, and there was no evidence at that time of warming or increased climate variability. Indeed, there had been a slight cooling trend. Yet the IPCC was established to produce a consensus in support of a treaty predicated on the assumption of dangerous anthropogenic warming and precaution, without, however, defining 'dangerous'. As we have seen, many of those active at this time were already convinced of the need for international action against fossil fuels.

The IPCC working group I consists largely of meteorologists and atmospheric physicists (some collecting and processing vast amounts of observational data), as well as computer and modelling experts attracted to climate, most assigned to it by government agencies. This is not surprising, since governments were attempting to assert some control over the issue, on which AGGG had had the running, by establishing the IPCC in the first place. But this exacerbated what became an institutionalization within the IPCC process of scientists, who were either government employees or working in government funded, often rather financially insecure, centres frequently associated with meteorological offices and institutes that had an interest in there being a climate problem which would justify further research. Few university scientists contributed to the IPCC process because they lacked the travel funds, access to the largest computers and the ability to attend meetings regularly, since they had classes to teach.[14] The IPCC process has therefore been dominated by scientists whose livelihoods depend upon direct government allocations for climate research, and thus on a belief now deeply entrenched even at the official level that dangerous climate change was both likely and subject to mitigation by policy.

To these systemic influences in the scientific drafting and review processes in the IPCC working groups we can add an explicitly political tone to the deliberations of the IPCC itself in its meetings. As the Chair of the World

Meteorological Organization has lamented, IPCC meetings are attended by government representatives as well as NGOs representing both industry and environment, and are not an arena in which disinterested scientists discuss scientific differences (Zillman, 1997). They are fora where lobbying occurs and participating scientists are placed under explicit political pressure. The extent of this differs between working groups, and is worst for the response people (WG II) where NGOs and business are happiest to lobby. Here 'pure' scientists and experts get their influence through the emission scenarios (cross-cutting issues and responses tend to be left alone), but simply find it easiest to work on the scenarios they are given (by WG III). And reports are invariably produced according to political needs, such as a looming climate change nego-tiation, rather than according to a scientific timetable. Special reports or briefings are prepared for UNCED or COPs, and convenient leaks of significant details have occurred on the eve of COPs – as happened with COP-6, which occurred before TAR had been finalized. There was very little new science in TAR over SAR, but there were some new results from modelling exercises into which had been fed some new scenarios likely to put pressure on negotiators.

'Peer Review' and the IPCC

A further problem arises with the 'peer review' process involved in the IPCC. Peer review is fundamental to the advance of science since it is a key means by which bias and error are guarded against, although it is also notoriously con-servative and corruptible. It is a process which is even more important in a world where reliance upon external funds and calls for policy relevance, social accountability and the responsibility of science raise the dangers of Lysenkoism. IPCC leaders lay claim to the use of peer review in the production of IPCC reports. For example, Sir John Houghton (co-chair of WG I) stated at the launch of TAR that: 'It had been reviewed by governments before we came here, and in fact it's probably one of the most peer-reviewed documents you could ever find' (*BBC News Online*, 22 January 2001). Aside from the reference to 'review by governments', this statement attempts to liken the IPCC document to the best science: peer-reviewed science. But the IPCC process falls short of the usual standards of peer review.

Peer review is criticized for embedding conservatism in science and for failing to prevent the publication of erroneous findings. While not foolproof, it nevertheless provides an important accepted quality check. The US Supreme Court, for example, in *Daubert* v. *Merrel Dow* sees publication only after peer review as a key criterion of what constitutes 'science'. But peer review in the usual process of evaluation before publication in scientific journals has important characteristics which are absent in the case of the IPCC. First, con-ventional peer review is *anonymous*. Papers submitted for publication are sent to reviewers in a form which makes identification of the authors impossible. This does allow power to be exercised by editors, who can exercise bias in selecting referees, and makes the existence of a pluralism in scientific publishing vital. And academic publications are available to the public without line-by-line approval that involves government officials.

Ideally, there are two or more reviewers, whose identity is not revealed to the authors. An editor, ideally also totally disinterested in the outcome of any debate among the protagonists, interprets the reports of the referees and decides to accept the paper for publication or reject it. Acceptance is sometimes conditional upon changes being made to meet the objections of referees, and where those objections are substantial the authors might be invited to revise the manuscript and resubmit it.

The IPCC process falls short of these standards in five important ways. First, the review process is conducted by the authors of a draft chapter of the IPCC report, the report having developed from a list of chapter headings laid down by a small group of researchers who then invite submissions from their colleagues, people whom they know directly or through the published literature. Second, the authors are themselves active researchers in the field, rather than being disinterested as are the editors of scientific journals in the case of most articles they are considering. Third, the lead authors choose the reviewers they will send the drafts to; and next, they themselves choose whether to accept or reject the criticisms offered. Finally, there is no possibility that the draft chapter will *not* be published. In these five ways, the IPCC process falls short of the accepted practice of 'peer review', and this is well known by those such as Sir John Houghton who attempt to secure acceptance and credibility for the reports by describing them as 'peer reviewed'.

IPCC drafts are first produced by lead authors who circulate them for 'peer review' among people of their own choice. These drafts might draw upon the research of the lead authors themselves. Only published material is included, and people (such as Lindzen) who have posed difficult questions for which no answers yet exist, as well as experts from distant disciplines with quite different approaches to the understanding of climate, are excluded from having any input. There also is a substantial level of self-citation, authors frequently citing their own work which has not yet been published. One analysis by a sceptic of the IPCC SAR draft sent out for comment found that 648 of the 1969 listed references (33 per cent) were improper when compared to the standards used by top-ranking scientific journals (Michaels and Knappenberger, 1996b, 162–3). The 648 included technical reports, book chapters, conference proceedings, previous IPCC reports, citations of work 'in press' or submitted for publication, or incomplete references provided. Authors cannot be expected to be dispassionate about their own work or criticisms of it by reviewers. Other scientists providing critical scrutiny must therefore argue to the lead authors, not some independent editor, that the interpretation of the scientific evidence (possibly including their own work) is erroneous. They are in the position of having to convince authors that they are wrong, rather than convincing editors that authors are wrong.

This is far removed from the usual canons of the peer review process. Even more serious is the lack of communication, if not in understanding, between different disciplines approaching the same fundamental questions. For example, solar physicists and paleogeologists are not likely even to read climate change modellers, but they may certainly question their conclusions when tested model predictions are compared to their own findings. The IPCC process remains essentially an exclusive and hence biased one, closer to the interests and funding claims of meteorology than it should be.

There are further problems. Critics have pointed to the use of 'in press' papers in IPCC reports. The problem here is not that such literature might not have been subjected to anonymous peer review, because in most cases they have been, but that the issue journal containing the paper has not yet appeared. Even the best of reviewers can get it wrong, or might have been selected for their particular views rather than critical expertise, and quite damning criticisms sometimes emerge only after papers have been published and considered by a wide range of scientists. This is particularly important because sometimes scientists working within a particular paradigm (and thus likely to be chosen as referees for publication) are likely to be too accepting of conclusions others might dispute. The passage of time after publication is important because this allows the opportunity for others to try to replicate the research or attempt to disprove it. One of our main worries is that of exclusion: geologists, solar physicists, oceanographers and biologists have had very little impact on the IPCC's understanding of climate. The reason for this exclusion will become clearer in Chapter 7.

CONCLUSION

The present authors are agnostic on the key questions of climate science and critical of the funding of IPCC related science. We note, for example, the general agreement that levels of CO_2 and other GHGs in the atmosphere have risen, but not at a constant rate that relates directly to rates of emissions, and we suspect considerable remaining unknown complexity. At least some of these increases are likely to be anthropogenic, though not everybody agrees. Climate is a product of feedbacks, not primarily radiative forcing. We also note a widespread agreement that there has been a small but not steady increase in the observed mean global temperatures since about 1850, though the global nature of this increase is in doubt and may relate to natural cycles or to where and how measurements are made. What is less clear is how closely emissions and climate are connected, and whether future GHG emissions are likely to lead to further global warming or other climate change at a rate which makes it prudent to take avoiding or mitigating action, or whether preparation for adaptation might be the wiser policy. We consider that the fundamental issue concerning how much of the observed past and possible future change in climate is either anthropogenic or natural, due to extraterrestrial or systemic causes, remains to be answered before policy measures can deliver the desired results. If climate change turns out to be driven primarily by factors such as solar variability, expensive policy measures would amount to a diversion of resources, for example from the more important priority of adaptation.

There is a chance that anthropogenic warming might require preventative action, and that therefore the case for voluntary 'no regrets' actions or seeking 'synergy' remains strong. But it should not be imposed equally on a world as unequal and non-uniform as the one we currently have. We see considerable uncertainty in the science of climate change and argue that this weakens the case for global compulsion which we consider to have been made primarily on grounds of economic interests rather than scientific reasoning. We argue that global blaming and talk of historical debts are premature and do not assist the development of international responses. On the contrary, we consider these factors have limited the development of effective instruments.

The one option widely advocated to decision-makers in the face of uncertainty is to undertake massive reductions in GHG emissions. This would entail substantial economic costs for many countries. While there is much scope for improvements in energy efficiency and some scope for renewable energy technologies, renewables cannot replace fossil fuels on a global scale because of inescapable physical constraints. No matter if photovoltaic cells achieve increases in efficiency from 15 to 20 per cent or higher, the amount of incoming solar radiation is effectively fixed and megawatt-scale solar energy requires substantial areas of land which would have to be withdrawn from other uses (or non-use options, such as wilderness). Policy restrictions on GHG emissions mean likely shifts from coal to gas for electricity generation and (more significantly) to nuclear generation. We also see only limited hope for major overall reductions in global energy demand arising from energy efficiency improvements or energy conservation.

Another option is to do nothing, but continue research and development of technologies which might provide greater conversion efficiencies, such as the fuel cell, which former Saudi oil minister and OPEC leader Sheik Ahmed Zaki Yamani fears will break the power of OPEC in a decade by providing conversion efficiencies in excess of 60 per cent. Such a response might seem reckless, but the decision is one of global risk management, of managing one risk against others that may already be much more apparent or devastating. To 'do nothing' in this arena while perhaps doing more elsewhere might arguably be preferable to incurring substantial economic costs in the face of uncertainty. This is especially the case because – even if the IPCC scientific consensus proves correct – the long residence period of CO_2 in the atmosphere (more than 100 years according to the IPCC, though some now say less) means that there will be elevated atmospheric CO_2 levels. The relevant policy question is whether it is preferable to generate the wealth needed to adapt or devote resources to trying to avoid what is 'inevitable' – and there are a host of distributional questions contained within this.

We do not presume to answer these questions, but wish in the next chapter to explore a number of these points of scientific controversy to provide evidence in support of our criticism of the IPCC claim to represent a scientific consensus in the usual sense of the expression. At most it represents a consensus among those able or selected to participate in the decision-making process. These are *some* of the very points at issue which weakened the power of 'IPPC science' to the extent that US President George W. Bush effectively killed his country's involvement in the Kyoto Protocol in March 2001. He specifically referred to uncertain science and then agreed to support a significant increase in US spending on climate science and R&D developments. US climate science had been hampered in the 1990s by a Commerce Department tariff of 450 per cent on Japanese supercomputers, which was lifted by the Bush Administration early in 2001 (*New York Times*, 3 July 2001).

We see merit in energy conservation and improved efficiency and even security, but have no particular like or dislike of nuclear energy but would not wish to foster it unnecessarily, for example. We consider, however, that the IPCC as an institution does not share our compunction; it does presume to answer such questions on society's behalf, because it has consistently supported interpretations of climate change science which accentuate the likelihood of rapid climate change, downplay the benefits of warming, and focus attention on emission reduction as the primary response to this scenario of climate catastrophe. The IPCC is made up of scientists with particular policy preferences, representatives of national governments and intergovernmental organizations – all with particular agendas they anticipate will be progressed by the development of a particular construction of the climate change issue.

As might be deduced from any commitment to precaution without known probability, worst case 'science' scenarios may turn into justifications for policies that advantage those who claim to have immediate solutions ready for 'saving the planet', such as phasing out fossil fuels and nuclear power. We do argue that some concessions were made in this direction during negotiations, but these were made without help from the IPCC. As we say, we are open minded (sceptical, in the best sense of the word) on these issues, and we believe such a position not only to be justified by the body of peer-reviewed science, but indeed *required* by scientific principles which see scepticism as vitally important.

The very notion of establishing an institution to produce a scientific consensus suggests that a certain kind of consensus was likely to emerge, because the only reason for producing a consensus lay in the belief that an international convention would not be developed unless there *was* such an ingredient. If one is not convinced of a need for a convention, there would be no need for consensus on the knowledge base because the existence of normal scientific controversy would be of no consequence. The very establishment of an institution to produce consensus can thus be seen as exerting a corrupting influence on the conduct of climate change research. We have described here the ways in which the IPCC makes possible systemic bias in a direction which key players such as Bolin, Houghton, Häfele, Flohn and Watson have always sought. We move in the next chapter to provide some examples which show just how the IPCC has dealt with uncertainty and scientific disputes.

NOTES

1. From the flyer for TAR, IPCC Third Assessment Report, Cambridge: Cambridge University Press, 2001.
2. IPCC research scientists now stress that the term 'projected' should be used instead. Given the many assumptions and uncertainties involved, the IPCC science group no longer claims to predict.
3. Bryson also argued that the time had come to do real interdisciplinary work at the international level 'rather than leave the science to the scientists and the social stuff to the social people: put them together and find a solution'.
4. Professor Bolin has worked on the carbon cycle and is a major advocate of earth systems science. He has published on climate change and energy policy since 1971. In 1980 he addressed the WMO on the subject of 'climatic changes and their effects on the biosphere' in which he concluded that 'it may take decades or centuries' before changes brought about by 'human interference' may be noted (1980, 47). He directed the Swedish International Meteorological Institute and was research director at the European Space Agency and collaborated closely with SCOPE and the Stockholm Environment Institute.
5. Climate change was accepted as a research issue at the 1972 Stockholm Conference. American–German Aspen Institute workshops then addressed climate change, producing forecasts very little different from those of the IPCC (see Kellogg and Schware, 1981).
6. Such scenarios have since been found to be quite unsuitable for policy-making, though useful for the testing of climate models.
7. Sir John accepted this post as chair of WG I (Science) when he was permanent UK representative to WMO on the condition that the UK government provided sufficient resources. As a former director of the UK Met Office and with a career in space and atmospheric physics he was extremely well placed to link national bodies to international ones. As chairman of the Royal Commission on Environmental Pollution and member of the UK government's Panel on Sustainable Development he has defended the IPCC on various occasions against attacks from other disciplines which want excluded areas of knowledge examined more closely, such as the roles of hydrology, solar forces, carbon dioxide chemistry and the impact of aerosols, such as minerals and carbon particles not included in current models.

8. Cited by Tim Patterson and Tom Harris, 'Profiting from panic', *Scripps Howard News Service/Nando Times*, 5 April 2001.
9. The Russians have been badly treated inside the IPCC, in part because of methodological differences (weak modelling capacity), in part because they have remained sceptics (on scientific grounds, e.g. Kirill Kondratyev who believes that the IPCC, by ignoring the complex effects of aerosols and weak observational inputs, has greatly exaggerated the 'danger' of warming); or welcoming the prospect of warming on the grounds that this would benefit mankind.
10. The brief of this group, however, widened rapidly in 1995. Mankind was still being treated largely as a single emitting and reproducing species that alters the nature of the terrestrial surface.
11. We have been informed, however, that lead authors on behalf of their set of authors may do so.
12. The number of individuals, institutions and countries involved varies with the subject being studied, which ranges from climate modelling (the dominant group), hydrology (speculations about the impact of changes in precipitation and rising sea levels), to agriculture, economics (predicting the impact of carbon taxes on global GNP), energy demand modelling and public health.
13. As this book was going to press, we became aware of a substantial critique of the Special Report on Emissions Scenarios and Working Group III, which are fundamental to the whole of the IPCC Third Assessment Report. (Recall that the SRES provides the scenarios for CO_2 emissions which are fed into, and thus determine the results coming out of the climate models providing estimates of future warming). In an e-mail to new IPCC Chair Dr. Rajendra Pachauri on 6 August, 2002, former President of the International Association of Official Statistics Ian Castles pointed to material errors in the SRES scenarios, particularly related to the incorrect use of exchange rate conversions rather than purchasing power parities in estimating past and future economic performance of non-Annex I countries. Economic performance is fundamental to forecasts of energy consumption, including fossil fuels.

These errors have the effect of vastly overstating likely future growth in these economies (and thus CO_2 emissions over the next century, and in the next two decades in particular. To give an illustrative comparison, real incomes in the US increased by a factor of 5 to 1 in the 19th century, and those in Japan by a factor of almost 20 to 1 in the 20th century. The SRES projects there will be a (barely credible) increase in average incomes for the entire Asian continent by a factor of between 70 and 140 to one over the next century.

As a result, the SRES scenario, which yields the lowest increase in temperature between 1990 and 2100 (1.98°C averaged across seven climate models), rather than being a 'low-growth' scenario, assumes rapid growth in global emissions of 1.6 billion tonnes between 2000 and 2010 and 1.5 billion tonnes between 2010 and 2020, compared with actual increases of only 0.8 billion tonnes in the 1980s and 0.7 billion tonnes in the 1990s. The SRES simply ignores the decarbonisation that is already under way and which has been apparent to bodies such as the World Energy Council for a decade, in order to produce scenarios which produce high figures for emissions and thus warming. We thank Ian Castles for sharing this critique.
14. Both the present authors have had some involvement with the IPCC process, but participation in meetings has not been possible for either author. Boehmer-Christiansen observed early meetings in the UK, has remained a reviewer of WG II reports and worked with one lead author; Kellow's effective participation in the activities of WG III was precluded by the arrival (by surface mail) of draft documents *after* the deadline for comments.

7. The suppression of scientific controversy

In this chapter we examine the ways in which climate change science has been selectively interpreted by the IPCC itself and even more so by its many 'users': environmental bureaucracies, NGOs and the media in particular, to promote consensus in favour of a particular policy direction. Here we focus on NGOs and the media as external users of IPCC advice, but provide some evidence that IPCC spokesmen acceded to what we consider to be unwarranted alarmism on the part of these actors.

We consider the IPCC (in its policy advisory role) and its users as a coalition of advocacy in favour of climate alarmism, with the IPCC as a research network possibly the more reluctant partner. To repeat, we accept the view reported to us by IPCC participants themselves that the underlying report is authored by the teams of scientists who have been nominated by governments and selected by the IPCC Bureau, with the Summary for Policy-makers representing a consensus document produced by government delegates at an IPCC Plenary Session. According to Richard Lindzen (and others), there is no scientific consensus supporting these SPMs.

Here we illustrate this contention with some examples of scientific controversies where the alarmist 'predisposition' of the IPCC process has resulted in interpretations supporting a more alarmist view of climate change science. We consider there are three stages in this process:

1. the production of assessment chapters that neglect challenges and uncertainties (the task of this chapter);
2. the production of the Summaries for Policy-makers (SPM), already dealt with in Chapter 6; and
3. the promulgation of this material in the popular media by the agents of influence referred to above, be these the IPCC spokesmen addressing policy-makers or industry, the environmental lobby, green investment funds or politicians. It needs to be stressed that environmental policy-makers (national and intergovernmental administrations and their expert advisers) now have become the major force driving the Kyoto process forward regardless of science or economic implications.

Media representation and uptake by politicians are important because much of the political 'spin' on climate science comes when political actors and journalists select, simplify or misrepresent evidence and theory to the public for effect. While the IPCC is active in contesting the claims of those who question its assessments, it remains strangely silent in relation to those who misrepresent its conclusions in ways which reinforce the construction of the issue preferred by energy-poor but technologically advanced countries. It is difficult to judge whether this is strategic or a reflection of genuinely held beliefs; probably both motivations are at work, with the latter more likely to prevail among bench scientists than the politically highly experienced IPCC leadership.

We wish to show that such silence is not justified by the available science, and that a more balanced and cautious tale could and should be told. What follows is a selection among many layers and levels of scientific controversy. We are neither able nor do we attempt to write a definitive critique of IPCC science, and must be selective to make our general points; also our information may not reflect the 'latest' state of knowledge. However, having followed several debates closely, we feel confident that we can show how the IPCC has tended towards generating a particular *kind* of consensus: one that would serve to bias policy towards emission reduction and hence attacks on coal and oil in particular.

The debates we have selected for examination here are: the attribution of observed climate change to anthropogenic emissions; the treatment of differences between surface and satellite observations of temperature (which has generated much empirical controversy over whether the earth is warming and by how much and over what time spans); the so-called hockey stick research, whereby a single paper which rewrote the climate history of the last millennium was accepted by the IPCC; and claims that global warming will lead to the spread of 'tropical' diseases such as malaria, which contributes to a negative construction of the effects of climate change. Together, we argue, the IPCC position on these debates has supported the construction of a view of climate science which downplays scientific uncertainty, accentuates likely warming (and sea level rise), attributes change primarily to human agency and depicts it in negative terms. To repeat, this serves both Baptists and bootleggers, as well as the research enterprise.

BASIC SCIENTIFIC DISPUTES: THE ATTRIBUTION CONTROVERSY

The claim that observed and model predicted global warming could be attributed primarily or even largely to anthropogenic activity related to radiative forcing (that is, changes in the composition of the atmosphere brought about by the combustion of fossil fuels rather than by other natural or human phenomena) was perhaps the most important message coming out of the IPCC Second Assessment Report (SAR), 1995. It was certainly the most important in a diplomatic sense. It overshadowed, at least to the public, the substantial lessening of prospective warming in IPCC literature itself. It is therefore important to examine the basis for the claim in the Policy-makers' Summary and the controversy over the way in which the conclusion was reached.

In 1990 and 1992 IPCC reports predicted (the IPCC now prefers the term 'projected') rises in mean global temperatures (relative to 1990) of 1.5–4.5°C by 2050; by 1995 the prediction was 1–3°C by 2100, a much less dramatic increase since it was both smaller and spread over almost twice the time period. Fred Singer, a leading sceptic, also argued that WG I (Climate Science) failed to make clear that an increase of 0.5°C by 2100 – the most likely, he argued, based on satellite data – would be well within the range of temperature fluctuations experienced historically (Singer, 1996, 153). Others complained that uncertainty ranges were not given. WG II downplayed the benefits of increased warming, increased carbon dioxide concentration or precipitation to some regions and plants in general, and the ability of humans to adjust to any adverse changes, such as disease, where good nutrition, sanitation, medical drugs and insecticides are more important than mere temperature. WG III (Response Strategies) was based upon the outdated temperature data from IPCC 1990 and 1992. Singer argued that if modest warming produced modest benefits rather than damages, the cost–benefit analyses were seriously off target. The SAR was therefore by no means as apocalyptic in its conclusions as the First Assessment Report (FAR), 1990, but claimed greater certainty over its conclusions. The world's media picked up its carefully constructed and internally much debated claim that: 'The balance of evidence suggests a discernible human influence on global climate', which tended to obscure the more than halving in the predicted rate of change and did not indicate that an influence on climate meant an increase in average global surface temperature. Interestingly, while warming is 'predicted' elsewhere in SAR, in this sentence the much more neutral 'influence on global climate' is used. Few could disagree!

This statement, however, was the subject of a fierce controversy which highlighted both the strengths and deficiencies of the IPCC process. Debate does take place, but the text of the key chapter of the SAR was altered after it had been agreed by WG I to downplay uncertainties which had previously been given greater prominence. Accused of altering the text without authorization to suit the politically agreed Summary for Policy-makers, the lead author of the chapter offered a defence which was just as worrisome, because it revealed that IPCC rules permitted such changes. Further, it was later revealed that the changes had been made at the instigation of the US government: the same government which funded the institutes that employed the chapter's lead authors. The US

State Department had carriage of this issue through Under-Secretary of State for Global Affairs, Timothy Wirth, who had been hand-picked for this post by Vice-President Al Gore. When Senator for Colorado, he had once stated: 'We've got to ride the global warming issue. Even if the theory of global warming is wrong, we will be doing the right thing, in terms of economic policy and environmental policy' (cited by Fumento, 1993, 362).

Under a concluding subhead of '8.6 When Will an Anthropogenic Effect of Climate be Identified?', the lead authors of Chapter 8 of SAR had stated: 'While there is already initial evidence for the existence of an anthropogenic climate signal, it is likely (if the model predictions are correct) that this signal will emerge more and more convincingly with time' (Santer *et al.*, 1996b, 438), and: 'evidence from the pattern-based studies reported on here suggests that an initial step has now been taken in the direction of attribution.' (ibid., 439). So they concluded that: 'The body of statistical evidence in Chapter 8, when examined in the context of our physical understanding of the climate system, now points towards a discernible human influence on global climate' (ibid.). 'Pointing toward' is not a term seriously suggesting causality. The internal science debate continued but the public could be assured by the users of IPCC pronouncements that policy intervention was urgent.

This somewhat cautious discussion of 'initial evidence' or an 'initial step' which 'points towards' attribution should be compared with the Summary for Policy-makers, where the subhead read: 'The balance of evidence suggests a discernible human influence on global climate.' A *body* of evidence pointing *towards* a discernible influence is not quite the same as a *balance* of evidence suggesting this. (In any legal trial, which is the origin of the language employed here, there is usually a 'body' of evidence pointing towards both guilt and innocence, but a 'balance' of evidence suggests one outcome is supported.)

When we combine this with the precautionary principle, an 'initial step in the direction of attribution' becomes either the basis for the imposition of substantial costs on industrial societies or an injunction for governments to force technological change via 'incentives'. And again, this initial step on the basis of pattern-based studies is described in the Summary as: 'More convincing recent evidence for the attribution of a human effect on climate is emerging from pattern-based studies.' Climate sceptics were livid, but could not assert their voices in the EU or globally; in the USA they appeared to have rather more success, where the Senate, but certainly not the EPA, remained unimpressed.

Despite containing much more cautious language than the Summary, this crucial Chapter 8 of SAR has itself been the subject of considerable controversy. Its authors were accused by William O'Keefe, Executive Vice-President of the American Petroleum Institute, of changing the text of Chapter 8 *after* it had been signed by Working Group I in Madrid and the full IPCC Plenary in

Rome in December 1995. Specifically, O'Keefe (1996) accused the lead authors of the deletion of the following two passages which had stressed uncertainty:

> Finally we come to the most difficult question of all: 'When will the detection and unambiguous attribution of climate change occur?' In light of the very large . . . uncertainties discussed in this Chapter, it is not surprising that the best answer to this question is 'We do not know.'

and:

> no study to date has positively attributed all or part of that [0.6°C rise in average global temperature during the past 100 years] to anthropogenic causes. Nor has any study quantified the magnitude of a greenhouse-gas effect or aerosol effect in the observed data – an issue that is of primary relevance to policymakers.

Lead author Benjamin Santer admitted altering the chapter, but claimed that the alterations were authorized and had the backing of the IPCC (Anon., 1996). O'Keefe represented the fossil fuel industry, so his criticisms were dismissed by the 'other side'. Herein lies the problem. The views of the fossil fuel industry are all too readily dismissed in the climate change debate as untrustworthy because motivated by interest, while those of environmentalists who often have, and play to, the ears and eyes of the media, tend to be believed. The more muted but structurally advantaged interests of the nuclear industry are therefore ignored by green activists and champions of solar power (see Leggett, 1999). Coal or oil interests are seeking to continue selling products for which limitations on GHG emissions are likely to involve market restrictions of one kind or another, with millions of jobs possibly at stake worldwide. After all, they have a very real interest in, even a duty, disputing the IPCC conclusions, because the latter claim to constitute the best available science provided by disinterested scientists. This view of climate change science as 'beyond interests' and 'beyond politics' is just not acceptable. Instead of leaving genuine debates publicly unresolved, science is either forced or persuaded by self-interest into taking up positions that support policy.

The fossil fuel industry and others were outraged by the attribution controversy, accusing Dr Santer of making the changes without authorization and against IPCC rules (see Seitz, 1996). The truth was perhaps even more disturbing, since IPCC rules of procedure permitted such changes. The US State Department, noting inconsistencies between the text of Chapter 8 and the Summary for Policy-makers, urged WG I chair Sir John Houghton in a letter on 15 November 1995 that the text not be finalized until these inconsistencies had been remedied. The letter read:

Finally, in comparing the text in the SPM and in the chapters, we have noted several inconsistencies, including some between different sections of the chapters. In keeping with past practice in WG I, it is essential that the chapters not be finalized prior to the completion of discussions at the IPCC WG I plenary in Madrid, and that chapter authors be prevailed upon to modify their text in an appropriate manner following discussion in Madrid.

As is the practice (see Chapter 6), the text of the Summary had been formally approved line-by-line by the Working Group and accepted by the IPCC and hence governments (see Zillman, 1997, 123). As an agreed document, the Summary could not be modified, and disturbingly the text of Chapter 8 – the detailed discussion of the science – was altered instead. An important issue of structural power is involved here, because Santer and his co-authors all worked at US government research institutes (Santer at Lawrence Livermore National Laboratory, Wigley at the National Center for Atmospheric Research, Barnett at Scripps Institution of Oceanography, and Anyamba at NASA/Goddard Space Flight Center), agencies which depended for financial support on the same government that was requesting that the science be brought into line with the politically negotiated summary.

The attribution issue was and remains a deeply divisive one, not least because the thrust of Chapter 8 depended upon research which was very recent and, in the case of a key paper by Santer and others, had not appeared in print at the time the IPCC report was finalized. In trying to bring the 'latest' research into the political domain, the authors relied not just on the merits of their *own* research, but research which (while it had been peer-reviewed for publication) had not stood the test of time once subjected to critical scrutiny. When it *was* published, the paper by Santer and others (Santer *et al.*, 1996b) immediately came under strong attack by sceptics (see Michaels and Knappenberger, 1996a).

EMPIRICAL DISPUTES: HOW MUCH WARMING?

One of the key points of criticism of the IPCC consensus has been its acceptance of the 'surface record' pattern of warming since 1850. This record, against which the general circulation models (GCM) used by climate researchers are calibrated, shows a warming up only until about 1940, followed by a flat period, and then some recent warming. This pattern does not reflect emissions and for many critics rather 'points towards' chaos: natural cyclical variations in the climate–ocean system, or even major (or cyclical) changes in the climate–ocean–biosphere–space system.

There are generally acknowledged problems with using this surface temperature record as a measure of mean global temperatures and even more so of change over time. The record of readings is short and, since 1850, is by no means global and is highly dependent on instruments and local environment. Reliable weather observations with anything like global coverage are not available, since weather observation stations only approached global coverage from the middle of the twentieth century. The addition of new stations and new measuring technologies means that adjustments must be made to allow for the changing mix of stations and their possible effect on the 'global mean'. There is a further problem: these land-based observations do not provide data for the two-thirds of the earth's surface which is covered by sea – a weakness to which we shall return. (Proxy measurements of changes in temperature disturb another nest of theoretical and methodological hornets, including increasingly those of statistical theory.)

Critics of the accuracy of the surface record also point out that the reliability of surface observations depends upon the constancy of factors at the observation site which might affect temperature readings. These include the possibility that the growth of trees or other factors might influence the microclimate at the observation site and (significantly) the growth of the so-called 'urban heat island effect' which blames increased temperature not on changes in the global atmosphere but on the direct release of heat by human activities near the point of measurement. Many meteorological observation sites are either in cities or on their verges and the measurement technology itself has changed over time, making comparisons difficult. Cities have spread geographically to envelop some former rural sites and their energy intensity has increased markedly, so they radiate waste heat. Maps of the earth at night give a visual indication of the vast amount of 'energy' emitted by mankind, as well as its pattern. Many sites are at airports, which are themselves significant sources of heat, and their numbers have increased rather than decreased. The reliability of temperature records also depends on the proper maintenance of equipment: if the standard white paint is allowed to discolour or ventilation is allowed to become blocked, then temperature readings will be elevated. Critics like to point out that warming has been least where the reliability of instruments is greatest, such as in the USA or Australia. There is still a major debate about the quality of Siberian data and the extent to which these might have been influenced by national politics and who did the measuring. Fuel allocations in the Soviet era were related to 'need' and there was a strong incentive to produce cold readings, which would overstate subsequent warming.

The accuracy of the surface record since 1850 therefore depends on a number of factors, including adjustments which need to be made to allow for such variability. Researchers are careful about how this is done, but it is an area where expectations that there *should* be a warming trend might influence the adjustment of data. But one problem with the warming indicated by the surface record for the last couple of decades of the twentieth century is that it is not supported by two other data sets that were arguably more accurate and more global in coverage. The fundamental problem appears to be that each of these instruments measures something slightly different, for temperature itself is by no means a simple phenomenon.

The first of these consists of measurements of atmospheric temperature above the earth's surface taken by remote sensing from orbiting satellites. These have provided a record since 1979 which is near global (95 per cent coverage) and which fails to show a marked warming trend in the temperature of this air (which should not be influenced by the factors that might affect surface temperatures). Indeed, until the mid-1990s, this record showed a slight cooling trend of 0.05°C per decade, but the error term for the data is ± 0.10°C, so it is consistent with a zero trend and no reliance should be placed on such a cooling 'trend'. Furthermore, these data are in broad agreement with the data taken from weather balloons, which also indicated a lack of warming.

These inconvenient data did not dissuade the authors of the IPCC SAR in 1995 from drawing their conclusions about warming, but (interestingly) once the data supported the warming hypothesis with some higher readings from the late 1990s, these were included as supporting the surface record, even though (correctly interpreted) they point to no statistically significant trend. It is interesting to note that the satellite data from 1979 to 2000 are reported in the Summary for Policy-makers of the Third Assessment Report (TAR) 2001, in the following terms:

> Since the start of the satellite record in 1979, both satellite and weather balloon measurements show that the global average temperature of the lowest 8 kilometres of the atmosphere has changed by +0.05±0.10°C per decade.

This means that the uncertainties are twice the measured value. As one of us explicitly acknowledged in 1997, the observed 'slight cooling of 0.05°C per decade' up to 1995 was compatible with a zero trend (Kellow, 1997), yet there is no comparable acknowledgement in the 2001 Summary for Policy-makers that the observed increase of 0.05°C per decade since 1979 was also compatible with a zero trend. On the contrary, the Summary approved by governments in January 2001 reported the satellite and weather balloon measurements since 1979 under the sub-heading 'Temperatures have risen during the past four decades in the lowest 8 kilometres of the atmosphere'.[1] 'Useful' evidence is clearly selected, while less useful material is ignored: this is politics, not science.

A research finding published in 2001 threw up further questions, and showed just how incomplete is our understanding of climate science. The historical surface record is heavily dependent on measurements from that two-thirds of the earth's surface that is water, where no meteorological stations are located. This absence of comparable data has been handled by employing data collected by ships, but clearly the reliability of air temperature readings on different ships is questionable. Instead, the surface record for the oceans has relied upon the use of *subsurface* temperatures: water temperatures were used as a proxy for air temperatures. Ships routinely log the water they take in to cool their engines, and since this is not affected by the numerous factors which might cause variation in air temperatures, it has been preferred. But just how reliable are these data? IPPC authors, when challenged, tend to reply that they are doing their best with the records that exist, an explanation that cannot be questioned. But is it good enough for policy, even a precautionary one? One problem is that the depth at which these temperatures are logged is variable, but the research published in 2001 questioned the very correspondence between air and water temperatures (Christy *et al.*, 2001). By actually comparing water temperatures with those of the air above them, this research suggested that a substantial element of the rise in global mean temperature could be an artefact of the unreliability of these proxy data. The implications of this would be profound. The models used to produce projections of future global mean temperatures, which are 'validated' by comparison with such data, would seriously overestimate future warming because they were constructed to produce a warming which was not in fact present on the historical record.

Similar stories could be told for sea level rises (currently hotly debated because measured variability is high because even this level is by no means constant in place and time without 'global warming'), ocean currents, aerosols and clouds, where the evidence remains inconclusive and often inconsistent, giving rise to one 'expert' view that climate is too chaotic and complex to be predictable! Others again predict future cooling; we are after all living in an interglacial period in which the cryosphere continues to melt, but temperature trends may naturally reverse. Our reading suggests that earth scientists, those who study the recent geological past, remain the most sceptical. They have evidence for so many large and rapid changes in climate long before the possibility of human impacts (see, for example, Berner and Streif, 2001).

THE HOCKEY STICK AND MANIC SUN

One important feature of the TAR was the claim that the 1990s was likely to have been the warmest decade of the millennium and 1998 the warmest year since records began. Previously, FAR and SAR statements about the high observed mean global temperatures in the late 1990s had been qualified with expressions such as the 'highest *recorded* temperature'. Since reasonably reliable records stretched back only a couple of centuries and 'global' records only for a little more than half a century, here was a qualification easily overlooked by the popular media and the relevant interests, but was hardly convincing for anyone aware of the best scientific *estimates* of the climate record for the millennium.

The TAR claim was much bolder than those in earlier Reports, and also of great significance. It had hitherto been accepted that a medieval warm period (or medieval climate optimum – MCO) between about AD 700 and 1300 had seen higher temperatures than anything the twentieth century produced. While the evidence that this period was global rather than regional is currently increasing, the IPCC tends to deny this, presumably because this would once again challenge the validity of the GCM models. However, SAR had accepted the MCO, along with the existence of a Little Ice Age (LIA) during the so-called Maunder Minimum between about AD 1560 and 1830.

The emergence from the LIA coincided with the development of industrial economies in Europe and North America leading to the massive increase in the combustion of fossil fuels and the somewhat lesser increase in carbon dioxide concentration in the atmosphere. Sceptics have always questioned whether the emission of CO_2 had produced the slight warming evident since the beginning of the nineteenth century or whether it had resulted from the end of an exceptionally cold period due to factors such as solar variability.

The MCO posed a further problem for the 'warming as man-made catastrophe' scenario, because it indicated a markedly warmer period *without* anthropogenic CO_2 emissions being implicated. Moreover, this was not a period of natural disasters and catastrophe, but an unusually fertile period: history records that grapes were grown in northern England, and a fertile Greenland was colonized by Vikings. Much early history is now being reinterpreted with climatic change, world-wide, in mind (Fagan, 2001). The accepted science was troublesome for the IPCC consensus. The TAR conclusion about the 1990s and 1998 represented a repudiation of the established scientific consensus and hence elevated model claims over observation. Some critics even alleged scientific fraud (Courtney, 1999).

As with the question of attribution in the SAR, the IPCC's conclusion was based primarily upon a paper which had been published only recently, again by a lead author of an IPCC assessment report chapter and a contributing author to other chapters, Michael Mann. (Recall that the key paper on attribution in SAR was co-authored by the lead author of the attribution chapter, Benjamin Santer.) Mann was lead author of the chapter titled 'Observed Climate Variability and Change'; he was hardly an established authority, having received his PhD only in 1998, but was establishing his career with this one publication. A paper published by Mann *et al.*, which appeared in the prestigious journal *Geophyscial Research Letters* in 1999 provided the basis for this rewriting of climate history on the part of the IPCC.

Using the growth rings of trees as a proxy and calibrating them against known temperature readings and other proxies from more recent centuries, this paper rewrote the climate history of the millennium. Gone was the MCO and the LIA, replaced by a slight cooling linear trend throughout the period until 1900. Then, the surface record for the twentieth century was grafted on to the end of the graph to produce a very sharp and steep upturn in future, the much-discussed 'hockey stick'. This indicated a sharp and (by implication) anthropogenic warming to new levels of mean global temperatures, and (by extrapolation) was highly suggestive of continued rapid warming. By January 2000, the 'hockey stick' had been widely accepted as the new orthodoxy with regard to the climate of the second millennium – without the flux of any reasonable time for critical evaluation. It was a remarkable rewriting of climate history, but one which has remained highly controversial and subject to critical contestation.

While there are indeed many difficulties with the science of dendrochronology, or tree rings, as a proxy for climate or mean global temperatures,[2] biological organisms adapt to climatic conditions and hence make difficult indicators of change. Mann *et al.* used tree ring width 'calibrated' against the temperature record, but there are indications from tree ring *density* that ring width might be anomalous (Briffa, 2000), which would invalidate the basis of the hockey stick research. The joining together of two different data sets is also of dubious validity. But even putting these objections aside, and assuming that the hockey stick were ultimately to be validated by subsequent science, the alacrity with which the paper became orthodoxy is remarkable – especially when compared with the determination to dismiss inconvenient satellite data and much other historical evidence.

The alacrity with which the validity of the 'hockey stick' was accepted by parties to the IPCC consensus also contrasts with their willingness to dismiss solar factors as an influence on climate change, which are taken as the likely cause of the MCO and LIA. Many see solar variability and the effects of solar wind as significant factors in driving climate variability (see Calder, 1997; Lockwood *et al.*, 1999; Svensmark and Friis-Christensen, 1997) and the statistical correlations are remarkable, but lack 'a testable hypothesis', as one author, Bob Watson, put it at a conference in London in 2001.

Those who subscribe to the IPPC consensus object that solar radiation has only increased by 0.7 per cent over the past 150 years and caused about 10 per cent of global warming, but Brekke argues that this ignores an extra 3 per cent UV light which generates more ozone and locks more heat into the atmosphere. In any case, according to the Svensmark theory, fewer cosmic rays may mean fewer dense, low-level clouds that shade the earth and therefore enhance warming. The Svensmark effect is not yet proven, but were it to exist, it means that the total effect of solar variability could account for at least 50 per cent of rising global temperatures. This would involve an effect that can be predicted to change direction, so cooling may set in again in a few decades. Until then, and if this were so, reducing GHG emissions would have much less effect in halting rising temperatures, according to Dr Paal Brekke of the European Space Agency.[3] This argument has in turn been publicly disputed by subscribers to the IPCC consensus such as Kevin Trenberth of the National Center for Atmospheric Research (NCAR) and James E. Hansen of NASA's Goddard Institute for Space Studies.[4] A number, including IPCC SAR Chapter 8 lead author Benjamin Santer, challenged a 'News and Views' article in *Nature* which they considered 'gave an exaggerated and misleading picture' of the effects of solar variability on terrestrial climate (Hoffert *et al.*, 1999).

The established scientific consensus supports the notion that, in the geological past, atmospheric CO_2 levels have reflected rather than driven climate change: that the changes in effective incoming solar radiation due to the variability of solar output or changes in the earth's orbit or alignment on its axis have been the drivers of climate variability (see, for example, Mudelsee, 2001; Naish *et al.*, 2001). Thus the period of low sunspot activity known as the Maunder Minimum is thought to indicate a solar cause for the Little Ice Age.

But the hockey stick was manna from heaven for pro-warming groups and was accepted immediately. While the original paper made explicit considerable uncertainty, the error bars were removed when it appeared shortly after the first draft of the TAR in June 2001 in the US National Assessment Synthesis (NAS). Moreover, while the Mann *et al.* paper had referred only to the northern hemisphere, the US NAS report labelled it as indicating *global* temperatures over the millennium. In a subtle twist, the TAR and the NAS document do not attempt to overturn the existence of the MCO and the LIA in Europe and Greenland, which are well verified by other proxy data and by historical accounts, but rather present them as regional events. These were seen as present in Europe but absent elsewhere in the world. Critics have been quick to cite evidence which challenges this conclusion.

The hockey stick was in effect a 'magic bullet' for alarmists. Not only did it permit the creation of the official reality that the 1990s were the hottest decade of the millennium, giving the strong appearance that the sharp temperature upturn was (*post hoc ergo propter*) anthropogenic in origin, it also weakened theories which suggested that various solar mechanisms (such as the absence of sunspot activity during the Maunder Minimum) were all relegated to secondary importance to human influences.

IMPACTS: THE MALARIA MYTH

The IPCC assessment reports have not only sought to play down the uncertainties surrounding climate science and to prefer data which appear to maximize rates of warming, they have also emphasized the negative impacts of any likely future warming.

A slightly warmer world with higher levels of atmospheric CO_2 is not universally regarded in necessarily negative terms. A slight warming might enhance agricultural productivity, as would elevated levels of CO_2, because plants photosynthesize CO_2 to produce food. It is the possible changes to rainfall patterns, sea level rises and frequency of storm events, rather than a modest warming *per se*, that are the concerns.

There have been attempts to create scenarios of more frequent heat waves causing thousands of deaths, but these are not credible because cold continues to be a much more significant cause of death in most places. Cold-related deaths are much more serious for Europe than heat-related deaths, with the former 78 times the latter in London, suggesting that there is little to fear from modest global warming (Keatinge *et al.*, 2000). Other kinds of extreme weather are supposed to be unambiguously catastrophic, but analysis suggests otherwise. The 1997–8 El Niño event has been estimated to have caused economic losses in the USA of approximately $4.5 billion plus 189 lives lost. On the other hand, it provided benefits of $19.5 billion and saved an estimated 850 lives due to a lack of bad winter weather (Changnon, 1999). Similarly, the impacts of El Niño periods in Australia appear to have been overestimated (Kuhnel and Coates, 2000).

But one scenario has been used effectively by politicians, including former US Vice-President Al Gore and the bureaucracy of the WHO (McMichael *et al.*, 1996). This is the prospect of tropical diseases moving towards the Poles, and even breaking out in the USA or Europe. The IPCC SAR section on human health impacts (admittedly using the higher FAR temperature increases of 3–5°C) estimated that there would be 50–80 million additional cases of malaria each year, an increase of 10–15 per cent on the background level. This was scary stuff, but it was based upon poor science. Malaria has come to be regarded as a 'tropical' disease because it is not usually found in temperate locations. Yet it was once endemic in such places and there were epidemics as far north as the Arctic Circle. The last endemic case was reported in England in the 1950s and in the Netherlands in 1961: the World Health Organization only declared Europe to be free of malaria in 1975 (Reiter, 2000). 'Marsh fever' or 'the ague' was rampant during the Little Ice Age (Dobson, 1997) and was eradicated during the period of warming since then as the result of various factors. These include swamp drainage and land reclamation, changes to agricultural practices, rural population decline, advances in house construction, better medical care, a rapid drop in the price of quinine – and, ultimately, the use of DDT after World War Two.

Unfortunately for the IPCC, weather and disease are related in complex, often perverse ways. In most parts of the world malaria is associated with rainfall, but in Sri Lanka *drought* causes malaria epidemics because it dries up rivers, leaving breeding pools. How this debilitating disease is spread by vectors depends on complex factors that include public health and other measures by which people manage their exposure to the risk. How then did the IPCC get it so wrong? The views of Paul Reiter, Chief Entomologist, US Centers for Disease Control and Prevention, San Juan, Puerto Rico are informative:

> The bibliographies of the nine lead authors of the health section show that between them they had only published six research papers on vector-borne diseases. Nevertheless, they devoted a third of their chapter to speculation on the future of those diseases. On the other hand, if you take those of us who don't toe their line, you will find that we have well over 600 publications on the subject. It beats me why the IPCC is given such credence while we are branded as sceptics. (Masood, 2000, 41)

USE OF CLIMATE CHANGE MODELS: MANUFACTURING CONSENSUS

These snapshots of the IPCC at work provide insights into how it systematically constructs the available science so as to downplay uncertainty, accentuate human causality, magnify the likely warming and depict it as harmful in its consequences. These are only brief vignettes, but we hold that they are typical and that they have important consequences. They raise the fundamental question as to why this has happened. Have the green beliefs of the authors and drafters themselves biased research, or was this bias strategic, required to ensure future funding? Empirical research here is difficult to conduct, but from observation over two decades we conclude that both factors were at work, with 'ethics' reinforcing interests – a powerful and dangerous 'narrative', or rather driving force, in the world of politics.

Central to the assumption that a scientific consensus would produce a political consensus for a particular kind of policy response has been a reliance on computer models to produce scenarios of future climate. While there is considerable disagreement over *actual* observations, there is a higher level of consensus between modellers over this *virtual* future reality. Climate models include all sorts of assumptions about the behaviour of the atmosphere and especially of the gases that are being 'enhanced' by human activities and which are said to have increased its energy retention by 0.8 per cent. The big question appears to be: Is climate, a highly complex, non-linear phenomenon, at all sensitive to this retention and if so, by how much? Opinions here vary, because we do not know and contested assumptions are built into models.

We shall not deal with this complex subject in any detail beyond pointing out that these general circulation models (GCM) are much improved weather forecasting tools. Their 'projections' cannot be any better than the science and data fed into them. In the language of research, the GCM, increasingly 'coupled' with the ocean and now even biosphere, are mathematical experiments using the most powerful computers available. They are the foundation of earth systems science, but their 'garbage in–garbage out' nature still concerns some scientists, particularly those wedded to other hypotheses about the 'driver' of climate and its changes. Two prominent sceptics from the solar school have recently argued that:

> Without computer models, there would be no evidence of global warming, no Kyoto. By simulating the climate on giant, ultra-fast computers, scholars try to find out how it will react to each new stimulus – like a doubling of CO_2. An ideal computer model, however, would have to track five million parameters over the surface of the earth and through the atmosphere, and incorporate all relevant interactions among land, sea, air, ice and vegetation. According to one researcher, such a model would demand ten million trillion degrees of freedom to solve a computational impossibility even on the most advanced supercomputer. (Glassman and Baliunas, 2001)[5]

While this probably overstates the case, much uncertainty remains in climate modelling, which remains a very inexact science, and Santer has admitted that attribution is 'not a done deal' (see Kerr, 1997). Most past models have had to be 'tweaked' because they tended to produce global warming even with constant atmospheric CO_2. Only recently have models been refined to the point where they can reproduce the existing climate over many iterations, and they suggest much more modest warming with a doubling of atmospheric CO_2 – about a degree over a century. This much less apocalyptic science was known to negotiators at Kyoto, but apocalyptic results were needed for the crucial negotiation in 2000–1.

Many computer models have produced warming even with stable atmospheric CO_2 levels: they include positive feedback loops in order to produce warming with rises in CO_2. It should be noted that CO_2 is not the most important naturally occurring GHG. Water vapour accounts for about 98 per cent of the natural and life-sustaining 'greenhouse' forcing. This raises mean global temperatures by about 33°C and makes the earth habitable at a mean global temperature of about 15°C. The average global temperature has typically varied roughly between 12°C and 22°C from the Precambrian era. Without the atmosphere and its ability to trap radiative heat at the surface, this temperature would be about –18°C. The popular view of the earth's atmosphere as a simple greenhouse, however, ignores other warming factors such as convection or the transport of heat by air currents. These factors actually restrict the impact of the greenhouse effect to about 25 per cent of what it would be in a totally radiative situation. The surface of the earth is cooled by various forms of air movements that carry heat upwards and towards the Poles, with rising air replaced by cool air from the Poles. Recent research (Lindzen *et al.*, 2001) has even suggested a kind of 'iris' in the clouds over the Pacific Ocean which might act as a corrective mechanism to cool the globe more as temperatures rise.

The greenhouse effect is mainly due to water vapour, not CO_2. The theoretical idea for forecasts of warming is that slight warming due to CO_2 will allow more water vapour to evaporate, and it is the water vapour which induces the major rise in temperature (Christy, 2000). There is little evidence for this 'theoretical idea', and the total water vapour/cloud feedback seems to be the worst source of uncertainty, as it may also be negative. This feedback cannot be modelled with any great confidence. Elevated CO_2 levels can therefore only produce worrisome degrees and rates of warming if it is assumed that they will be accentuated by the behaviour of clouds and water vapour, the major GHG. Critics have questioned whether this assumption is valid. Clouds reflect about 75 watts of incoming solar radiation per square meter, whereas a doubling of atmospheric CO_2 would only contribute about 2 watts/m^{-2}. So the results of climate modelling exercises depend crucially on what assumptions are made about water vapour and cloud behaviour at various heights. High altitude clouds can contribute to warming, but others shield the earth from the sun and high clouds transport heat from the surface and help cool the earth. Major climate models assume that warming will raise concentrations of water vapour in the upper troposphere (5–12 km altitude) and only in this way can they produce warming scenarios in excess of about 1.7°C. This area remains one of uncertainty, though much research is in progress.

The limitations of the models themselves cause fundamental problems. They consist of vast numbers of mathematical equations representing physical and chemical processes that are combined with numerical data either measuring or estimating 'facts' about change. They cannot be more 'truthful' than the scientific theories and data sets they compute. The GCMs currently in use require expensive supercomputers, but even they cannot incorporate all of the complexity to be found in the global climate system. The best models can only provide a resolution down to a 300 km grid, so each grid square must be treated as a unit, when we know what is happening below that level is enormously complex. This is especially so for small-scale phenomena, such as water vapour and cloud behaviour. Another crucial factor in the equation is the effect of sulphate aerosols and other pollutants produced when fossil fuels are burned, or when dust and particulates are added from a variety of sources. Only one of these has been modelled and their net effect on 'radiative forcing' is by no means fully understood. It was the increase in such 'dust' that caused the initial concerns that mankind might be cooling the earth. Aerosols have a cooling effect by screening incoming radiation, and are used to explain one inconvenient fact in the surface record: most of the observed warming since 1850 occurred between 1850 and about 1940, whereas most fossil fuel combustion has occurred since 1940. But then, there are always convenient lags in the system.

It is not just these isolated difficulties outlined above which make climate science problematic, but the way in which they are interrelated in an uncertain, chaotic and perhaps unpredictable complexity. Paltridge, a scientist summarizing climate science for a general readership, has concluded that: 'the science of climate change is plagued by uncertainty. At least part of that uncertainty, and perhaps most of it, will never be resolved' (Paltridge, 2001, 9). He points out that the atmosphere and oceans are turbulent, so very small fluctuations can grow in size and alter the large-scale processes within the system; and no matter how detailed are our measurements, there can be undetected fluctuations smaller than the distance between the measurements. A further problem is the very short run we have of data against which to test forecasting techniques. The aim of the GCMs has been to simulate today's climate on the assumption that they will therefore also be good at simulating future climate – a questionable assumption when dealing with turbulent complex systems.

Paltridge concludes that we can have some confidence, but by no means certainty, that over the next century, as a result of anthropogenic GHG emissions, the earth's average temperature might rise between 1 and 3°C above the temperature it would have been otherwise: 'With much lesser confidence we might accept that the temperature will rise a degree or three above that of today' (ibid., 10). The lesser confidence results from the possibility of rapid change that might result from other factors. He speculates that such an increase might be greater at the polar regions than at the equator, perhaps by a factor of two, and that overall global sea level might rise by a few tens of centimetres per century and global average rainfall might increase by 10 or 20 per cent. He concludes: 'No confidence can be placed in forecasts of climate change at any greater level of detail' (ibid., 10). Yet, as Paltridge and others have long noted, it is regional and local climate changes that matter to policy. It is at these levels that adaptation will in any case have to be the major response.

Paltridge further points out that it is not the mean global temperature that is important, but the possibility of a change in the extremes of weather: the 'tails' of the frequency distributions of rainfall, temperature and other climate variables. A rise in mean temperatures will affect the 'tails', but: 'We usually do not know the shapes of the "tails" as they are now, let alone the way they might change with change of climate' (ibid.). If the shape of the distribution and its tails remain the same, the relative change in the number of extreme events is always greater than the change in the average. This is what allows dire predictions to be made on the basis of relatively small changes in average temperatures, but as Paltridge cautions: 'There is no particular reason to assume the shapes of frequency distributions and their "tails" will remain the same in a slightly warmer world' (ibid., 11). Bearing this in mind, the caveat provided with some regional climate change scenarios by the Australian climate research institution CSIRO's Climate Impacts Group in its projections for Australia is worth noting:

> The projections are based on results from computer models that involve simplifica-tions of real physical processes that are not fully understood. Accordingly, no responsibility will be accepted by CSIRO for the accuracy of the projections inferred from this brochure or any person's interpretations, deductions, conclusions or actions in reliance on this information. (CSIRO, 2001, 8)

This would appear to be a frank caveat justified by the state of scientific knowledge, but it is not the kind of statement one finds scattered liberally throughout reports of the IPCC, and certainly not in the Summaries for Policy-makers of the IPCC main Assessment Reports. The documents are about all that policy-makers and NGOs are likely to read and can be expected to comprehend. Nevertheless, buried away in an IPCC Special Report on Emissions Scenarios, the socio-economic data which was used to drive the climate models to produce the scenarios for TAR, one can find the following caveat:

> Any scenario necessarily includes subjective elements and is open to various inter-pretations. Preferences for the scenarios presented here vary among users. No judgement is offered in this report as to the preference for any of the scenarios and they are not assigned probabilities of occurrence, neither must they be interpreted as policy recommendations. (IPCC, 2000)

But the point, of course, is that, once fed through the supercomputers and the IPCC process, they are stripped of caveats and uncertainties and *do* serve as the basis for policy recommendations and major political efforts to persuade the doubtful or reluctant.

The power of extreme scenarios to influence negotiations was apparent in the projections produced by WG I for TAR, where a wider range of possible warming scenarios than in SAR was generated. The resultant projected increase of 1.4–5.8°C over the next century was not the result of scientific advances or substantial improvements in computing skills, but of feeding 35 different scenarios into seven different climate models. These produced a number of scenarios for the usually assumed doubling of CO_2 from pre-industrial levels. The resulting range was calculated by the available equations as amounting to average global warming for the whole surface between 1.7°C and 4.2°C. The 5.8°C rise, however, was produced by a scenario which combined high CO_2 emissions with very low emissions of (selected) aerosols. In other words, this scenario assumed that CO_2 emissions would not be effectively reduced, but that the included aerosols would be slashed by regulation. The obvious question was how likely this scenario was to occur, a question the IPCC did not answer but for which we have some sympathy. Fossil fuel use is not likely to be reduced by Kyoto while local and regional air pollution may become more tightly controlled because of concerns over health effects. However, this should have been clearly spelt out and only throws the whole debate back to attribution and the nature and predictability of climate.

The changes in the range of global warming predicted since Arrhenius did his simple black-body calculation and suggested between 4°C and 6°C in 1896 is illuminating, because the most recent results are close to those from his estimates. The first draft of the WG I TAR, which was produced on 6 November 1999, showed a figure with a range of 1.5–4.0°C. In the second draft of 16 April 2000 the range had increased to 1.3–5.0°C, and by the third and final draft of the report of 22 October 2000 (after the main scientific review process had been completed, and in time to be leaked to the media and revealed by IPCC Chair Watson at COP-6 in The Hague) it had risen to 1.4–5.8°C. The later, higher results reflected subsequent 'tuning' of models using more scenarios.

The IPCC TAR indeed reported a range for the predicted global mean surface temperature rise but did not provide likelihood estimates for this key finding, although it did for others. One such analysis subsequently found that the upper limit of the IPCC range was highly improbable, with far less than a 1 per cent likelihood of a rise in mean global temperature as large as 5.8°C by 2100 (Webster *et al.*, 2001). This research suggested the mean projection was only 2.5°C, yet the 5.8°C figure attracted all the headlines, often rounded up to 6°C. And Dr Watson told COP-6 that the earth's surface temperature was now higher than for 1,000 years and new forecasts (*sic*) put the expected (*sic*) temperature rises until 2100 at between 1.5°C and 6.0°C – double the previous estimates.[6] These amendments did not reflect any changes in our understanding of climate, but were attributable entirely to differences in the selection of models and the socio-economic assumptions employed in the form of various scenarios. The latter were based on 'storylines' developed by futurologists and economists rather than climate scientists. No probabilities were attached to them, and while their authors are quick to point out that these are neither predictions nor forecasts, politicians, journalists and even some scientists often treat them precisely as such (as far as we can tell) without any IPCC spokesman correcting them on this significant point (for example, the BBC's use of 'forecast' and 'expected' when reporting Dr Watson at COP-6, above). The upper limit was widely reported as a *prediction*, and a likely one at that: a headline in *The Times* warned: 'Global warming "will be twice as bad".'[7]

We consider that such evidence shows that the IPCC process is an institutionalized means of policy support: downplaying the uncertainties while intensifying the perception of threat and thus encouraging a particular consensus. This, it is hoped, is to produce the appropriate response: the conclusion of international agreements to limit the emission of CO_2 (especially) and other GHGs. The FCCC depends for its progress upon there being dangerous, anthropogenic warming that can be mitigated by emission reduction. As the perception of those dangers is enhanced, so is the potential success of assorted strategies that have been attracted to the Kyoto process.

To understand this, it is necessary to consider each of the stages in the process by which the IPCC consensus is produced and the dangers associated with funding policy relevant science. At one level, there is the science being conducted by 'bench scientists'. As we noted in the previous chapter, some of this will turn out to have been good science and some of it will prove ultimately to have been mistaken – its results will not be replicated by numerous subsequent studies. With climate science, a risk lies in the very success the science politicians have enjoyed in securing resources for the bench scientists. For research agendas and globally managed research programmes like GARP, IGBP and GEC, the risk is that the ability of the science politicians to secure these resources has become dependent on their ability to convince governments that there is an urgent need to conduct 'their' science instead of or in addition to other scientific endeavours. But the other steps in the IPCC consensus process are more worrisome. After the production of a consensus view of the current state of knowledge in one area of climate science comes the production of a précis of all of those understandings in a Summary for Policy-makers. It is this summary that is meant to be 'used' and thus becomes the major policy input. The uses to which this statement of conclusions for the lay reader is put is just as important politically, and it is frequently misused – without correction by IPCC spokesmen.

THE EXTERNAL USE OF IPCC REPORTS

The writing of the individual chapters and Policy-makers' Summaries of IPCC assessment reports may have received critical attention from insiders, but from a policy perspective the next stage is even more important: that is the use of the IPCC reports by 'stakeholders' – its own spokesmen, the media, NGOs, politicians, public servants and other political actors.

What is apparent here and cannot but be known to 'science' is that these actors, especially dedicated bureaucracies and NGOs – be they environmentalist or commercial – strip away all caveats and quote the science selectively for political effect. To give one example, the IPCC talks guardedly about 'scenarios' and 'projections'; NGOs talk of these as 'predictions' and real futures. This is not unusual, but what is worrying is that the IPCC leadership does not correct this misrepresentation. Rather, its representatives have made numerous efforts to impugn the credibility of those scientists who dissent from the consensus, but are silent on the errors committed by those who support it. To give one recent example, Sir John Houghton, chair of WG I, stated as TAR was finalized: 'I think there are very few scientists who'd disagree with the IPCC. And most of those who do disagree have not published much.'[8] Questions and doubts invite research, and papers cannot be written without research that may take many years, as the climate change specialists know only too well. Once implementable policy is made, funding dries up. Our point is that the IPCC type of scientific organization, now being called for in other environmental policy areas such as forestry, whether deliberately or not stifles such research and in the longer term will harm science more than policy, and lobbies will lose their credibility.

Remarks such as Sir John's are aimed at producing and bolstering, through the IPCC, a consensus in favour of a more certain and negative view of climate change than is warranted by the evidence – at least by our reading. We have given several examples of how IPCC consensus has favoured interpretations of science that helped create scenarios which would support a view that there was a need for political action to limit GHG emissions. Others relate to the dismissal of paleoclimate data, solar and cosmic ray forcings and the roles of assorted aerosols. We therefore interpret Houghton's remark as an attempt to stifle dissent and thus as profoundly anti-scientific, though it may serve to keep the UK climate change modelling efforts at the front of the pack and Sir John from losing face, for he has succeeded in making a whole range of UK policies dependent on his version of global warming.

Yet he may well be doing a considerable disservice to the many scientists who differ from the IPCC consensus in some way, large or small. Reputable scientists disputed the conclusions of the TAR of WG I as soon as it was released. Statements to that effect were made by Andrew Weaver of the University of Victoria in Canada and a lead author of the report, and by Gordon McBean, a professor at the University of Western Ontario.[9] Leading critics such as John Christy from the University of Alabama and Richard Lindzen of MIT now contribute to the IPCC while disputing the consensus view and have impressive research credentials as 'bench scientists'. Roger Pocklington, a former oceanographer with Canada's Bedford Institute of Oceanography, reports that he published contrary findings in the scientific literature but has had them ignored by policy-makers. Dr Chris De Freitas, of the University of Auckland, is both sceptical and an editor of *Climate Research*. Dr Tim Ball, formerly of the University of Winnipeg also dissents.[10] There are countless critics from numerous branches of science, such as Professor Phillip Stott, University of London; Professor David Unwin, Birkbeck College, London; and Piers Corbyn, of the private company Weather Action. Again some have published in *Energy and Environment*, at times in anger: Kirill Kondratyev, Richard Courtney, Heinz Hug, Vincent Gray, Jarl Ahlbeck, Per Brekke (ESA, Norway), Sallie Baliunas (Harvard-Smithsonian Center for Astrophysics) and Sherwood Idso (US Water Conservation Laboratory). The EU media in particular have paid little attention to such sceptics and, of necessity, their objections often come from positions of more limited specialist knowledge but broad reading, often profound experience and complete neutrality as far as funding is concerned. However, they are not all members of the 'climate community'. Such communities, whether religious, political or scientific, cannot but have common interests in maintaining themselves and, hopefully, growing. Their punishment is exclusion.

Perfectly reputable scientists are publicly sceptical about various signs which are commonly taken as indications of global warming. For example, the shrinking of the Breidamerkurjokull glacier in southern Iceland (Europe's largest) was interpreted by Dr David Evans of Glasgow University as resulting from the end of the LIA rather than anthropogenic warming.[11] Coral reef 'bleaching', as evidence of response to the temperature and sea level rises associated with El Niño events, is understood by field geographers as either natural or a response to regional and local changes, and might in fact be beneficial and simply part of the adaptation processes, as corals expel one kind of algae (which provide colour) before taking on others adapted to the new conditions (Baker, 2001).

Behind the IPCC consensus there is indeed a large body of scientific literature. Like any body of scientific literature, its quality and reliability are variable. What is accepted by the IPCC and what is rejected is therefore of crucial importance. In the case of the satellite data (and the other data referred to), the IPCC can be seen to have rejected some scientific findings in 1995 because they did not support the consensus, but included them in 2001 because, with the addition of further observations, the data supported it. The satellite, balloon and surface data (including sea water and the air above it) collectively point to the need to understand further the relationship between the many factors affecting climate. The IPCC was *required* to reach a consensus despite this substantial lack of understanding. The idea, once mooted, that there might be minority reports was not adopted.

There is a wide consensus that the world has warmed a little and even the sceptics most critical of the IPCC consensus grant that human activity has been a factor, however small, in this warming. But the sceptics point out that the observed warming began before the widespread use of fossil fuel which accompanied the Industrial Revolution, as the world emerged from the 'Little Ice Age', and might not be harmful. These events are usually explained in terms of solar variability, which is an order of magnitude greater than CO_2 forcing. Some sceptics tend to see solar variability, via cosmic ray effects, as much more significant in explaining climate change.

NGO 'Science' and the Media

Beyond the workings of the IPCC comes the eventual distillation of 'the facts' by NGOs and the media. NGOs produce their own 'scientific evidence', usually in support of 'eco-catastrophe' for it is by promising to defend mankind against disaster that they gather supporters and income. (Again, we can only give glimpses here, but the genre is exemplified by books by Leggett, 1999, and Gelbspan, 1997). For example, in February 1997 Greenpeace researchers reported to the media massive cracks in Antarctic sea ice which, they claimed, were evidence of global warming. Greenpeace had despatched its research team to the area precisely to look for evidence to highlight global warming to the public, and was indeed able to provide dramatic video footage to a hungry media. This was not peer-reviewed science but a media event supporting a political campaign. In contrast, the rebuttal of the claim by glaciologists – pointing out that warming would affect the rate of melting, whereas cracking was a natural phenomenon related to shearing pressures – received but a few column centimetres in the print media.

The likelihood of substantial rises in sea levels as a result of global warming induced melting of the cryosphere appear to be exaggerated. In a statement issued on 10 February 2000, the Antarctic Cooperative Research Centre at the University of Tasmania argued that there would be little rise in sea levels over the next century or two were there to be warming of a few degrees melting the Greenland or Antarctic ice sheets (Antarctic CRC, 2000). Melting the Greenland ice sheet would contribute substantially to sea level rise, but would take one or two thousand years. The Antarctic ice sheet could make a much larger contribution to sea level rise, but temperatures are well below the melting point of ice in Antarctica, and warming of two or three degrees would not be sufficient for melting. Indeed, warming is thought to be likely to increase snowfall in Antarctica and thus thicken the ice sheet. Any sea level rise would come from non-polar glaciers and thermal expansion of the oceans and would be only of the order of 'several tens of centimeters per century': a rate already experienced in several places because of geological changes causing the relative sea level to rise (by 80 cm per century on the east coast of Japan, to 10 cm per century on some Pacific Islands or the eastern USA).

Another television report while Kyoto was being negotiated linked the appearance of coloured frogs in the United Kingdom (after earlier widespread but not uncommon floods) to global warming. Newspaper reports simply had scientists wondering aloud whether global warming *might* be responsible: a discrepancy that tells us much about the way in which the visual media treat such information. Similar claims are made for almost any unwanted climate-related event. (The press even blamed an increase in badgers on the same cause.)

Flash floods in Italy, slope failure from deforestation in Latin America, hurricane damage in the USA, as well as serious flooding and very high rainfall in the UK on the eve of COP-6 in 2000 were all attributed to climate change rather than land-use practices or neglect. Any short-term variation tends to be attributed to *anthropogenic* climate change even if it is a normal part of climatic variation. May not industry or the USA be to blame? The exceedingly cold winter in the northern hemisphere in 2000–1 (strangely) received little comment. In fact, the rain which caused Britain's flooding was not attributable to global warming but to the North Atlantic Oscillation,[12] and land-use changes played a role in the severity of its impact.

The frequently asserted increase in storm frequency and severity as a result of recent observed warming has a dubious basis, because (as the IPCC acknowledges) data available thus far on both counts do not seem to support the hypothesis, and damage is not more severe, despite more building near exposed coastlines. Tillinghurst-Towers Perrin released the first comprehensive study of hurricane damage for the entire twentieth century in July 2001. It found that, when actual insured hurricane damages are adjusted to reflect current property values and the increase in the number of people living close to the coast, insured damages in the 1990s were not unusually high. Further, while Atlantic hurricane frequency did increase in the second half of the 1990s, the number of such storms striking the USA in the decade was actually the second-lowest of the twentieth century; and the most expensive storm was not Hurricane Andrew in 1996, but a September 1926 Miami hurricane which was twice as expensive (*Business Wire Features*, 11 July 2001).

We need to beware of selecting only the data which confirm our preferred theories, and this applies equally to the public communication of science and to the conduct of science itself. This is where the deficiencies of the IPCC consensus-generating process become important. Greenpeace specializes in politicized science, often committing the cardinal scientific sin of bringing the evidence to the theory, usually in the form of dramatic visual footage supplied to the media from some remote location. Newspapers pick up the upper range of the IPCC scenarios, treat them as predictions, and add appropriate spin. For example, the UK newspaper the *Independent* announced the release of the TAR from WG I under the headline 'UN delivers apocalyptic warning on climate; Global warming: increase in storms, floods, droughts, failed farms and raging pestilence will hit poor hardest, claim scientists.'[13] The *Independent* used language such as 'can be expected' and 'the world's average temperature will rise by up to 6°C by 2100'. There would be a rise in deaths from the onset of 'once-tropical' diseases such as malaria. It quoted Friends of the Earth senior climate campaigner Roger Higman as describing this as a 'catastrophe': 'Governments in industrial countries must agree radical cuts in our use of coal, oil, and gas, and big increases in the use of renewable power.'

The tacit coalition between a scientific community and news media all wanting bad news has had embarrassing results. On 19 August 2000 the *New York Times* published a story by reputable science journalist John Noble Wilford based on accounts of several scientists who had just returned from the North Pole. They included oceanographer James McCarthy, director of the Museum of Comparative Zoology at Harvard University and an IPCC member. They were shocked by the thin polar ice and the open water they found at the Pole. 'The North Pole is melting', declared the *Times*. Global warming was to blame. A week later, the *Times* had to admit that that ice-free areas were not unusual, and Arctic Ocean ice fluctuated in a 60–70-year cycle.[14] A decline in Arctic ice was a feature of TAR, based upon an analysis published in 1999 (Rothrock *et al.*, 1999). A re-analysis using the same data supplemented by a further three years of submarine data suggested that this interpretation was in error (Winsor, 2001), again demonstrating the tentative nature of scientific evidence.

IPCC representatives not only fail to correct the excesses of NGOs and journalists, at times they actively add to the alarmism. For example, IPCC Chair Watson stated at the launch of WG I TAR that the implications of global warming on human health included increases in heat stress mortality in the summer and diseases such as malaria and dengue fever (*Reuters*, 22 January 2001; see also malaria story, pp. 159–161 above). Many of the alarmist claims which have become established climate change 'facts' in the public mind, such as sea level rise from melting polar ice caps, are similarly contestable. A research programme in the Pacific found that, while the oceans were warming, there was no evidence of sea level rise, according to Dr Wolfgang Schere, director of Australia's National Tidal Facility, which had conducted the research for the South Pacific Regional Environment Program and reported to the South Pacific Forum meeting in Kiribati. Greenpeace representatives responded to these results by claiming that sea level rises in the past century were 10 times greater than during the previous 3,000 years and high sea levels would threaten reefs and entire atoll nations among the 14 nations gathered for the South Pacific summit.[15]

The fate of these atoll nations depends on numerous complex factors, including the rates at which they mine their reefs for construction material, but they have an interest in deflecting attention from factors for which they might have responsibility. At the 2001 Pacific Forum, the President of Nauru described the current inundation of islands as a 'holocaust', ignoring a further report to the same Forum by Dr Schere of an absence of evidence of sea level rise. Some geologically unstable islands are indeed *sinking*, but nobody is to blame for this nor to seek compensation from – except on the basis of humanitarian aid, which should be reason enough.

CONCLUSION

Much of the science supporting climate change alarms ignores not only the natural variablity of the many factors shaping climate and our still weak quantitative understanding of the many feed-backs this involves, but also the complex social and scientific factors which affect any impacts of changing climate. While all science depends upon some degree of reductionism, because it cannot deal with too much complexity, this reduces policy relevance. In climate science this loss of relevance should be particularly worrying to environmentalists, given that environmental science lays claims to holism. We cannot develop this point here. We believe that the uncertainties and limitations in all climate sciences, especially knowledge about sources and sinks from land-use activities, remain a major gap and that appeals to precaution in such a context tend to lead to the politicization of research, as demonstrated by the IPCC.

There are many factors driving climate science that are not scientific in nature, including the funding issues (science itself is an interest). IPCC reports are intended by the science politicians and environment politicians to persuade nations to accept the need for action of a particular kind: reduction of emissions from energy utilization (although increasingly there are indications of an acceptance of the need for adaptation strategies). IPCC climate science, however, reinforces national economic priorities in some countries (such as Germany and the UK) while threatening them in others (USA, Australia). Rather than producing a political consensus on the need for a particular kind of policy response, IPCC science has divided nations as much as it has brought them together, and each can select a 'reading' of the science which bolsters its own interests.

The IPCC reports are quite explicitly expected to play a political role in bringing about international consensus on the need for action of a particular kind. The statements made by IPCC and UNEP officials at the release of the WG I TAR clearly illustrate this. For example, Klaus Töpfer (UNEP Secretary-General and former German environment minister): 'The scientific consensus presented in this comprehensive report about human-induced climate change should sound alarm bells in every national capital and in every local community' (*Panafrican News Agency*, 22 January 2001). Michael Zammit Cutajar, Executive Secretary of the UNFCCC: 'The scientific findings being reported today should convince governments of the need to take constructive steps towards resuming the climate change talks that stalled last November in The Hague' (*Environmental News Service*, 22 January 2001). IPCC scientists too are prepared to use the Assessment Reports to exert special pressure on those nations that resist dominant negotiating positions. Again, Sir John Houghton tried to put 'scientific' pressure on the USA: 'I hope the White House will read the report very carefully, and realise that it's been put together by leading scientists. They need to take it very seriously and to begin to lead the world into taking action' (*BBC News Online*, 22 January 2001). He has also stated quite clearly that nothing but legally mandated emission reductions within countries is acceptable, and that no gain is possible without this pain:

The whole problem with carbon trading is it can be used as a cop out by some countries who find they can suddenly manage to fill their books in ways that are too easy and don't really do what we need to do in the end is to make sure that on a global, long-term basis we actually reduce the amount of carbon dioxide that gets into the atmosphere. (*Four Corners*, 1999)

Again, this is politics, not science.

The desired response as far as key figures such as Houghton and Töpfer are concerned is primarily emission abatement rather than either adaptation, sink creation or carbon trading, although TAR has seen more emphasis upon adaptation and Töpfer has granted a place for it (but not sinks): 'We must now move ahead boldly with clean energy technologies, and start preparing ourselves for the rising sea levels, changing rain patterns, and other impacts of global warming' (*Panafrican News Agency*, 22 January 2001).

Yet, at the time of writing (October 2001), even these best efforts of the IPCC and its supporters to create a scientific consensus had failed to produce full political consensus behind the kind of Kyoto outcome favoured by environmentalists, the EU and G-77. We suggest the answer is two-fold.

First, cutting edge research science is not a reliable basis for policy; rather it tends to be used as a political weapon. In the EU the case for climate action is made strongly by having faith in the application of the precautionary principle as interpreted by bureaucracies and their allies. The approach allows for a *de facto* risk–benefit equation for the EU that depends crucially upon its interests but hides behind science. This risk–benefit equation differs substantially from that of other Annex I parties, and no attempt to increase the pressure on parties by selectively citing science is likely to take consensus very far. Further, the precautionary principle encourages a degree of policy ambition which takes action beyond the limits of the science, encouraging the development of calls for action when there is still so much uncertainty in the science that the modalities of key elements of policy responses cannot be spelled out. Uncertain scientific knowledge cannot deliver sufficient policy certainty.

Second, it is improbable that science can provide the 'underpinning' for agreement on *any* major environmental issue. An absence of significant disagreement over science might be an important factor in facilitating agreement, but (as climate science shows) it is possible to reach apparent agreement on the science but find substantial, perhaps intractable, differences over policy prescriptions. This is shown most clearly by Hansen *et al.*,'s (2000) paper which was important in the US decision to withdraw. As far as we know, Hansen *et al.* believe fully in the IPCC consensus yet their analysis shows that there are various ways in which any political system might sensibly respond to the risk, mitigating any number of GHGs (not to mention various sink options).

Especially when interests are powerful, scientific (or epistemic) consensus appears at best to be a necessary rather than sufficient condition for political agreement, unlikely to reconstruct interests sufficiently to avoid a negotiation of interests if international policy responses are to be developed. As Underdal and Hanf (2000) argue, science and normative arguments probably helped initiate the Kyoto process, but when it comes to developing detailed policy responses, a negotiation of interests is inescapable and only an 'equal cost' solution is likely to achieve overall consensus. Instead, we observe competition for commercial advantage. Moreover, because this was not appreciated in the 'metapolicy' of the Kyoto process (the selection of the appropriate process), the outcome has probably been more modest than if the whole process had simply focused on interests from the outset.

The 'blame and shame' rhetoric of CAN and its members, and even of some leading politicians, and the belief that science would produce unity has *de facto* weakened the Protocol as agreed so far, which no longer includes the most significant party, the USA. Further negotiations are needed on many issues, including the flexible mechanisms and future commitments, but compulsion has largely gone and sinks have been accepted. Ratification and entry into force remain problematic, as does the value of the Protocol, both as a response to the putative risk of climate change and for the other purposes it is intended to serve, such as justifying energy taxes and supporting energy technologies which will remain uncompetitive as long as fossil fuels are plentiful and relatively cheap.

NOTES

1. We are grateful for Ian Castles for drawing this point to our attention.
2. Trees do not grow on the more than two-thirds of the earth's surface covered by water, nor on deserts or in many other areas. Tree rings indicate growth during the day during the growing season (largely summer), so tell us little about winter or night temperatures. They are affected by rainfall, sunlight, pests and nutrients. Further, calibrating rings against the recent surface record might be problematic if that record is influenced by the urban heat island effect.
3. Paal Brekke, 'Viewpoint: The Sun and climate change', *BBC News*, 16 November 2000.
4. 'Sun Studies May Shed Light on Global Warming', *Washington Post*, 9 October 2000.
5. IPCC supporters value these models much more highly. While the above may ignore that many variables involved are interrelated by a very few basic conservation laws and that models are never perfect, the question remains of whether they are good enough for policy guidance.
6. 'Climate Talks Told of "Mounting Evidence" ', *BBC News*, 13 November 2000.
7. See 'Global Warming "Will be Twice as Bad" ', *The Times*, 22 January 2001.
8. Alex Kirby, 'Human Effect on Climate "Beyond Doubt" ', *BBC News Online*, 22 January 2001 <http://news.bbc.co.uk/hi/english/sci/technewsid_1130000/1130501.stm>
9. 'Top Scientists Call UN Report on Climate Change Misleading', *Toronto Star*, 23 January 2001.
10. *Toronto Star,* 7 April 2001.
11. 'Europe's Biggest Glacier Shrinks', *CNN.com*, 23 October 2000.
12. 'Britain's Flooding "Not Caused by Global Warming", Say Scientists', *The Daily Telegraph*, 26 November 2000.
13. *Independent*, 20 February 2001.
14. See 'Fixing the Hole in the North Pole', *Anchorage Daily News*, 4 September 2000.
15. 'Pacific Sea Levels Not Rising: New Research', *Age*, 28 October 2000.

8. Baptists, bootleggers and the Kyoto process

With the release of the TAR of WG I in January 2001, UNEP Secretary-General Klaus Töpfer, former German environment minister, hoped that the 'science' in the report would drive the parties together in the negotiations which had stalled in the previous year and were about to resume in Bonn in July 2001.

In September, various EU policy-makers, meeting in London in preparation for COP-7 in Marrakech in October 2001, pleaded with a reluctant USA to return to the fold and rejoin this major global effort – in spite or because of the World Trade Center terrorist attacks on September 11 – ready for ratification at the Rio +10 conference in Johannesburg in 2002. Yet the many experts also present, while they had lived off the climate threats for over a decade, remained uncertain and gave ratification a 50:50 chance. Some suggested that sufficient parties would never ratify; others expressed doubts unless more concessions were made. There was much concern about likely carbon prices if the USA would not return. The pressure for something to be ratified remained great, in particular from the EU and many developing countries (expecting major new investment and aid streams), and this might result after Marrakech because the negotiations are increasingly adjusting to interests and hence equalizing 'burden-sharing' or opportunities.

As we noted in the previous chapter, Töpfer had stated that he considered the scientific findings of the IPCC's Third Assessment Report should convince governments of the need to 'take constructive steps' towards resuming the stalled climate change negotiations. At the time of writing, COP-6 Part II in Bonn had come and gone, resulting in a substantial watering down of Kyoto commitments in the face of interests in order to secure agreement. Negotiations resumed in October 2001 in Morocco (COP-7). A vast investment by national and international bureaucracies in these negotiations and their underlying expertise needed to be salvaged. Töpfer had repeatedly argued that changes in energy systems and adaptation were needed, stating that: 'We must now move ahead boldly with clean energy technologies, and start preparing ourselves for the rising sea levels, changing rain patterns, and other impacts of global warming.' (Panafrican News Agency, 22 January 2001).

Just as his predecessor Mustafa Tolba had done at the outset of the international politics of climate change, Töpfer had clearly hoped that the science and strong normative injunctions would override the interests which had kept the parties apart in The Hague. UNEP (and Germany) wanted a global agreement in support of 'clean energy technologies' along the lines envisaged by the European Union and its supporters in business and 'civil society'. Yet not long after Töpfer made his statement at the release of IPCC TAR, the negotiations degenerated into acrimonious finger-pointing by the European Union and repeated assurances from the USA that, while it considered climate change to be an important issue, Kyoto was the wrong solution. The USA then withdrew from the process, and at the end of the day the EU was prepared to accept in Bonn most of what it had rejected in The Hague, to the extent that it is questionable from an environmental perspective whether the whole process was worth the effort.

Many have questioned the value of the bargain struck in Bonn, as a clear compromise between interests. Even then, the agreement was a decision of the COP, which could only be binding once adopted by the Meeting of the Parties to the Kyoto Protocol had entered into force, after it had received the requisite ratifications by 55 per cent of parties that accounted for 55 per cent of Annex I emissions. As David Victor put it in an op-ed piece, 'A Deal Rescuing Nothing' (*Los Angeles Times* on 19 August 2001): what was agreed in Bonn would allow countries to claim credits for the carbon dioxide absorbed when their forests grow, even though most forest restoration predated the Kyoto Protocol and was unrelated to forest-management programmes that will be used to justify the credits. Furthermore, he noted, nobody knew how to verify carbon fluxes.

The EU finally accepted largely what it had rejected because the requirements for entry into force gave substantial bargaining power to those whose ratification would notionally push the total over the 55 per cent of Annex I ratifications required, after the withdrawal of the USA, which accounted for 36 per cent. If Russia joined the EU, Switzerland, Estonia, Latvia and Norway in ratifying, ratifications would account for 49.7 per cent of 1990 emissions, and Japan's ratification (8.5 per cent) would raise it to 58.25 per cent and the Protocol would enter into force. Japan was therefore the crucial party, and it was the one which would find it most difficult to meet its target because of the progress it had made towards energy efficiency before 1990, and which remained most reluctant to submit to mandatory compliance measures on cultural grounds.

Interests dominated in this end-game, not just the interests of the Umbrella Group nations, which wanted to ensure that the advantage to the EU implicit in the original Protocol was reined back in, but the interests of the EU itself. The EU secured international obligations which would legitimate (indeed, require) official support for taxes, clean energy and energy efficiency, and hence provide a strong push towards 'decarbonization' and improved energy security. This would also serve the cause of EU political integration by establishing new competences for the European Commission.

Victor's first point illustrates that, when it came to the crunch, the Umbrella Group demanded (and won) the same kind of advantage that the EU had received by virtue of the selection of 1990 as the base year, thanks to energy restructuring in the UK and Germany, which were equally unrelated to climate change action. And his second point highlights the near impossibility of undertaking action of the complexity and difficulty of climate change on the basis of the precautionary principle, because such fluxes form part of the problem (inasmuch as they were included in national inventories) but were difficult to include as part of the solution, except as the basis of the Bonn compromise. By what Victor described as 'political logrolling', the Kyoto cut of 5.2 per cent became a mere 2 per cent cut, with those most reluctant to proceed without US participation, especially Japan, receiving the most generous concessions. Even more concessions were gained by these parties at Marrakesh at COP-7, with Russia able to increase its allowance for sinks from 17 to 33 megatons of carbon.

This outcome also sees the USA, with almost 40 per cent of Annex I emissions, outside the deal, and its absence made it easier for all other parties to meet their targets, because the largest buyer had effectively quit the market for emission credits that was being established. Whereas the USA had accepted a target of –7 per cent at Kyoto, it was looking at the likely reality of a +30 per cent performance by the time the commitment period was reached, with it needing to purchase credits on the newly formed international market in order to bridge the gap. Russia and Ukraine were potentially (on paper at least) the biggest sellers, thanks to post-communist economic collapse, but the exit of the USA removed their largest potential customer and drove down the value of credits. Other Annex I parties will now be able to pick up credits at low prices and avoid any costly measures to meet targets. Victor estimates that the 38 Annex I parties will, on average, be able to increase emissions by 8 per cent, so that emission levels will be no different if Kyoto never enters into force. Moreover, by driving down the value of credits, the Bonn compromise diminishes substantially the value of creating credits in developing countries, creating little incentive for investment in clean energy technologies.

Ironically, the exit of the USA made Kyoto much easier for the remaining parties, with the discounted value of world abatement costs falling, according to one analysis, from over \$2 trillion to about \$250 billion, and drove down the value of a ton of carbon in 2010 in the original Kyoto agreement from \$55 to \$15 after Bonn, and even less after Marrakesh (Nordhaus, 2001).

Since the 5.2 per cent Kyoto reduction target for Annex I parties now amounts to perhaps a 2 per cent reduction in emissions, and trading will allow most Annex I parties some increases, it is germane to ask whether this (or an even greater result) might have been achieved if parties had simply signed on for future reductions that they thought they could afford, ignoring the structural advantage of 1990 as a base year. The USA might well still have been in the process and there would have been considerably more goodwill than exists now, after the many insults levelled by environmentalists championing the EU cause, and after a US delegate has been hit in the face with a cream pie, as occurred in The Hague. (The leader of the Scottish Liberal Democrats even labelled George W. Bush a mass murderer after the US withdrawal.) Developing countries must have been watching in amazement, but also with some concern as the expected flows of aid money receded and the demands that they should join the emission reduction club increased.

Instead of an unrealistic Protocol that probably would never have entered into force, we now have a still incomplete agreement that will make little difference globally as far as emission reduction by international *diktat* is concerned. In addition, the strong principled discourse, with a heavy reliance upon rhetoric that can best be described as 'blame and shame', has – ironically – almost certainly harmed the development of the shared norms which are usually regarded as central to the development of successful regimes (Young, 1994). Such shared norms usually develop over time as parties work together, but accusations of 'climate criminal' can hardly be seen as contributing to their development.

We have suggested that this outcome was the result of paradigmatic differences between the parties, particularly the EU and the Umbrella Group, of which the USA was the leader. The EU (supported by most NGOs) was essentially operating within a principled discourse that masked its interests, while the Umbrella Group was operating more openly on the basis of interests, or within what Mitchell referred to as an instrumental discourse. The EU and its supporters attempted to harness the causal discourse of science to their cause through an essentially eco-centric epistemology of ethics. Developing countries, on the other hand, could not be persuaded that the threat of climate change outweighed the more immediate and real dangers arising from any curtailment of development efforts.

We can now ask whether negotiations where differences in interests are made explicit and respected by the parties might not achieve more. While we are more sceptical of the science than many, the issue of climatic deterioration, however caused, remains important, because the creation of a regime which provides the framework for a future response is ultimately the kind of 'insurance institution' that is needed, regardless of cause.

One prominent sceptic, Patrick Michaels, suggested earlier that the Kyoto Protocol was a poor investment as an 'insurance institution' for preventing climate change because it would have shaved only 0.14°C off the 2.2°C average warming predicted by the GCMs: a reduction of about 6.4 per cent. The cost of implementing Kyoto had been estimated at about 2 or 3 per cent of Annex I GDP. So the 'insurance policy' was expensive for the return if the risk eventuated (Michaels, 2001). The Kyoto targets, even if achieved in reality and not just on paper (always a danger, given measurement problems), were effectively meaningless, since they would make an infinitessimal difference if the worst fears prove justified. But defenders say it is only a first step and that agreement on a second commitment period must be reached soon for the process to continue.

What seems more important to us is whether the regime exists to respond adequately if these fears do turn out to be appropriate (and technological change and other factors do not substantially decarbonize the global economy over the next half-century or so). Moreover, might it not be wiser to retain 3 per cent of GDP and invest it in non-carbon technology and strategies to adapt to the change the IPCC is said to consider inevitable, regardless of whether it is attributable to anthropogenic causes?

This suggests that the establishment of a regime in which shared norms could evolve to facilitate the development of future responses was more important than the targets and measures in Kyoto themselves. Yet the strongly principled rhetoric employed (largely unsuccessfully) during the Kyoto process and the related insistence on a punitive compliance mechanism may have set back the prospects for the evolution of such a regime, a regime the Japanese have in fact pleaded for most, given their high costs of further emission reduction and limited prospects for planting more 'biomass' at home.

Perspectives on the questions we pose above differ according to the specific interests and needs of the parties. Regardless of whether 2 or 3 per cent was an accurate estimate of the costs to the USA and other economies, that was the kind of ballpark figure which featured in US national interest calculations. Significantly, it was two orders of magnitude greater than that in the EU, which Environment Commissioner Margot Wallström estimated at 'only 0.06' per cent of GDP. Again, the accuracy of this figure is not important. What is important is that major protagonists viewed the costs involved in meeting Kyoto commitments as differing by two orders of magnitude and yet some expected agreement to result because of science and normative arguments! Following a process which assumed that science and normative injunctions would overcome such differences in interests (and burdens) was a major error in judgement unless there had been prior agreement that environmental negotiations were also to serve the objectives of a global redistribution of wealth or economic competitiveness. Disguised interests – bootleggers masked by the efforts of Baptists – dominated the whole Kyoto process and thus condemned it to failure.

As we have seen here, the EU wanted climate change to be seen as an issue about CO_2 emissions and therefore about energy technologies, fuels and demand. It wanted uniform targets and mandatory policies, and therefore sought to use the issue to address its lack of energy competitiveness and to overcome resistance to the Europeanization of energy policy. As with issues such as the selection of the base year of 1990, which was favourable to Germany and the UK and thus (thanks to the Bubble) the EU as a whole, it sought to maximize its advantage in negotiations. There were all manner of subtexts: support was created for reducing German coal subsidies; the nuclear and gas sectors each received a boost; so too did research; support was generated for unpopular taxes; the EU Commission gained competence in the energy sector. While the EU has achieved its aims at home, whether international competitiveness will follow is now more doubtful. With the USA dropping out of the futures market for carbon credits, this market will have an oversupply. The sellers of 'hot air' (or sinks) have already been advised not to sell because of likely low prices (Jepma, 2001).

The USA and its allies in the Umbrella Group were of course also seeking to protect and advance their interests, particularly flexibility in the use of sinks to achieve net reductions rather than having to reduce emissions at source, and in having the policy approach encompass the full range of GHGs, including those not related to energy. The Umbrella Group also saw the importance of at least some commitment from developing countries to slow future growth in emissions if the very small gains of Kyoto were not rapidly to be offset and amount to an expensive and futile gesture.

The EU was prepared to leave aside this issue of future emission growth in non-Annex I parties in order to secure the support of G-77 for its approach, but this also sat well with the moral posturing of the EU bureaucrats, politicians and environmentalists. Its position was supported by the plausible rationale that Annex I parties had caused the problem through historical emissions. But the EU did not extend this argument within Annex I, where, as the Brazilian proposal indicated, it would have asked for the greatest sacrifice by those countries such as the UK and Germany which had industrialized early and had been burning substantial quantities of fossil fuels for a century and a half. Similarly, global emissions trading was condemned by the EU, at least before COP-6 Part II in Bonn, while 'political' trading within the EU Bubble was somehow morally acceptable.

What distinguished the positions of the two main negotiating blocs most of all was the extent to which the EU position appeared to be reinforced by the moral and other non-economic arguments, such as those which assumed that the science and professional expertise demanded particular responses. While in domestic politics such coalitions of interests and moral justifications may become sufficiently powerful to ensure that the policy proposals they support are adopted, in international politics regime theory suggests that norms are important, although more likely to be successful when agreements reflect and foster the evolution of norms rather than seek to impose them where they are not held. With Kyoto, however, we suggest that the 'moral resources' were asymmetrically distributed and that this contributed significantly to the failure of the process. The green lobby, as the main provider of these arguments, must therefore bear much of the blame for what must, for it, constitute a major failure.

The asymmetrical distribution of moral arguments that we find with the climate change case, where the EU was portrayed as acting in a principled manner while the Umbrella Group appeared to be acting out of 'mere selfish interests', illustrates what Bruce Yandle (1989), at the domestic level, has referred to as 'Baptist and bootlegger' coalitions. These can be found behind many successfully adopted regulatory policies. The 'Baptists' are those who consider a certain activity to be regulated morally wrong. (In Yandle's metaphor, Baptists consider the sale of alcohol on a Sunday to be wrong.) The 'bootleggers' are indifferent to the moral arguments, but have an economic interest which will be advantaged by the regulation. (Bootleggers support the prohibition of alcohol sales because they can only make money if it cannot be bought from legitimate outlets.)

Coalitions between Baptists and bootleggers are frequently powerful enough to sweep aside their opposition. They are particularly important in political systems such as the United States because of cultural factors and very weak party discipline in the legislature, and majorities in favour of legislation must usually be built effectively from scratch. As Charles Lindblom (1959, 1979) noted in arguing for his incrementalist theory of the policy process, the distinction between ends and means is difficult to maintain, and actors can support (or oppose) policies because they are concerned with the ends or concerned with the means. These conditions obtain at multilateral level. Given this tradition in the USA, its relative weakness in getting its case across in the public principled disourse should not surprise. The Baptists were strong at home and inside the administration; the bootleggers hardly dared to challenge them; the EU therefore possessed a 'third' column supporter in US politics, and yet failed.

Theodore J. Lowi (1987) has pointed out that a distinction between ends and means may also serve as the basis for distinguishing between 'mainstream' or liberal politics and the 'radical' politics to which environmentalism belongs. 'Liberal' politics concentrates on interests and a concern with regulating things which are wrong in their consequences. Radical politics tends to eschew interests, and focuses on things which are wrong in themselves. Sometimes these 'paradigms' are in conflict: economic interests line up against the higher moral calling of environmental groups, which argue that 'priceless' wilderness cannot be sacrificed to Mammon or the protection of human life cannot be measured in 'mere money'. Frequently, however (and this is Yandle's point), the moral discourse supports and masks economic interests, and the masking is just as important in increasing their influence as the reinforcement they provide. And where the coincidence between norms and interests is asymmetrical, where one side does not have strong moral arguments it can muster, the Baptist and bootlegger coalition is almost unstoppable – but not quite.

A coincidence between moral justifications and economic interests does more than just add more support of numbers to that side, it also acts as a political tool to undermine the opponent. The addition of a strong moral rationale weakens opponents who are accused of relying solely upon self-interest. As Shue puts it, norms make liars of those unable to tackle them head-on. Beyond that, however, a moral cloak makes it legitimate to do what would otherwise be unacceptable: to provide support (financial or political) to causes that would otherwise lack legitimacy.

We noted a good example of this from outside the climate issue in Chapter 5: from the NGO action against the WTO Ministerial Meeting in Seattle in 1999, at which the Group Public Citizen Trade Watch was pushing for a kind of 'social tariff' to protect against imports where cheap labour has been employed. This is a contentious area: on the one hand, sweatshop labour is hard to defend; on the other, most developing countries have few advantages other than cheap labour. But the claim for a social tariff would also provide protection for US labour (and capital). (Such protection against 'exploitation' should be requested by the workers being 'exploited' rather than those who would simultaneously benefit from the protection.) It was later revealed that this campaign had been supported and financed by US cotton manufacturing magnate Roger Milliken, who could not have achieved as much influence if he had simply sought to limit trade liberalization by lobbying on the grounds of economic self-interest. As we have seen, Climate Network Europe and other NGOs active on the climate issue have been supported financially by the European Union. Their actions have both masked and assisted the various interests both outside and within the EU.

So there are many reasons for scepticism over the activities of NGOs in international environmental and development politics. Overwhelmingly, they originate in the North, and their activities in the South should always be subject to critical scrutiny; and global bootleggers may well find them attractive allies whose naivety they can exploit. There is a case to be made for a 'democratic' role for global civil society when they are championing human rights in non-democratic states, for example, but they frequently simply play Baptist to bootlegger interests. Sometimes, as with EU funding for the Climate Action Network, the links between NGOs and those pushing particular interests are quite clear. In other examples, such as the distribution of support for Greenpeace, support for the NGO also manifests itself in national interests, even if the NGO eschews explicit government support, because the same support which feeds into the NGO also helps construct national interests.

Such melding of normative and interest-based cases is typical of politics. While environmentalists might be indifferent to such coalitions on the basis that means do not matter so long as the 'end' that is the negotiated outcome is 'correct', they would do well to note that a 'correct' outcome is by no means always guaranteed. Their dreaded nuclear power might well be a big winner from Kyoto, global poverty may increase and the poorest might be expected to bear most of the costs of 'enhanced competitiveness' in the North (Boehmer-Christiansen, 2002).

In another example of a Baptist and bootlegger coalition, the EU also uses the notion of 'multifunctionality' to defend its protectionist agricultural trade regime. This involves arguing for trade restrictions on the basis that traditional (inefficient) agriculture preserves landscapes, hedgerows and 'traditional' village lifestyles. But, aside from higher prices for consumers, it also encourages higher levels of fertilizer and pesticide use in trying to produce crops where comparative advantage would suggest they should not be; serious problems such as nitrate pollution of groundwater result.

We suggest that in the Kyoto process this coincidence between norms and interests helped to sustain the EU in what Lowi would term a discourse of 'radical' politics. The Umbrella Group instead had moved on to the 'mainstream' (or interest-based) discourse which Hanf and Underdal suggest is necessary to progress beyond the initiation or 'framework convention' stage of the international policy process. The support of morality-based advocates in the form of NGOs and strong linkage with development politics (and thus issues of distributive justice) helped bolster this position. So, too, was the 'science' of the IPCC intended to override interests and tip the balance back in favour of morals, thanks to the use of ecocentric ethical arguments, where scientific evidence of anthropogenic interference with climate was expected to be persuasive. Clearly, this did not happen, because the science and expertise were themselves too contaminated by interests (including their own) and were used selectively by interests in application. The idea of science reconstructing interests remained a chimera. The IPCC had always been reflective of numerous interests: energy conservation, alternative energy, nuclear energy, developing countries, and so on, not to mention climate science itself. Rather than facilitating the negotiation of a protocol, these factors sustaining the EU and G-77 in a discourse more suited to the development of a framework convention simply delayed the inevitable interest-based negotiation, for which an instrumental discourse was appropriate.

While possibilities for norms and knowledge to sustain ultimately non-productive discourses probably exist everywhere, it may well be that the nature and the ambitions of the EU bureaucracy facilitated this result. While the 'decomposition' of issues to different directorates in the EU Commission limits the integration of environmental and economic interests which occurs elsewhere, international agreements, however weak, strengthen the Commission *vis-à-vis* the other EU institutions and member states. Many EU policies appear inconsistent to the outside observer, with different Directorates-General appealing to their individual constituencies without having to consider trade-offs between issues (recall that the case was being made for continuing coal subsidies throughout the Kyoto process). Continuing international negotiations are part of the creation of competences for EU DGs, and this helps create bargaining power for (generally weak) environment ministries within national governments.

These rationales for action simply add to the likelihood of a vertical disintegration of policy, already enhanced by the spillover of principled and causal discourses from policy initiation into subsequent stages of the international policy process, where they marginalize those actors employing instrumental discourses – except those with interests which coincide, rather than conflict, with those principled and causal discourses. While, in this case, the establishment of energy competence for the EU coincided with the fiscal interests of treasuries, the EU was essentially able to 'harvest the green vote', as Skolnikoff has put it, without having to integrate its climate change polices fully into a 'whole-of-government' stance. As we have seen, there are signs at both EU level and domestic level that energy policy is not tightly aligned *de facto* with environmental policy, except where one serves to disguise the other, as in the UK and Germany.

This lack of alignment may be assisted by differences in the relative influence of business and environment groups at the level of the nation-state and at the supranational level. This means that the relative marginalization of business generally at the supranational level is accentuated by *both* the propitious circumstances afforded environment NGOs in the EU and the wider multilateral system *and* the way in which the principled discourse reinforces *some* interests at that level. Since the circumstances at supranational level are not propitious for business generally, those interests that are able to secure influence at this level are all the more likely to be those that can find coalition partners who can lend convincing principled discourses. With some environmental issues, such as hazardous waste, the 'bootlegger' interests might be small and lacking in economic significance – waste treatment operators advantaged by export bans, for example – so we need not be overly concerned about their influence over policy. But with climate change policy, there are diverse interests on both (or, perhaps, all) sides of the issue, and the myth that economic interests exist on only the side resisting certain proposals works to the considerable advantage of those who stand to benefit and who are perhaps only incidentally interested in the ends of the policy. This point, and that there are also interests among scientists and among bureaucrats seeking advantage, is fundamental to an understanding of the course of the Kyoto process.

In conclusion we suggest that a more prominent, explicit and respectable place should be found for interests broadly defined in the international environmental policy process. This view is supported by developments in other areas of high normative content, such as whaling and toxic waste regulation. Science, too, must be admitted to have legitimate interests typical of a global enterprise dependent on national funding and which thrives on uncertainty, as well as future threats, to justify more research. But science must be acknowledged to have limited ability to redefine interests in ways which are conducive to the development of detailed, 'low politics' environmental agreements. While that also holds for whaling, it is a perhaps surprising conclusion, given the importance of science in exploring and perhaps one day understanding climate and how it changes over different time scales.

Certainly, if the causal discourse of science is to play a substantial role in overcoming the interests involved in the climate change issue and in the instrumental discourse central to the development of international policy responses, it will have to be more authoritative and less tied to principled discourses that thus far have done little more than mask the interests of others, limiting the effectiveness of some, and making the Kyoto process less productive than it might otherwise have been.

Bibliography

Adams, John (1995), *Risk*, London: UCL Press.

Agarwal A. and S. Narain (1991), *Global Warming in an Unequal World*, New Delhi: Centre for Science and Environment.

Albin, Cecilia (1995), 'Rethinking justice and fairness: the case of acid rain emission reductions', *Review of International Studies* **21**: 119–43.

Ambio (1994), 'Integrating earth systems', **23** (1) (Special Issue).

Anderson, Kym (1995), 'The political economy of coal subsidies in Europe', *Energy Policy* **23**: 485–96.

—— and Warwick J. McKibbin (1997), 'Reducing coal subsidies and trade barriers: their contribution to greenhouse gas emissions', Adelaide: Centre for International Economic Studies, University of Adelaide (Seminar Paper 97–07).

Anon. (1996), 'Climate change debate hots up', *Tomorrow* **6**(5), 32–3.

Antarctic Cooperative Research Centre, University of Tasmania (2000), Position statement: 'Polar ice sheets, climate and sea level rise', 10 February.

Auer, Matthew R. (1996), 'Negotiating toxic risks: a case from the Nordic countries', *Environmental Politics* **5**, 687–99.

Australia. Department of Foreign Affairs and Trade (1997), *Australia and Climate Negotiations: An Issues Paper,* Canberra: DFAT, September.

Australian Bureau of Agricultural and Resource Economics (ABARE) (1997), *The Economic Impact of International Climate Change Policy*, (Research Report 97.4), Canberra: Australian Government Printing Service.

Baker, Andrew C. (2001), 'Ecosystems: reef corals bleach to survive change', *Nature* **411**, 765–6.

Bantock, J. and J. Longhurst (1995), 'UK electricity requirements and the environmental and economic aspects of the development of the combined cycle power station', *Environmentalist* **15**, 122–38.

Barrow, J.D. (1991), *Theories of Everything,* Oxford: Oxford University Press.

Barry, Brian (1967), 'The public interest', in Anthony Quinton (ed.) *Political Philosophy*, Oxford: Oxford University Press.

BBC News Online <http://news.bbc.co.uk/hi/english>.

Beitz, Charles R. (1983), 'Cosmopolitan ideals and national sentiment', *Journal of Philosophy* **80**, 591–600.

Benedick, Richard (1991), *Ozone Diplomacy*, Cambridge, Mass.: Harvard University Press.

Berner, U. and H. Streif (eds) (2001), *Klimafakten: Der Rückblick, ein Schlüssel für die Zukunft* (Climate facts: the past as one key to the future), E. Schweizerbart.

Boehmer-Christiansen, Sonja (1988), 'Pollution control or *Umweltschutz?*', *European Environment Review* **2** (1), 6–10.

—— (1990), 'Energy policy and public opinion: manipulation of environmental threats by vested interests in the UK and West Germany', *Energy Policy* **18**, 9.

—— (1992a), 'Environmentalism and nuclear power: Anglo-German comparison', *Energy and Environment* **3**(1), 1–28.

—— (1992b), 'Anglo-German contrasts in environmental policy-making', *International Environmental Affairs* **4**, 295–322.

—— (1993), 'Science policy, the IPCC and the Climate Convention: the codification of a global research agenda', *Energy and Environment* **4** (4), 362–406.

—–— (1994a), 'The precautionary principle in Germany: enabling government', in Timothy O'Riordan and James Cameron (eds) *Interpreting the Precautionary Principle*, London: Earthscan.

—— (1994b), 'Global climate protection policy: the limits of scientific advice, Part I', *Global Environmental Change* **4** (2), 140–59.

—— (1994c), 'Global climate protection policy: the limits of scientific advice, Part II', *Global Environmental Change* **4** (3), 185–200.

—— (1994d), 'A scientific agenda for climate policy?', *Nature* **372**, (6505), 400.

—— (1995a), 'Britain and the International Panel on Climate Change: the impacts of scientific advice on global warming. Part I: Integrated policy analysis and the global dimension', *Environmental Politics* **4**, 1–18.

—— (1995b), 'Britain and the International Panel on Climate Change: The impacts of scientific advice on global warming. Part II: The domestic story of the British response to climate change', *Environmental Politics* **4**, 175–96.

—— (1996), 'The international research enterprise and global environmental change: climate change policy as a research process', in John Vogler and Mark F. Imber (eds) *The Environment and International Relations*, London: Routledge.

—— (1999a), 'Climate change and the World Bank: opportunity for global governance?', *Energy & Environment* **10**, 27–50.

—— (1999b), 'Epilogue: Scientific advice in the world of power politics', in Pim Martens and Jan Rotmans (eds), *Climate Change: An Integrated Approach*, Dordrecht: Kluwer.

—— (2002), 'The geopolitics of sustainable development: bureaucracies and politicians in search of the Holy Grail', *Geoforum*, forthcoming.

—— and Jim Skea (1991), 'The operation and impact of the IPCC: results of a survey of participants and users', Centre for Science, Technology, Energy and Environment Policy, Discussion Paper no. 16, Brighton: SPRU.

—— and —— (1993), *Acid Politics: Environmental and Energy Politics in Britain and Germany*, London: Belhaven.

—— and Zoe Young (1997), 'The global environment facility: Is institutional innovation in need of guidance?', *Environmental Politics* **6** (1), 193–202.

——, D. Merten, J. Meissner and D. Ufer (1993), 'Ecological restructuring or environment friendly deindustrialisation: the fate of the East German energy sector and society since 1990', *Energy Policy* **21**(4), 355–73.

Bolin, B. (1980), 'Climatic changes and their effects on the biosphere', *Fourth WMO lecture*, WMO-No. 542, Geneva: World Meteorological Organization.

—— (1993), 'Energy and climate change', *WEC Journal* July: 42.

—— (1994), 'Science and policy-making', *Ambio* **23** (1), 25–9.

—— (1998), The Kyoto negotiations on climate change: a science perspective, *Science* **279**: 330–1.

—— (1999), 'Knowledge and controversies in the climate change issue', in Tor Ragnar Gerholm (ed.) *Climate Policy After Kyoto*, Brentwood: Multi-Science.

——, B.R. Döös, Jill Jäger and Richard A. Warwick (eds) (1986), *The Greenhouse Effect, Climatic Change and Ecosystems* published on behalf of the Scientific Committee on the Problems of the Environment (SCOPE) of the International Council of Scientific Unions (ICSU) and the World Meteorological Organization, Chichester, Sussex: John Wiley.

Brazil (1997), Proposed Elements of a Protocol, paper tabled at meeting of Ad Hoc Group on the Berlin Mandate FCCC/AGBM/1997/Misc.1/Add.3.

Brenton, Tony (1994), *The Greening of Machiavelli: The Evolution of International Environmental Politics*, London: Earthscan.

Briffa, K.R. (2000), 'Annual climate variability in the Holocene: interpreting the message of ancient trees', *Quaternary Science Reviews* **19**, 87–105.

Bryson, R.A. (1972), 'Climatic modification by air pollution', in N. Polunin, *The Environmental Future*, London: Macmillan.

Budiansky, Stephen (1995), *Nature's Keepers: The New Science of Nature Management,* New York: The Free Press.

Calder, Nigel (1997), *The Manic Sun: Weather Theories Confounded*, London: Pilkington Press.

—— (1999), 'The carbon dioxide thermometer and the cause of global warming', *Energy & Environment* **10**, 1–18.

Cavander, Jeannine and Jill Jäger (1993), 'The history of Germany's response to climate change', *International Environmental Affairs* **5**, 3–18.

Changnon, S.A. (1999), 'Impacts of 1997–98 El Niño-generated weather in the United States', *Bulletin of the American Meteorological Society* **80**,1819–27.

Chichilnisky, Graciela and Geoffrey Heal (1994), 'Who should abate carbon emissions? An international viewpoint', *Economics Letters* **44**, 443–9.

Christy, J.R., (2000), 'Global climate change: scientific and social impacts', *Bridges* **7**, 39–57.

——, David E. Parker, Simon J. Brown, Ian Macadam, Martin Stendel and William B. Norris (2001), 'Differential trends in tropical sea surface and atmospheric temperatures since 1979', *Geophysical Research Letters* **28**, 183.

Churchill, R. and Freestone D. (1992), *International Law and Global Climate Change*, London: Graham & Trotman/Nijhoff.

Claus, G. and K. Bolander (1977), *Ecological Sanity*, New York: David McKay.

Clover, C. (1993), *The Daily Telegraph*, April.

Cohen, Michael D., James G. March and Johan P. Olsen (1972), 'A garbage can model of organizational choice', *Administrative Science Quarterly* **17**(1), 1–25.

Cole, Leonard A. (1983), *Politics and the Restraint of Science*, Totowa: Rowman and Allenheld.

Cole, S. (1992), *Making Science*, Cambridge, Mass.: Harvard University Press.

Collier, Ute (1996), 'The European Union's climate change policy: limiting emissions or limiting powers?', *Journal of European Public Policy* **3**, 122–38.

Courtney, Richard (1999), 'An assessment of validation experiments conducted on GCMs using the GCM of the Hadley Centre', *Energy and Environment* **10**(5), 491–502.

Courtney, Richard (2001), personal comment to Sonja Boehmer-Christiansen.

CSIRO (2001), *Climate Change Projections for Australia*, Climate Impact Group, Melbourne: CSIRO Division of Atmospheric Research.

Dasgupta, C. (1994), 'The climate change negotiations', in I.M. Mintzer and J.A. Leonard (eds), *Negotiating Climate Change: The Inside Story of the Rio Convention*, Cambridge: Cambridge University Press.

Daubert v. *Merrel Dow Pharmaceuticals Inc.* (1993), 113 S Ct 2786.

Deutsche Physikalische Gesellschaft (DPG) (1985), Presseinformation: 'Zur Warnung des Arbeitskreises Energie der Deutschen Physikalischen Gesellschaft vor einer drohenden, weltweiten Klimakatastrophe', Prof. Dr K. Heinloth, Universität Bonn, press conference, December 1985, Bonn, Hotel Tulpenfeld.

Dobson, M.J. (1997), *Contours of Disease and Death in Early Modern England*, Cambridge: Cambridge University Press.

Dornbusch, R. and J.M. Poterba (1991), *Global Warming: Economic Policy Responses*, London: MIT Press.

Douglas, Mary (1966), *Purity and Danger: An Analysis of Concepts of Pollution and Taboo*, London: Routledge & Kegan Paul.

—— (1992), *Risk and Blame*, London: Routledge.

Earth Negotiations Bulletin (1997), 'Report of the Third Conference of the Parties to the United Nations Framework Convention on Climate Change: 1–11 December 1997', *Earth Negotiations Bulletin* **12** (76).

Edelman, Murray (1964), *The Symbolic Uses of Politics*, Urbana, Ill.: University of Illinois Press.

Edin, Karl-Axel (1999), 'Swedish climate policy', in Tor Ragnar Gerholm (ed.) *Climate Policy After Kyoto*, Brentwood: Multi-Science.

Eichner, Volker (1997), 'Effective European problem-solving: lessons from the regulation of occupational safety and environmental protection', *Journal of European Public Policy* **4**, 591–608.

Emsley, J. (ed.) (1996), *The Global Warming Debate: The Report of the European Science Forum*, Bournemouth, Dorset: Bournemouth Press.

Environmental News Service <html://ens.lycos.com.ens/html>.

Estrada-Oyuela, R. (1993), 'UN/UNEP/WMO', *Climate Change Bulletin*,1.1 3rd quarter, 1.

Fagan, Brian (2001), *The Little Ice Age: How Climate Made History*, New York: Basic Books.

FCCC (United Nations Framework Convention on Climate Change) (1992), (New York) 9 May 1992, in force 24 March 1994; 31 I.L.M. 1992.

Feigenbaum, H.B. (1985), *The Politics of Public Enterprise: Oil and the French State*, Princeton, N.J: Princeton University Press.

Feldman, David Lewis (1995), 'Iterative functionalism and climate management organizations: from Intergovernmental Panel on Climate Change to Inter-governmental Negotiating Committee', in Robert V. Bartlett, Priya A. Kurian and Madhu Malik (eds) *International Organizations and Environmental Policy*, Westport, Conn: Greenwood Press.

Finnemore, Martha (1996), 'Norms, culture, and world politics: insights from sociology's institutionalism', *International Organization* **50**, 325–47.

Fischer, W. (1992), *Climate Protection and International Policy*, Forschungszentrum Jülich, Jul-2695, November, 33.

Fleming, James Rodger (1998), *Historical Perspectives on Climate Change*, Oxford: Oxford University Press.

Flohn, H. (1981), *Life on a Warmer Earth: Possible Climatic Consequences of Man-made Global Warming*, Laxenburg, Austria: International Institute of Applied Systems Analysis.

Four Corners (1999), 'Emission impossible', Sydney: Australian Broadcasting Corporation, broadcast on 8 November.

Franck, T.M. (1990), *The Power of Legitimacy Among Nations*, Oxford: Oxford University Press.

Frankhauser, S. (1993), *Global Warming Economics: Issues and State of the Art*, CSERGE Working Paper GEC1993–28, London: University College London and Norwich: University of East Anglia.

French, Hilary (1996), 'The role of non-state actors', in Jacob Werksman (ed.) *Greening International Institutions*, London: Earthscan.

Fumento, Michael (1993), *Science Under Siege: Balancing Technology and the Environment*, New York: William Morrow.

Gailus, Jeff (1996), 'That glow in the eastern sky', *Tomorrow*, **6**(4), 30.

Gelbspan, Ross (1997), *The Heat is On: The High Stakes Battle Over Earth's Threatened Climate*, Reading, Mass.: Addison-Wesley.

German Advisory Council on Global Change (GACGC) (1998), *The Accounting of Biological Sinks and Sources Under the Kyoto Protocol: A Step Forwards or Backwards for Global Environmental Protection?*, Bremerhaven: WBGU.

Gibbons, Michael and Bjorn Wittrock (1985), *Science as a Commodity: Threats to the Open Community of Scholars*, Harlow: Longman.

Glassman, James K. and Sallie L. Baliunas (2001), 'Bush Is Right on Global Warming' (*On The Issues*) Washington: American Institute for Public Policy Research, June. (*http://www.aei.org/oti/13068.htm*)

Goldemberg, J. (1994), 'The road to Rio', in I.M. Mintzer and J.A. Leonard (eds) *Negotiating Climate Change: The Inside Story of the Rio Convention*, Cambridge: Cambridge University Press.

Goldstein, Judith and Robert Keohane (eds) (1993), *Ideas and Foreign Policy: Beliefs, Institutions, and Political Change*, Ithaca, N.Y.: Cornell University Press.

Goodin, Robert E. (1992), *Green Political Theory*, Cambridge: Polity Press.

Gorshkov V.G. and V.V Gorshkov (1998), *Biotic Regulation of the Environment: Key Issues of Global Change*, Chichester, Sussex: Springer-praxis.

Gosovic, Branislav (1992), *The Quest for World Environmental Cooperation: The Case of the UN Global Environmental Monitoring System*, London: Routledge.

Greenpeace International (1996), *Annual Report*, London: Greenpeace.

Grubb, Michael (1995), 'Seeking fair weather: ethics and the international debate on climate change', *International Affairs* **71**, 463–96.

Gummer, John and Robert Moreland (2000), *The European Union and Global Climate Change: A Review of Five National Programs*, Washington: Pew Center on Global Climate Change.

Gupta, J. (2000), 'North–South aspects of the climate change issue: towards a negotiating theory and strategy for developing countries', *International Journal of Sustainable Development* **3**, 115–35.

Haas, E.B. (1990), *When Knowledge is Power*, Berkeley, Cal.: University of California Press.

Haas, Peter M. (1990), 'Obtaining international environmental protection through epistemic consensus', *Millennium: Journal of International Studies* **19**(3), 347–64.

Häfele, W. (ed.) (1981), *Modelling of Large-scale Energy Systems,* Oxford: Pergamon (IIASA Proceedings series, vol. 12).

Haigh, Nigel (1996), 'Climate change policies and politics in the European Community', in Timothy O'Riordan and Jill Jäger (eds) *The Politics of Climate Change: A European Perspective*, London: Routledge.

Hammond, A.L., E. Rodenburg and W.R. Moomaw (1991), 'Calculating national accountability for climate change', *Environment* **33**, 11–15, 33–5.

Hanf, Kenneth and Arild Underdal, (1998), 'Domesticating international commitments: linking national and international decision-making', in Arild Underdal (ed.) *The Politics of International Environmental Management,* Dordrecht: Kluwer.

Hansen, J., M. Sato, R. Ruedy, A. Lacis, and V. Oinas (2000), 'Global warming in the twenty-first century: an alternative scenario', *Proceedings of the National Academy of Sciences* **97**, 9875–80.

Hart, D. and D. Victor (1993), 'Scientific elites and the making of US policy for climate change research 1957–1974', *Social Studies of Science* **23** (4), 643–80.

Hatch, Michael T. (1995), 'The politics of global warming in Germany', *Environmental Politics* **4**, 415–40.

Her Majesty's Treasury (1992), *The Economics of Man-made Climate Change*, London: HMSO.

Hirschman, Albert O. (1970), *Exit, Voice and Loyalty,* Cambridge, Mass.: Harvard University Press.

Hoffert, Martin I., Ken Caldera, Curt Covey, Philip B. Duffy, and Benjamin D. Santer (1999), 'Solar variability and the Earth's climate', *Nature* **401**, 764.

Hoffman, Stanley (1966), 'Obstinate or obsolete: the fate of the nation state and the case of Western Europe', *Daedalus* **95** (3), 862–915.

Houghton, J.T. (1993), 'Energy for tomorrow's world – the realities, the real options and the agenda for achievement', *WEC Journal*, July, 47.

——, B.A. Callander and S.K. Varney (eds) (1992), *Climate Change 1992: The Supplementary Report to the IPCC Scientific Assessment*, Cambridge: Cambridge University Press.

——, G.J. Jenkins and J.J. Ephraums (eds) (1990), *Climate Change: The IPCC Scientific Assessment*, Cambridge and New York: Cambridge University Press.

——, L.G. Meira Filho, B.A. Callander, N. Harris, A. Kattenberg and K. Maskell (eds) (1996), *Climate Change 1995: The Science of Climate Change*, Cambridge: Cambridge University Press.

Hoyt, Douglas V. and Kenneth H. Shatten (1997), *The Role of the Sun in Climate Change*, Oxford: Oxford University Press.

IGBP (1994), *Global Change Newsletter* 17, March.

International Council of Scientific Unions (ICSU) and International Geosphere Biosphere Project (IGBP) (1992), *Reducing Uncertainties*, Stockholm: Royal Swedish Academy of Sciences.

—— (1994), 'IGBP in action: work plan 1994–1998', *Global Change Report* no. 38, Stockholm.

International Panel on Climate Change (IPCC) (1994), *IPCC Technical Guidelines for Assessing Climate Change Impacts and Adaptations*, CGER-1015-94, London: Department of Geography, University College London and the Centre for Global Environmental Research.

—— (2000), *Special Report on Emissions Scenarios*, <http://www.grida.no/climate/ipcc/emission/002.htm.anc3> (accessed 20 August 2001).

Jacobson, Arnold K. (1984), *Networks of Interdependence: International Organizations and the Global Political System*, New York: McGraw-Hill.

Jacobson, H.K. and Price, M.F. (1990), *A Framework for Research on the Human Dimension of Global Environmental Change*, Vienna: ISSC/UNESCO.

Jäger, J. and H.L. Ferguson, (eds) (1991), *Climate Change: Science, Impacts, Policy: Proceedings of the Second World Climate Conference*, Cambridge: Cambridge University Press.

—— and O'Riordan, Timothy (1996), 'The history of climate change science and politics', in Timothy O'Riordan and Jill Jäger (eds) *The Politics of Climate Change: A European Perspective*, London: Routledge.

Jasanoff, Sheila (1998), 'Harmonization: the politics of reasoning together', in Roland Bal and Willem Halffman (eds) *The Politics of Chemical Risk: Scenarios for a Regulatory Future*, Dordrecht: Kluwer.

Jepma, C.J. (2001), 'Hot air at bargain prices?', *Joint Implementation Quarterly*, **7**(2), 1.

Jokinen, Pekka and Keijo Koskinen (1998), 'Unity in environmental discourse? The role of decision makers, experts and citizens in developing Finnish environmental policy', *Policy and Politics* **26**, 55–70.

Jordan, A, (1994), 'Financing the UNCED agenda: the controversy over additionality', *Environment* **36**, 3.

Kalkstein, L.S. and Greene, J.S. (1997), 'An evaluation of climate/mortality relationships in large US cities and the possible impacts of a climate change', *Environmental Health Perspectives* **105**, 84–93.

Kaufmann, Johan (1988), *Conference Diplomacy: An Introductory Analysis*, 2nd edn, Dordrecht: Martinus Nijhoff.

Keatinge, W.R., G.C. Donaldson, E. Cordioli, M. Martinelli, A.E. Kunst, J.P. Mackenbach *et al.* (2000), 'Heat related mortality in warm and cold regions of Europe: observational study', *British Medical Journal* **321**, 670–703.

Keck, Margaret E. and Kathryn Sikkink (1998), *Activists Beyond Borders: Advocacy Networks in International Politics*, Ithaca, N.Y.: Cornell University Press.

Kellogg, W.W. and R. Schware (1981), *Climate Change and Society: Consequences of Increasing Carbon Dioxide*, Boulder, CO: Westview Press.

Kellow, Aynsley (1988), 'Promoting elegance in policy theory: simplifying Lowi's arenas of power', *Policy Studies Journal* **16**, 713–24.

—— (1996), *Transforming Power: The Politics of Electricity Planning*, Cambridge: Cambridge University Press.

—— (1997), 'The politics of climate change: problem definition, precaution, and the international policy process', paper presented to the National Academies Forum: 'The Challenge for Australia on Global Climate Change', Canberra, 29–30 April.

—— (1999), *International Toxic Risk Management: Ideals, Interests and Implementation*, Cambridge: Cambridge University Press.

—— (2000), 'Norms, interests and environment NGOs: the limits of cosmopolitanism', *Environmental Politics* **9**, 1–22.

—— (2002), 'Comparing business and public interest associability at the international level', *International Political Science Review*, **23**, 175–86.

Kennedy, Paul (1993), *Preparing for the Twenty-first Century*, New York: Random House.

Kerr, Richard A. (1997), 'Greenhouse forecasting still cloudy', *Science* **276**,1040–42.

Kirsch, Guy (1986), 'Solidarity between generations: intergenerational distributional problems in environmental and resource policy', in Allan Schnaiberg, Nicholas Watts and Klaus Zimmerman (eds) *Distributional Conflicts in Environmental-resource Policy*, Aldershot, Hants.: Gower.

Klotz, Audie (1995), 'Norms reconstituting interests: global racial equality and US sanctions against South Africa', *International Organization* **49**, 451–78.

Kohler-Koch, B. (1994), 'The evolution of organized interests in the EC: driving forces, co-evolution or new type of governance?', paper given at the XVth World Congress of the International Political Science Association, 21–25 August, Berlin.

Korten, David (1996), *When Corporations Rule the World*, London: Earthscan.

Koskenniemi, Martti (1996), 'New institutions and procedures for implementation control and reaction', in Jacob Werksman (ed.) *Greening International Institutions*, London: Earthscan.

Kuhnel, I. and I. Coates (2000), 'El Niño–Southern Oscillation: related probabilities of fatalities from natural perils in Australia', *Natural Hazards* **22**, 117–38.

Kyoto Protocol to the United Nations Framework Convention on Climate Change (1997), 37 I.L.M. 22; the corrected text is available at the website of the FCCC Secretariat, <http://www.unfccc.int>.

Laferrière, Eric (1996), 'Emancipating international relations theory: an ecological perspective', *Millennium: Journal of International Studies* **25**, 53–75.

Lal, Depak (1995), 'Eco-fundamentalism', *International Affairs* **71**, 515–28.

Leggett, Jeremy K. (ed.) (1990), *Global Warming: The Greenpeace Report*, Oxford: Oxford University Press.

Leggett, Jeremy (1999), *The Carbon War: Global Warming and the End of the Oil Era*, Harmondsworth, Middlesex: Penguin.

Lester, James P. and Elfar Loftsson (1993), 'The ecological movement and green parties in Scandinavia: problems and prospects', in Sheldon Kamieniecki (ed.) *Environmental Politics in the International Arena: Movements, Parties, Organizations, and Policy*, Albany, N.Y.: State University of New York Press.

Levy, David L. and Daniel Egan (1998), 'Capital contests: national and transnational channels of corporate influence on the climate change negotiations', *Politics and Society* **26**, 337–61.

Lindblom, Charles E. (1959), 'The science of "muddling through" ', *Public Administration Review* **19**(2), 79–88.

—— (1977), *Politics and Markets,* New York: Basic Books.

—— (1979), 'Still muddling, not yet through', *Public Administration Review* **29**(6), 517–26.

Lindzen, R. (1992), 'Global warming: the origin and nature of the alleged scientific consensus', Special Issue of Energy and Environment, Proceedings of OPEC Seminar, Vienna, April, Brentwood: Multi-Science.

Lindzen, Richard (2001), Testimony of Richard S. Lindzen before the US Senate Environment and Public Works Committee on 2 May 2001, unpublished submission.

——, Ming-Dah Chou and Arthur Y. Hou (2001), 'Does the earth have an adaptive infrared iris?', *Bulletin of the American Meteorological Society* **82**(3), 417–32.

Lipschutz, Ronnie D. (1992), 'Reconstructing world politics: the emergence of global civil society', *Millennium: Journal of International Studies* **21**, 389–420.

Litfin, Karen (1994), *Ozone Discourses: Science and Politics in Global Environmental Cooperation*, New York: Columbia University Press.

—— (1995), 'Framing science: precautionary discourse and the ozone treaties', *Millennium: Journal of International Studies* **24**, 251–77.

Lockwood, M., R. Stamper and M.N. Wild (1999), 'A doubling of the Sun's coronal magnetic field during the past 100 years', *Nature* **399**, 3 June, 437–9.

Lowe, Ian (1998), 'Surprise finding on land clearance', *New Scientist* 3 January, 45.

Lowi, Theodore J. (1964), 'American business, public policy, case studies, and political theory', *World Politics* **16**, 677–715.

—— (1987), 'New dimensions in policy and politics', Foreword in R. Tatalovich and B. Daynes (eds) *Social Regulatory Policy*, Boulder, Co: Westview Press.

—— (1993), 'Risks and Rights in the History of American Governments', in Edward J. Burger, Jr., (ed.) *Risk*, Ann Arbor, MI: The University of Michigan Press.

Lumsdaine, David (1993), *Moral Vision in International Politics*, Princeton, N.J.: Princeton University Press.

Lundgren, L.J. (1998), *Acid Rain on the Agenda: 1966–1968*, Lund: Lund University Press.

Mabey, N., Hall, S., Smith, C. and Gupta, S. (1997), *Argument in the Greenhouse*, London: Routledge.

Maloney, Michael T. and Gordon L. Brady (1988), 'Capital turnover and marketable pollution permits', *Journal of Law and Economics* **31**.

Mann, M.E., R.S Bradley and M.K. Hughes (1999), 'Northern hemisphere temperatures during the past millennium: inferences, uncertainties and limitations', *Geophysical Research Letters* **26**, 759–62.

Marshall Institute (1992), *Global Warming Update: Recent Scientific Findings*, Washinton, D.C.: George C. Marshall Institute.

Masood, Ehsan (1996), 'Sparks fly over climate report', *Nature* **381**, 639.

—— (2000), 'Biting back: opinion interview' [with Paul Reiter, Chief Entomologist, US Centers for Disease Control and Prevention, San Juan, Puerto Rico], *New Scientist* 23 September, 41–3.

Maxwell, J.H and S.L. Weiner (1993), 'Green consciousness or dollar diplomacy? The British response to the threat of ocean depletion', *International Environmental Affairs* **5**(1), 19–41.

McCormick, J. (1999), 'The role of environmental NGOs in international regimes', in N.J. Vig and R.S. Axelrod (eds) *The Global Environment: Institutions, Law, and Policy*, London: Earthscan.

McCracken, M. (1992), quoted in S. Veggeberg 'Global warming researchers say they need breathing room', *The Scientist* **6**, 2.

McMichael, A.J., A. Haines, R. Slooff and S. Kovats (eds) (1996), *Climate Change and Human Health*, Geneva: World Health Organization, World Meteorological Organization, and United Nations Environment Programme.

McMullan, J.T. (1996), 'The uncertainty of CO_2 disposal and the impact this may have on global warming', in John Emsley (ed.) *The Global Warming Debate*, London: European Science and Environment Forum.

McTegart, W.T. and W.J. Zillman (1990), 'The International Panel on Climate Change', Melbourne, unpublished, cited with permission.

Michaels, Patrick J. (1992), *Sound and Fury: The Science and Politics of Global Warming*, Washington: Cato Institute.

—— (2001), 'Kyoto: do the math', *Cato: Today's Commentary*, 30 March <http://cato.org/dailys/03–30–01.html>.

—— and Paul C. Knappenberger (1996a), 'Human effect on global climate?', *Nature* **384**, 522–3.

—— and —— (1996b), 'The United Nations Intergovernmental Panel on Climate Change and the scientific "consensus" on global warming', in John Emsley (ed.) *The Global Warming Debate*, London: European Science and Environment Forum.

Miller, Clark A. and Paul N. Edwards (eds) (2001), *Changing the Atmosphere: Expert Knowledge and Environmental Governance*, Cambridge, Mass.: MIT Press.

Mitchell, Ronald B. (1998), 'Discourse and sovereignty: interests, science, and morality in the regulation of whaling', *Global Governance* **4**, 275–93.

Moore, B. and B.H. Braswell (1994), 'Planetary metabolism: understanding the carbon cycle', in *Ambio Special Issue*.

Mudelsee, M. (2001), 'The phase relations among atmospheric CO_2 content, temperature and global ice volume over the past 420 ka', *Quaternary Science Reviews* **20**, 583–9.

Mukerji, C. (1989), *A Fragile Power: Scientists and the State*, Princeton, NJ: Princeton University Press.

Nadelmann, Ethan A. (1990), 'Global prohibition regimes: the evolution of norms in international society', *International Organization* **44**, 479–526.

Naish, Tim R., Ken J. Woolfe, Peter J. Barrett *et al.* (2001), 'Orbitally induced oscillations in the East Antarctic ice sheet at the Oligocene/Miocen boundary', *Nature* **413**, 719–23.

Nordhaus, William D. (2001), 'Global warming economics', *Science* **294**, 1283–4.

Oberthür, S. and H.E. Ott (1999), *The Kyoto Protocol: International Climate Policy for the 21st Century*, Berlin: Springer Verlag.

O'Keefe, W.F. (1996), 'Letter: Climate science conspiracy', *Tomorrow* **6**(4), 59.

Ostrom, Elinor (1990), *Governing the Commons: The Evolution of Institutions for Collective Action*, Cambridge: Cambridge University Press.

Ott, Herman E. (2001), 'Climate change: an important foreign policy issue', *International Affairs* **77**, 277–96.

Paltridge, Garth (2001), 'Climate change: a short primer', *Quadrant* **44**(4), 9–13.

Panafrican News Agency <http://allafrica.com/stories/html>.

Parker, E.N. (1999), 'Solar physics – sunny side of global warming', *Nature* **399**, 416–17.

Pearce, F. (1995), 'Price of life sends temperatures soaring', *New Scientist* 1 April.

Pogge, Thomas W. (1992), 'Cosmopolitanism and sovereignty', *Ethics* **103**, 48–75.

Polunin, N. (1972), *The Environmental Future*, London: Macmillan.

Ponte, L. (1976), *The Cooling*, Englewood Cliffs, N.J.: Prentice-Hall.

Porter, T. (1995), *Trust in Numbers*, Princeton, N.J.: Princeton University Press.

Princen, Thomas and Matthias Finger (1994), *Environmental NGOs in World Politics: Linking the Local and the Global*, London: Routledge.

Proctor, R. (1991), *Value Free Science? Purity and Power in Modern Knowledge*, Cambridge, Mass.: Harvard University Press.

Putnam, Robert D. (1988), 'Diplomacy and domestic politics: the logic of two-level games', *International Organization* **42**, 427–60.

Rayner, S. (1994), *Governance and the Global Common*, London: London School of Economics, Centre for the Study of the Global Governance (Discussion Paper 8).

Reiter, Paul (2000), 'From Shakespeare to Defoe: malaria in England in the Little Ice Age', *Emerging Infectious Diseases* **6**(1) January–February.

—— (2001), 'Climate change and mosquito-borne disease', *Environmental Health Perspectives* **109**, 141–61.

Reynolds, Anna (1998), 'An immoral victory: greenhouse greed is simply putting off the inevitable', *Arena* **33**, 9.

Rosenau, James N. (1995), 'Governance in the twenty-first century', *Global Governance* **1**(1), 13–43.

Rotblat, Joseph (ed.) (1997), *World Citizenship: Allegiance to Humanity*, London: Macmillan.

Rothrock, D.A., Y. Yu and G.A. Maykut (1999), 'Thinning of the Arctic sea-ice cover', *Geophysical Research Letters* **26**, 3469–72.

Rowlands, Ian H. (1997), 'International fairness and justice in addressing global climate change', *Environmental Politics* **6**, 1–30.

Rüdig, W. (1993), 'Sources of technical controversy', in A. Barker and B. Peters (eds) *The Politics of Expert Advice*, Edinburgh: Edinburgh University Press.

Sand, Peter H. (1990), *Lessons Learned in Global Environmental Governance*, Washington, D.C.: World Resources Institute.

Sandbrook, Richard (1997), 'UNGASS has run out of steam', *International Affairs* **73**, 641–54.

Santer, B.D., K.E. Taylor, T.M.L. Wigley, T.C. Johns, P.D. Jones, D.J. Karoly, J.F.B. Mitchell, A.H. Oort, J.E. Penner, V. Ramaswamy, M.D. Schwarzkopf, R.J. Stouffer and S. Tetts, (1996a), 'A search for human influences on the thermal structure of the atmosphere', *Nature* **382**, 39–46.

Santer, B.D., T.M.L. Wigley, T.P. Barnett and E. Anyamba, (1996b), 'Detection of climate change and attribution of causes', in J.T. Houghton, L.G. Meira

Filho, B.A. Callander, N. Harris, A. Kattenberg and K. Maskell (eds) *Climate Change 1995: The Science of Climate Change*, Cambridge: Cambridge University Press for the IPCC (IPCC Second Assessment Report).

Schell, Jonathon (1989), 'Our fragile earth', *Discover* October, 47.

Schneider, Stephen (1976), *The Genesis Strategy: Climate and Global Survival*, New York: Plenum.

Sebenius, James K. (1992), 'Challenging conventional explanations of international cooperation: negotiation analysis of the case of epistemic communities', *International Organization* **46**, 323–65.

—— (1993), 'The Law of the Sea Conference: lessons for negotiations to control global warming', in G. Sjostedt (ed.) *International Environment Negotiations*, Laxenberg: International Institute for Advanced Systems Analysis.

Seitz, Frederick (1996), 'A major deception on global warming', *Wall Street Journal*, 12 June.

Shue, Henry (1992), 'The unavoidability of justice', in Andrew Hurrell and Benedict Kingsbury (eds) *The International Politics of the Environment: Actors, Interests and Institutions*, Oxford: Clarendon Press.

—— (1995), 'Ethics, the environment and the changing international order', *International Affairs* **71**, 453–61.

Sikkink, Kathryn (1993), 'Human rights, principled issue-networks, and sovereignty in Latin America', *International Organization* **47**, 411–41.

Sinclair Knight Merz (1998), *Millmerran Power Project: Draft Impact Assessment Study*, vol. 1, Brisbane: Sinclair Knight Merz.

Singer, Fred (1996), 'A preliminary critique of the IPCC's second assessment of climate change', in John Emsley (ed.) *The Global Warming Debate*, London: European Science and Environment Forum.

Skodvin, T. and Underdal, A. (1994), 'The science–politics interface', paper given at the International Studies Association meeting, Washington, D.C., 29 March–1 April.

Skolnikoff, Eugene B. (1993), *The Elusive Transformation: Science, Technology, and the Evolution of International Politics*, Princeton, N.J.: Princeton University Press.

—— (1999), *From Science to Policy: The Science-related Politics of Climate Change Policy in the United States*, Cambridge, Mass.: MIT Joint Program on the Science and Policy of Global Change (Report no. 46).

Slovic, P. and B. Fischhoff (1983), 'How safe is safe enough?', in C.A. Walker, L.C. Gould and E.J. Woodhouse, *Too Hot to Handle*, New York: Yale University Press.

Soroos, Marvin S. (1986), *Beyond Sovereignty: The Challenge of Global Policy*, Columbia: University of South Carolina Press.

—— and Elena N. Nikitina (1995), 'The World Meteorological Organization as a purveyor of global public goods', in Robert V. Bartlett, Priya A. Kurian and Madhu Malik (eds) *International Organizations and Environmental Policy*, Westport, Conn.: Greenwood Press.

Sprinz, Detlef and Tapani Vaahtoranta (1994), 'The interest-based explanation of international environmental policy', *International Organization* **48**, 77–105.

Stokke, O.S. and D. Vidas (1996), 'Effectiveness and legitimacy of international regimes', in O.S. Stokke and D. Vidas (eds) *Governing the Antarctic: The Effectiveness and Legitimacy of the Antarctic Treaty System*, Cambridge: Cambridge University Press.

Subak, S. (1991), 'Commentary on the greenhouse index', *Environment* **33**, 2–3.

Svensmark, Henrik and Eigil Friis-Christensen (1997), 'Variation of cosmic ray flux and global cloud coverage – a missing link in solar-climate relationships', *Journal of Atmospheric and Solar-terrestrial Physics*, **59** (11), 1225–32.

Thorsrud, E. (1972), 'Policy-making as a learning process', in A.B. Cherns, R. Sinclair and W.I. Jenkins (eds), *Social Science and Government*, London: Tavistock.

Tolba, M. (1982), *Development Without Destruction*, Dublin: Yycool.

Turner, B.L *et al.* (eds) (1990), *The Earth as Transformed by Human Action*, Cambridge: Cambridge University Press.

Underdal, Arild (1979), 'Issues determine politics determine policies', *Cooperation and Conflict* **14**: 1–9.

—— (1989), 'Conclusion' in S. Andresen and W. Ostreng (eds), *International Resources Management: The Role of Science and Politics*, London: Belhaven Press.

—— and Kenneth Hanf (2000), *International Environmental Agreements and Domestic Politics: The Case of Acid Rain*, Aldershot, Hants.: Gower.

United States National Research Council (1983), *Towards an International Geosphere–Biosphere Program: A Study of Global Change*, Washington, D.C.: National Science Foundation.

—— (1990), *Research Strategies for the US Global Change Research Program*, Washington, D.C.: National Academy Press.

van der Lugt, Cornelis (2000), *State Sovereignty or Ecological Sovereignty? A Study of the Regulation of Acid Rain Within the European Union*, Baden-Baden: NOMOS.

Veggeberg, S. (1992), 'Global warming researchers say they need breathing room,' *Scientist*, 11 May.

Victor, David G. (2001), *The Collapse of the Kyoto Protocol and the Struggle to Slow Global Warming*, Princeton, N.J.: Princeton University Press.

—— and J.E. Salt (1994), 'From Rio to Berlin: managing climate change', *Environment* **36** (10).

Vogel, David (1995), *Trading Up: Consumer and Environmental Regulation in a Global Economy*, Cambridge, Mass.: Harvard University Press.

—— (1997), 'Trading up and governing across: transnational governance and environmental protection', *Journal of European Public Policy* **4**, 556–71.

Walker, R.B.J. (1994), 'Social movements/world politics', *Millennium: Journal of International Studies* **23**, 669–700.

Wapner, Paul (1995), 'Politics beyond the state: environmental activism and world civic politics', *World Politics* **47**, 311–40.

—— (1996), *Environmental Activism and World Civic Politics*, Albany, N.Y.: SUNY Press.

Warrick, R.A. and P.D. Jones (1988), 'The greenhouse effect: impacts and policies', *Forum for Applied Research and Public Policy* **3** (3), 48–62.

Waterton, Claire and Brian Wynne (1996), 'Building the European Union: science and the cultural dimensions of environmental policy', *Journal of European Public Policy* **3**, 421–40.

Watson, R.T. (1998), Climate change: the challenge for energy supply', *Energy & Environment* **10** (1), 19–26.

Watson, Robert T. (ed.) (2002), Climate Change 2001: Synthesis Report: Third Assessment Report of the Intergovernmental Panel on Climate Change (IPPC), Cambridge University Press, UK.

Weart, S. (1992), 'From the nuclear frying pan into the global fire', *Bulletin of Atomic Scientists* **48** (5), 18–27.

Webster, Mort D., Chris E. Forest, John M. Reilly, Andrei P. Sokolov, Peter H. Stone, Henry D. Jacoby and Ronald G. Prinn (2001), 'Uncertainty analysis of global climate change projections', Cambridge, Mass: MIT Joint Program on the Science and Policy of Global Change Report no. 73.

Weiler, Joseph H.H. (1988), 'The White Paper and the application of Community law', in R. Beiber, D. Dehousse, J. Pinder and J.H.H. Weiler (eds) *One European Market?*, Baden-Baden: Nomos.

Werksman, Jacob (1996), 'The Conference of Parties to Environmental Treaties', in Jacob Werksman (ed.) *Greening International Institutions*, London, Earthscan.

—— (1998), 'The Clean Development Mechanism: unwrapping the "Kyoto Surprise",' *Review of European Community and International Environmental Law* **7**, 147–58.

Wildavsky, Aaron (1984), *The Politics of the Budgetary Process*, Boston, Mass.: Little, Brown.

—— (1987), *Speaking Truth to Power: The Art and Craft of Policy Analysis*, New Brunswick, N.J.: Transaction Books.

—— and Mary Douglas (1981), *Risk and Culture*, Berkeley, Cal.: University of California Press.

Willetts, Peter (1982), 'The impact of promotional pressure groups on global politics', in Peter Willetts (ed.) *Pressure Groups in the Global System: The Transnational Relations of Issue-orientated Non-governmental Organizations*, London, Frances Pinter.

—— (1996), 'From Stockholm to Rio and beyond: the impact of the environmental movement on the United Nations consultative arrangements for NGOs', *Review of International Studies* **22**, 57–80.

—— (2000), 'From "consultative arrangements" to "partnership": the changing status of NGOs in diplomacy at the UN', *Global Governance* **6**(2), 191–212.

Wilson, James Q. (1973), *Political Organizations*, New York: Basic Books.

Winner, Langdon (1977), *Autonomous Technology: Technics-out-of-control as a Theme in Political Thought*, Cambridge, Mass., MIT Press.

Winsor, P. (2001), 'Arctic sea ice thickness remained constant during the 1990s', *Geophysical Research Letters* **28**, 1039–41.

World Commission on Environment and Development (WCED) (1987), *Our Common Future*, Oxford: Oxford University Press.

World Energy Council (WEC) (1993), 'Energy and climate change', *World Energy Council Journal*, July: 26.

World Meteorological Organization (WMO) (1986), *Report of the International Conference on the Assessment of Carbon Dioxide and Other Greenhouse Gases in Climate Variations and Associated Impacts*, Villach, 9–15 October 1985, WMO no. 661, Geneva: WMO.

—— (1990), *Report of the Sixth Session of CAS/JSC, Numerical Experimentation* (WCRP-53) Geneva: WMO.

—— (1991a), *Report on the Global Climate Observing System* (WCRP-56), Winchester, Hants.: WMO.

—— (1991b), *Eleventh World Meteorological Congress, Abridged Report* (WMO-No. 756), Geneva: WMO.

—— (WMO) (1992), *The World Climate Programme 1992–2001*, WMO no. 762), Geneva: WMO.

—— and International Council of Scientific Unions (ICSU) (1990), *Global Climate Change: A Scientific Review Presented by the World Climate Research Programme*, Geneva: WMO.

Wynne, Brian (1987), *Risk Management and Hazardous Waste: Implementation and the Dialectics of Credibility,* Berlin: Springer-Verlag.

—— (1992), 'Global environmental change: human and policy dimensions, *Global Environmental Change* **2** (2), 11–27.

Yamin, F. (1998), 'The Kyoto Protocol: origins, assessment and future challenges', *Review of European Community and International Environmental Law* **7**: 113–27.

Yandle, Bruce (1989), *The Political Limits of Environmental Regulation,* New York: Quorum Books.

—— (2001), 'Bootleggers, baptists and global warming', in Terry L. Anderson and Henry I. Miller (eds) *The Greening of US Foreign Policy*, Stanford, Cal.: Hoover Press.

Young, Oran (1994), *International Governance: Protecting the Environment in a Stateless Society*, Ithaca, N.Y.: Cornell University Press.

Zillman, John (1997), 'The IPCC: a view from inside', in Alan Oxley (ed.) *Managing Climate Change: Key Issues*, Proceedings of the Conference 'Countdown to Kyoto', Canberra: Australian APEC Studies Centre.

Index

ABC News Online (Australia)
  Greenpeace and nuclear phase-out
    difficulties 42
Adams, John 106
Advisory Group on Greenhouse Gases
    (AGGG)
  formation of 128–9, 130
  work of 128–31
Agarwal, Anil 85
AGGG *see* Advisory Group on
    Greenhouse Gases
Anderson, David 81
Anderson, Kym 45
Anonymous 152
Antarctic Cooperative Research Centre
  sea levels and global warming 170
Anyamba, E. 151, 153
Arrhenius, Svente 121, 166
Associated Press
  nuclear power and ethical debate 115
Australia
  Department of Foreign Affairs and
    Trade 45, 58
  emissions 35
  emissions targets 63–4
  fossil fuel sector 42–3
  Greenpeace and nuclear phase-out
    difficulties 42
  Greenpeace protest pre COP-3 96–7
  international agreements and 113
  John Houghton broadcast 174
  Kyoto process and 73, 74
  renewable energy sector 47–8
Austria
  Villach Conference 128–30

Baker, Andrew C. 169
Baliunas, Sallie L. 162, 168
Ball, Tim 168
Bantock, J. 51
Baptists and bootleggers

ethical debate 109–12
  Kyoto process and 182–5
Barnett, T. P. 151, 153
Barrett, Peter J. 159
Barry, Brian 111
BBC News Online
  external use of IPCC reports 173
  IPCC 'peer review' 141
Beitz, Charles R. 90
Benedick, Richard 4, 5
Berlin Mandate
  aims 59–60
  compliance and monitoring 70
  coverage 60–62
  emissions trading 64–7
  joint implementation 67–8
  national policies and measures 68–9
  negotiations under 60
  targets 62–4
Berlusconi, Silvio 81
Berner, U. 8, 156
Blair, Tony 49, 81
Boehmer-Christiansen, Sonja
  acid rain concerns preceding global
    warming concerns 39, 123
  economic change in post-unification
    Germany 51
  environmental language in Germany
    94
  green politics in Germany 46–7
  interests and international policy
    process 20, 22
  IPCC research and procedures 131,
    139
  multilateral environment agreement
    problems 18
  nuclear science lobby in Germany
    127
  scientific and political consensus 5
  winners and losers from Kyoto
    process 184

Bolin, Bert
  climate change research and 119, 120,
    122
  genetic fallacy 118
  *The Greenhouse Effect, Climate
    Change and Ecosystems*, 124
  institutionalising international climate
    research 129
Bradley, R. S. 157, 158, 159
Brady, Gordon L. 65
Brekke, Paal 158, 159, 168
Brenton, Tony 3–4, 4, 11, 18–19
Briffa, K. R. 158
Brown, Simon J. 156
Bryson, R. A. 122, 123
Budiansky, Stephen 105
Bush, George W.
  election as President 77
  Kyoto Protocol withdrawal and 36–7,
    78, 80, 138, 145
  "mass murderer", labelled as 179
Business Wire Features
  Atlantic hurricane damage 171

Calder, Nigel 158
Caldera, Ken 159
Callander, B. A. 136
Callendar, Guy 121
CAN *see* Climate Action Network
Canada
  international agreements and 113
  nuclear power 38–9
  renewable energy sector 46
  Toronto Conference (1988) 53
Cavander, Jeannine 39, 125
CDM *see* Clean Development
  Mechanism
Changnon, S. A. 160
Chichilnisky, Graciela 111
Chou, Ming-Dah 33, 162–3
Christensen, Eigil Friis- *see* Friis-
  Christensen, Eigil
Christiansen, Sonja Boehmer- *see*
  Boehmer-Christiansen, Sonja
Christy, John R. 156, 163, 168
Churchill, R. 132
Clark, William 129
Clean Development Mechanism (CDM)
  Emissions reductions and 103
  exclusions sought from 100, 101

Climate Action Network (CAN)
  Eco case study 98–104
  moral agent, as 96, 97
  moral discourse employed by 89, 112
climate change *see* global warming
Coates, I. 160
Cohen, Michael D. 10, 120
Collier, Ute 57
Commonwealth Scientific and Industrial
    Research Organization (CSIRO)
  Climate Impacts Group, 165
Corbyn, Piers 168
Cordioli, E. 160
Courtney, Richard 135, 157, 168
Covey, Curt 159
Craig, Senator 37, 80
CSIRO *see* Commonwealth Scientific
    and Industrial Research
    Organization
Cutajar, Michael Zammit 71, 173

The Daily Telegraph
  German Green Party and nuclear
    phase-out difficulties 41–2
  sinks and COP-6 78–9
De Freitas, Chris 168
de Palacio, Loyola *see* Palacio, Loyola
  de
Department of Foreign Affairs and Trade
    (Australia)
  emissions reduction 58
  energy interests and opportunities 45
Deutsche Physikalische Gesellschaft
    (DPG)
  industrial solutions and economy 127
Dobson, M. J. 160
Donaldson, G. C. 160
Döös, B. R. 124, 129
Douglas, Mary 94, 104, 108
DPG *see* Deutsche Physikalische
  Gesellschaft
Duffy, Philip B. 159

Eco (CAN Newsletter)
  CAN moral discourse and 98–104
  funding of 96
Edelman, Murray 27
Edin, Karl-Axel 127–8
Egan, Daniel, 21–2, 23, 24
Ehrlich, Paul 119

Eichner, Volker 10
emissions
  ethical debate 85–8
  levels in EU 35, 51–2
emissions targets
  see also quantified emission limitation
      and reduction objectives
  Australia 63–4
  Berlin Mandate and 62–4
  EU 57–8, 62–3
  Germany 40
  Japan 63
  Norway 63
  Switzerland 63
  USA 63, 64
emissions trading
  Berlin Mandate and 64–7
  EU 66–7
  Kyoto Protocol and 74–5, 76
  Russia 35–6, 66–7, 82
  USA 61, 65–6, 67
energy sector
  see also fossil fuel energy; nuclear
      power; renewable energy
  carbon taxes 49–50
  policy and climate change science
      119, 145–6
Environment News Service
  climate change policy, as moral basis
      for spreading energy and security
      costs 50
  external use of IPCC reports 173
environmentalism
  see also international environmental
      policy
  moral crusade, as 104–09
Estrada-Oyuela, Raúl 71, 72, 73, 75
ethical debate
  Baptists and bootleggers 109–12
  civil society and its representatives
      88–9
  emissions and 85–8
  environmentalism as moral crusade
      104–09
  global society 90–92
  Kyoto Protocol, after 98–104, 112–15
  norms and interests 92–8
European Union (EU)
  *see also individually named member
      states*
  Baptists and bootleggers and 181–2,
      184–5
  Bonn Agreement and 177–8
  compliance and monitoring 70
  emission levels in 35, 51–2
  emissions targets 57–8, 62–3, 64
  emissions trading 66–7
  environment ministers' strengths and
      weaknesses 30
  environment policy inconsistencies of
      114
  'European Bubble' 56–7
  flexibility mechanisms 79–80
  fossil fuel sector 45
  international agreements and 114
  Kyoto process and 71, 75, 76
    advantages sought by 58–9, 60–61
    costs 34, 180–81
    interests 52
    joint implementation 67–8
    national policies and measures 68–9
    US withdrawal from 80–81
  nuclear politics in 38–42
  sinks 61, 78–9, 81–2
Evans, David 169

Fagan, Brian 157
FCCC *see* Framework Convention on
      Climate Change
Feigenbaum, H. B. 45
Feldman, David Lewis 4, 19
Ferguson, H. L. 131
Filho, Luis Gylvan Meira *see* Meira
      Filho, Luis Gylvan
The Financial Times
  'dash to gas' in UK 51
  nuclear revival in UK 42
  nuclear revival in USA 41
Finger, Matthias 24
Finland
  First International Conference on
      Environmental Futures (1971) 122
  nuclear revival in 41
Finnemore, Martha 90–91
Flohn, Herman 119–20, 121–2, 125
Forest, Chris E. 166
fossil fuel energy
  see also energy sector
  climate change science and 125, 126
  gas, UK 51
  security and 42–5

Four Corners (Australian Broadcasting
        Corporation broadcast)
    carbon trading and emissions
        reduction 174
Fourier, Joseph 121
Framework Convention on Climate
        Change (FCCC)
    see also Berlin Mandate; Kyoto
        process; Kyoto Protocol
    1990 base year and 57
    extrabudgetary sources 95
    objective 54
    principles 54–6
Frank, T. M. 87
Frankfurter Allgemeine Zeitung
    'ecological modernization' in
        Germany 47
    national and energy interests in USA
        34
Freestone, D. 132
Freitas, Chris De *see* De Freitas, Chris
French, Hilary 46
Friis-Christensen, Eigil 158
Fumento, Michael 118, 151

GACGC *see* German Advisory
        Committee on Global Change
Gailus, Jeff 40
Galileo (Galileo Galilei) 118
gas *see* fossil fuel energy
Gelbspan, Ross 118, 170
German Advisory Committee on Global
        Change (GACGC)
    sinks ratios 36
Germany
    see also European Union
    Advisory Council on Global Change
        36
    climate change research 121–2, 125
    Deutsche Physikalische Gesellschaft
        127
    'ecological modernization' in 47
    'ecology tax' in 49
    emission levels 51–2
    emission targets 40
    energy policy and climate change
        science 125–7
    Green Party 41–2
    Kyoto Protocol ratification 80
    nuclear power 38, 39–40, 41–2

climate change and 126–7
    ethical debate and 115
    renewable energy sector 46–7
Gibbons, Michael 119
Glassman, James 162
global policy *see* international
        environmental policy
global warming
    see also Intergovernmental Panel on
        Climate Change
    acid rain precedes 123–4
    alarmist view of science 148–9
    attribution controversy 149–53
    challenges in developing responses to
        3–4
    climate change models and,
        manufacturing scientific
        consensus with 161–7
    global governance needed to combat 2
    "hockey stick" and 156–8
    how much? 153–6
    legal context for mitigation efforts
        1–2
    malaria myth 159–61
    research
        brief history 121–3
        institutionalising 128–32
        nuclear power and 125–7
    scientific and political consensus and
        4–5, 116–17
    solar radiation and 158–9
    threat prevails 124–8
Goldstein, Judith 9
Goodin, Robert E. 104
Goodman, Gordon 130–31
Gore, Al 36, 71–2, 78, 160
Gorshkov, V. G. 8
Gorshkov, V. V. 8
Gosovic, Branislav 95
Green Party (Germany)
    nuclear phase-out difficulties and
        41–2
Greenpeace
    climate change alarmism by 171
    environmentalism as moral crusade
        and 105
    moral agent, as 93–4, 96–7
    nuclear phase-out difficulties and 42
Grubb, Michael 91

The Guardian
national and energy interests in USA
36
nuclear revival in Finland 41
sinks and COP-6 79
Gummer, John 35

Haas, Ernst B. 4, 20, 109
Haas, Peter M. 4, 6, 19, 109
Häfele, Wolf 38, 53, 119–20, 125
Hagel, Chuck 37, 77, 80
Haines, A. 160
Halopainen, E. 122
Hammond, A. L. 85
Hanf, Kenneth
interests
framework agreement and protocol
negotiations compared 89
scientific consensus and 175
international environmental policy
process, model 26–9
mainstream politics discourse, EU and
Kyoto process and 184
multilateral environmental agreement
problems 17
policy, vertical disintegration of 11
science and norms, importance of 10
Hansen, James E. 37, 80, 130, 159, 174
Hart, D. 123
Hatch, Michael T. 39, 126
Heal, Geoffrey 111
Helms, Senator 37, 80
Hill, Robert 73
Hirschman, Albert O. 2
Hoffert, Martin I. 159
Hoffman, Stanley 10, 13
Hou, Arthur Y. 33, 162–3
Houghton, John T.
climate change research and 119, 120,
132
IPCC assessment reports and research
base 136
IPCC 'peer review' and 141, 142
IPCC reports and, external use of
167–8
letter from US State Department to
152–3
pressure on United States government
by 173–4
WG I co-chairman, as 133

Hughes, M. K. 157, 158, 159

The Independent
climate change alarmism 171
Climate Change Levy in UK 49
nuclear revival in UK 41
sinks and COP-6 79
interests
carbon taxes and 49–50
energy, opportunities and 33–4
fossil fuel, energy security and 42–5
political, European nuclear 38–42
influence of on international
environmental policy 21–6
Kyoto process and 34–8, 52, 177–9,
185–6
norms and, ethical debate 92–8
renewable energy, efficiency and 46–9
technology, economic change and
50–52
Intergovernmental Panel on Climate
Change (IPCC)
assessment reports and research base
136–9
attribution controversy and 150–53
climate alarmism and 148–9, 173–5
climate change models and,
manufacturing scientific
consensus with 161, 165–7
formation of 132–4
"hockey stick" and 156, 157–8
how much warming and 155–6
institutionalization of science of
climate change in 116, 117,
143–6
logical fallacies and 118–19
negative impact emphasis by 159,
160–61
organisation and membership of
134–5
origins of 123
'peer review' and 141–3
reports, external use of 167–72
solar radiation and 158–9
Special Report on Emissions 165
systemic bias in 139–41
international environmental policy
see also environmentalism
ambivalent science and 18–21, 30–32
climate change

moral basis for spreading energy
    and security costs, as 50
    negotiations, complexity of 13–15
inconsistencies of EU 114
influence of interests and 21–6
model of process 26–30
multilateral environmental
    agreements, problems with
    16–18, 30–32
IPCC *see* Intergovernmental Panel on
    Climate Change

Jacobson, Arnold K. 94
Jacoby, Henry D. 166
Jäger, Jill
    acid rain concerns preceding global
        warming concerns 124
    institutionalising international climate
        research 129, 131
    nuclear power and global warming 39,
        125
Japan
    emissions targets 63
    sinks 61, 81, 82
Jasanoff, Sheila 85
Jepma, C. J. 181

Kaufmann, Johan 95
Keating, W. R. 160
Keck, Margaret E. 92
Keeling, Charles 122
Kellogg, W. W. 123, 125
Kellow, Aynsley
    empirical disputes, global warming
        and 155
    energy efficiency and renewables 46
    interests and international policy
        process 20, 22
    international environmental policy
        process, model 27
    NGOs as moral agents 31, 93
    nuclear capacity in Canada 39
Kennedy, Paul 86
Keohane, Robert 9
Kerr, Richard A. 162
Kirsch, Guy 92
Klotz, Audie 91
Knappenberger, Paul C. 142, 153
Kohl, Helmut, 38, 46–7, 112, 114, 126–7
Korten, David 24, 89

Koskenniemie, Martti 15
Kovats, S. 160
Kuhnel, I. 160
Kunst, A. E. 160
Kyoto News
    USA and sinks concessions 81
Kyoto process
    see also Berlin Mandate; Framework
        Convention on Climate Change
    annual opportunity cost 33
    Australia and 73, 74
    Baptists and bootleggers and 182–5
    COP-4 to COP-6 76–80
    EU and 34, 71, 75, 76
    failure of 34–8, 82–4
    FCCC principles and 54–9
    impact assessment of 33–4
    insurance policy, as 33, 179–80
    interest and negotiating positions 53–4
    interests and 34–8, 52, 177–9, 185–6
    New Zealand and 75
    NGOs and 183–4
    nuclear revival justified by 41
    outline of 11–12
    régime of shared norms important for
        180–82
    Russia and 73
    science, norms and 5–11
    USA and 71–2, 73–4, 75
        pressed to rejoin 176–7
        withdrawal from 34–5, 36–7, 77,
            80–82
Kyoto Protocol
    conclusion of 70–71
    coverage 71, 72
    differentiation 71–2
    emissions trading 74–5, 76
    ethical debate after 98–104, 112–15
    German ratification 80
    QELROs 71, 72, 73–4
    sinks 71, 72–3
    USA and
        ratification stumbling blocks 75–6
        signed by 77

La Viña, Antonio 71, 72
Lacis, A. 37, 80, 174
Laferrière, Eric 19, 90
Lal, Depak 111
Leggett, Jeremy K. 96, 118, 152, 170

Lester, James P. 94
Levy, David L. 21–2, 23, 24
Lindblom, Charles E. 4, 21, 22, 111, 182
Lindzen, Richard 33, 138–9, 148, 162–3, 168
Lipschutz, Ronnie D. 90
Lockwood, M. 158
Loftsson, Elfar 94
Longhurst, J. 51
The Los Angeles Times
  carbon credits 177
Lovins, Amory 119
Lowi, Theodore J.
  'functional prerequisites' 66
  radical politics 106, 182
  radical politics discourse, EU and Kyoto process and 184
  regulatory policy 22, 26, 27
Lugt, Cornelius van der 16
Lumsdaine, David 3
Lundgren, L. J. 122
Luther, Martin 104
Lysenko, Trofim 7

Macadam, Ian 156
Mackenbach, J. P. 160
Maloney, Michael T. 65
Mann, Michael E. 157, 158, 159
March, James G. 10, 120
Marshall Institute
  scientific opposition to IPCC and 138
Martinelli, M. 160
Masood, Ehsan 161
Maykut, G. A. 172
McBean, Gordon 168
McCarthy, John 171–2
McCracken, 123
McKibbin, Warwick J. 45
McMichael, A. J. 160
McMullan, J. T. 44
McTegart, W. T. 131
MEA *see* multilateral environmental agreement
Meacher, Michael 79
media
  see also individually named newspapers and broadcasters
  NGO 'science' and 169–72
Meira Filho, Luis Gylvan 71
Meissner, J. 51

Menem, Carlos 77
Merten, D. 51
Michaels, Patrick J. 142, 153, 179–80
Milliken, Roger 112, 183
Ming-Dah Chou *see* Chou, Ming-Dah
Mintzer, Irving 124
Mitchell, Ronald B. 9–10, 14, 179
Moomaw, W. R. 85
moral discourse *see* ethical debate
Moreland, Robert 35
The Moscow Times
  emission trading by Russia 35–6, 82
Mudelsee, M. 106–7, 159
Mueller, Werner 39–40
multilateral environmental agreement (MEA)
  ambivalent science and 18–21, 30–32
  problems with 16–18, 30–32
  role of ethics in 89

Nadelmann, Ethan A. 4, 92
Nader, Ralph 37, 111
Naish, Tim R. 159
Narain, Sunita 85
The New York Times
  energy policy and climate change science in USA 145
New Zealand
  Kyoto process and 75
NGOs *see* non-governmental organizations
Nikitina, Elena N. 124
non-governmental organizations (NGOs)
  see also Climate Action Network; Greenpeace
  Baptists and bootleggers and 183
  environmental negotiation effectiveness 22–4, 25
  Kyoto process and 183–4
  moral agents, as 92–8
  moral discourse employed by 89
  representatives of civil society, as 88
  'science', media and 169–72
Nordhaus, William D. 178
norms
  interests and, ethical debate 92–8
  science and, Kyoto process 5–11
  US domestic, South Africa and 91
Norris, William B. 156

Norway
  emissions targets 63
nuclear power
  see also energy sector
  climate change debate and 120–21
  climate change science and 125–6
  ethical debate in Germany 115
  politics in EU 38–42

The Observer
  nuclear revival in UK 41
Oinas, V. 37, 80, 174
O'Keefe, William F. 151–2
Olsen, Johan P. 10, 120
Ostrom, Elinor 16
Oyuela, Raúl Estrada- *see* Estrada-
  Oyuela, Raúl

Paavola, Mauno 41
Palacio, Loyola de 114
Paltridge, Garth 164
Panafrican News Agency
  climate change models, manufacturing
    scientific consensus with 174
  external use of IPCC reports 173
  need to prepare for global warming
    176
Parker, David E. 156
Persson, Goran 80
Pocklington, Roger 168
political consensus
  scientific consensus and, global
    warming 4–5, 116–17, 146
Polunin, N. 122
Ponte, L. 123
Porter, T. 20
Prescott, John 78, 79
Princen, Thomas 24
Prinn, Ronald G. 166
Prodi, Romano 80
Pronk, Jan 79–80, 81
Putnam, Robert D. 13, 15, 113

quantified emission limitation and
    reduction objectives (QUELROs)
  see also emissions targets
  Kyoto Protocol 71, 72, 73–4

Reilly, John M. 166
Reiter, Paul 160, 161

renewable energy
  see also energy sector
  efficiency and 46–9
  technology and economic change and
    50–52
Reuters
  climate change alarmism 172
  'ecology tax' in Germany 49
  emission levels in EU 35
  emission targets in Germany 40
  environment policy inconsistencies of
    EU 114
  nuclear revival in Finland 41
  nuclear revival in UK 41
  nuclear revival in USA 41
  sinks concessions to Russia 81
  US withdrawal from Kyoto process
    80, 81
Roberts, Senator 37, 80
Rodenburg, E. 85
Rosenau, James N. 2
Rotblat, Joseph 86
Rothrock, D. A. 172
Rüdig, W. 127
Ruedy, R. 37, 80, 174
Russia
  Bonn Agreement and 178
  emission trading by 35–6, 66–7, 82
  Kyoto process and 73
  sinks 81, 82

Sand, Peter H. 3, 16
Sandbrook, Richard 16, 23, 24, 87, 89
Santer, Benjamin D. 151, 152, 153, 159,
    162
Sato, M. 37, 80, 174
Schell, Jonathon 119
Schere, Wolfgang 172
Schmidt, Helmut 126
Schneider, Stephen 119, 123
Schroeder, Gerhard 49, 80
Schumacher, E. E. 119
Schware, R. 123, 125
science
  see also global warming;
    Intergovernmental Panel on
    Climate Change
  ambivalent, multilateral environmental
    agreements and 18–21, 30–32
  nature of 117–21

NGO, media and 169–72
norms and, Kyoto process 5–11
scientific consensus
    manufacturing, with climate change
        models 161–7
    political consensus and, global
        warming 4–5, 116–17, 146
scientific controversy
    alarmist view of science 148–9
    attribution 149–53
    climate change models and,
        manufacturing scientific
        consensus with 161–7
    "hockey stick" and 156–8
    how much global warming? 153–6
    malaria myth 159–61
    solar radiation 158–9
Sebenius, James K. 20
Seitz, Frederick 152
Shue, Henry
    interests and ethics 25, 88, 90, 91,
        109–10
    moral justification and economic self-
        interest and, 183
Sikkink, Kathryn 9, 92
Sinclair Knight Merz 42
sinks
    EU 61, 78–9, 81–2
    Japan 61, 81, 82
    Russia 81, 82
    COP-5 78
    COP-6 78–9
    Kyoto Protocol 71, 72–3
    ratios in Germany 36
    US withdrawal and COP-6 Part II 81,
        82
Skea, Jim 20, 39, 123, 139
Skodvin, T. 135
Skolnikoff, Eugene B. 20, 109, 116, 185
Sloof, R. 160
Sokolov, Andrei P. 166
Soroos, Marvin S. 10, 14, 15, 124
South Africa
    US domestic norms and 91
Sprinz, Detlef 20, 57
Stamper, R. 158
Stendel, Martin 156
Stokke, O. S. 87
Stone, Peter H. 166
Stott, Phillip 168

Streif, H. 8, 156
Strong, Franz Joseph 127
Strong, Maurice 24
Subak, S. 85
The Sunday Times
    nuclear revival in UK 41
Svensmark, Henrik 158
Sweden
    energy policy and climate change
        science 127
Switzerland
    emissions targets 63

taxation
    carbon, energy sector and 49–50
Thatcher, Margaret 45, 51, 112, 120, 122
The Times
    climate change alarmism 172
    emission levels in EU 51–2
    Kyoto process annual opportunity cost
        33
    nuclear revival in Finland 41
Tolba, Mustafa 5, 18, 124, 130, 177
Töpfer, Klaus 95, 173, 174, 176–7
Trenberth, Kevin 159
Trittin, Juergen 52

Ufer, D 51
Underdal, Arild
    institutionalizing scientific advice 135
    interests
        framework agreement and protocol
            negotiations compared 89
        scientific consensus and 175
    international environmental policy
        process, model 26–9
    mainstream politics discourse, EU and
        Kyoto process and 184
    multilateral environmental agreement
        problems 17
    policy, vertical disintegration of 11
    science and norms, importance of 10
UNEP *see* United Nations Environment
    Programme
United Kingdom
    Climate Change Levy 49
    climate change research 121
    'dash to gas' 51
    nuclear revival in 41, 42

United Nations Environment Programme
(UNEP)
  climate change research and 124
  moral agent, as 95
  Villach Conference and 130
United States of America
  Bonn Agreement and 178
  climate change research 121–2, 123
  domestic norms, South Africa and 91
  emissions targets 63, 64
  emissions trading 61, 65–6, 67
  energy policy and climate change
    science 145
  Kyoto process and 71–2, 73–4, 75
    compliance and monitoring 70
    withdrawal from 34–5, 36–7, 77,
      80–82
  Kyoto Protocol and
    ratification stumbling blocks 75–6
    signed by 77
  national and energy interests in 34, 36
  nuclear power
    climate change and 125–6
    revival in 41
  renewable energy sector 46, 48
Unwin, David 168

Vaahtoranta, Tapani 20, 57
van der Lugt, Cornelius *see* Lugt,
  Cornelius van der
Varney, S. K. 136
Victor, David G. 102, 123, 177, 178
Vidas, D. 87
Viña, Antonio La *see* La Viña, Antonio
Vogel, David 17, 23
Voynet, Dominique 79, 80

Walker, R. B. J. 25, 90
Wallström, Margot 34, 114, 180
Wapner, Paul 90
Warwick, Richard A. 124, 129
Waterton, Claire 20
Watson, Robert T.
  COP-6 and 166
  energy policy and 119, 120

  IPCC chair, as 133
  IPCC TAR and, 11, 136
  Kyoto process and Japan 70
  solar radiation 158
WCED *see* World Commission on
  Environment and Development
Weaver, Andrew 168
Webster, Mort D. 166
WEC *see* World Energy Conference
Weiler, Joseph H. H. 10
Wigley, T. M. L. 151, 153
Wild, M. N. 158
Wiłdavsky, Aaron 94, 108
Wilford, John Noble 171
Willetts, Peter 23–4, 97
Winner, Langdon 10
Winsor, P. 172
Wirth, Timothy 151
Wittrock, Bjorn 119
WMO *see* World Meteorological
  Organization
Woolfe, Ken J. 159
World Commission on Environment and
  Development (WCED)
  acid rain concerns preceding global
    warming concerns 124
World Energy Conference (WEC)
  energy policy and climate change
    science 119
World Meteorological Organization
  (WMO)
  climate change research and 124
  IPCC formation and 132
  Villach Conference and 129
World Resources Institute (WRI)
  scientific experts' conflicts 85
Wynne, Brian 16, 20

Yamani, Sheik Ahmed Zaki 144
Yandle, Bruce 112, 182
Young, Oran 179
Young, Zoe 18
Yu, Y. 172

Zillman, W. J. 131, 135, 141, 153